GW00357721

THE IRISH SCHOOL OF ECUMENICS

For

The Original ISE Patrons

John W. Armstrong (Church of Ireland)
John M. Barkley (Presbyterian)
Cecil McGarry (Roman Catholic)
Robert A. Nelson (Methodist)

In gratitude
for their
confidence and encouragement

Edited by Michael Hurley SJ

The Irish School of Ecumenics
(1970 – 2007)

'Like wheat that springs up green'

the columba press

First published in 2008 by
the columba press
55A Spruce Avenue, Stillorgan Industrial Park,
Blackrock, Co Dublin

Cover by Bill Bolger
Origination by The Columba Press
Printed by Athenaeum Press Ltd., Gateshead

ISBN 978 1 85607 613-5

Copyright © 2008, The Contributors

Table of Contents

Editor's Preface

Michael Hurley

Michael Hurley grew up in the seaside village of Ardmore, Co Waterford, was educated by the Cistercian monks in Mount Melleray, and then in 1940 joined the Jesuits. He graduated in classics from University College, Dublin in 1945 and later studied theology in Louvain and in Rome where he obtained a doctorate in 1960 from the Gregorian University. From 1958 until 1970 he taught theology at the Jesuit Theological Faculty in Dublin and established there the Milltown Park Public Lectures. He founded the Irish School of Ecumenics in 1970 and remained as Director until 1980. In 1983 he founded the residential Columbanus Community of Reconciliation in Belfast and remained a member until 1993. His publications include *Church and Eucharist* (ed 1966), *Theology of Ecumenism* (1969) *Irish Anglicanism* (ed 1970), *Reconciliation in Religion and Society* (ed 1994), *Church Unity: An Ecumenical Second Spring* (1998) and an autobiographical memoir *Healing and Hope* (2003). He received an honorary doctorate (LLD) from Queen's University, Belfast in 1993 and from Trinity College Dublin in 1995.

As the title indicates, this book proposes to tell the story of the Irish School of Ecumenics (ISE), founded in Dublin just under forty years ago. It begins with an introductory chapter on how the School began and then gives all its Directors the opportunity and space to tell their individual stories in print for the first time. One by one, chapter by chapter they share their memories. The book therefore is more a memoir than a history; and so it is sparing with footnotes.

Like wheat that springs up green
Despite the difficulties and set backs we each have to record, this book is for all of us a success story; and that is the point of our sub-title: 'Like wheat that springs up green'. This many readers will recognise as the refrain from the hymn 'Now the Green Blade rises'. It is sung at Easter time here in the West by congregations both Catholic and Protestant and it seems appropriate in our book because it tells the story of a rising. At the beginning we had nothing but goodwill and hope; with these we have risen, if not to glory, at least to be a 'living and life-giving' academic body; we are at least a partial success.

Our subtitle recalls ISE's emblem or logo. This was devised by Mr Gerard Slevin, a friend who was Chief Herald at Dublin Castle at the time of our inauguration. The flourishing and perishing of our motto (*'Floreat ut Pereat'*; 'May it Flourish in order to Perish', *'Tagadh Blath chun go dTagadh Feo'*[1]) reminded him of the dying and rising involved not only in the glorification of Jesus but also in natural growth and in the sacrament of the eucharist. He remembered the Johannine verse which says: 'Unless a grain of wheat falls into the earth and dies, it remains just a single grain; but if it dies, it bears much fruit' (Jn 12:24). And the wheat reminded him of the bread which in the eucharist becomes for us the sacramental body of Christ; he saw each in its

1. For this long overdue Irish version of our ISE motto I am grateful to some of my Jesuit friends, specially to Fr Leon Ó Giolláin, one of the chaplains at University, College, Dublin (UCD) and to Professor Seosamh Watson also of UCD.

own mysterious way illustrating the miracle of change, of dying to rise, and gave us an ear of wheat as our logo.

Our subtitle also recalls the very unusual but very consoling gift which at the beginning some Presbyterian friends gave to the School: a crucifix found by a World War I Irish Presbyterian chaplain in the mud and rubble of an unidentified French village and brought back by him and given a place of honour in his manse for the rest of his life. The fourth gospel sees the crucifixion of Jesus as an elevation into glory as well as an elevation on a cross. The Presbyterian crucifix encouraged us to believe that the School must in due course have an Easter experience.

Rising to die

In the 60s this idea of dying to rise had become part of the churches' ecumenical thought and language. At its New Delhi Assembly in 1961 the World Council of Churches stated that:

> The achievement of unity will involve nothing less than a death and rebirth of many forms of church life as we have known them. We believe that nothing less costly can finally suffice.

Vatican II in its *Decree on Ecumenism* also stressed that the church 'which bears in her own body the humility and dying of Jesus' needs to be 'more purified and renewed'.

Paradoxically, however, the School's motto is not about dying to rise but about rising to die. Ecumenical institutions, I wrote at the beginning, 'live to die as soon as ever possible, as soon as the task is completed of reconciling the churches in the unity which is God's will for his people'. And in the 80s some Anglicans did not hesitate to think in a similar vein about their own church/communion. They wrote of its 'provisional character', of its eventual 'disappearance', even quoting the ISE motto as an appropriate expression. (cf Michael Hurley, *Christian Unity: An Ecumenical Second Spring?* Veritas, Dublin 1998, pp183-6).

Education in Ecumenism

But in 1970 the ISE motto was more a criticism of the existing ecumenical movement. This had begun in 1910 and by the 60s and 70s had numerous achievements to its credit but only too obviously had still failed in its efforts to encourage and energise the churches to die and rise, to become one. At the press conference to announce the establishment of ISE, I took the liberty of stating that 'the scandal of disunity has become the scandal of ecumenism' and I expressed the hope that the encouragement of ecumenics as a discipline and the creation of departments or institutes of ecumenics would, by providing opportunities for relevant research and study, 'help to remedy, at its real source, the present worldwide ecumenical malaise'.

This was to identify a lack of emphasis on facilities for education in ecumenism at all levels as a significant factor in the failure to date of the ecumenical movement. In the following decades the Vatican's Pontifical Council for the Promotion of Christian Unity and the Joint Working Group of the Roman Catholic Church and the World Council of Churches would both publish documents which recognised the need. They provided suggestions and directives and in particular insisted on 'the strategic importance of giving priority to the ecumenical formation of those who have special responsibility for ministry and leadership in the churches'.

But this new emphasis on education and formation, on research and study has not been sufficient to reanimate and reactivate the churches into a more dynamic movement for unity. The movement has in fact slowed down. Millennium hopes were not realised; the old, cynical remark that 'the churches will say and do everything about unity except unite' sadly remains only too true. As institutions, as corporate bodies, the churches do not wish to die any more than individual persons do: like ourselves they fear death and resist it. But ecumenical bodies themselves, the School of Ecumenics included, can also become institutionalised. And the longer they live the greater perhaps the danger that they lose their memories, that they forget who they are and

as a result become less inclined to, less able to change and reform, to adopt new strategies and tactics. For the School our
motto encourages us to be on our guard against this process of
institutionalisation; it is an encouragement to believe that eventually to flourish, to be a complete and not only a partial success
will mean making ourselves redundant, freeing ourselves for
the greater things which remain to be revealed. It is also an encouragement to believe that being already a partial success,
having already helped to bring unity and peace somewhat nearer,
entails a readiness to die, to perish, to sacrifice the particular
achievements of the present but only to build on them in order
to bring unity and peace still nearer in the now emerging post-
secular society.

The emerging post-secular society

The process of secularisation which has overtaken our world in
recent times did bring us many benefits, not least perhaps a tam-
ing of the churches. But I now look forward to the post-secular
culture which a number of thinkers see emerging, though more
slowly here in Europe than elsewhere. This 'post-secularism'
has a positive attitude to religious belief and believers, 'rescuing
the importance of religion from both fundamentalist assertion
and liberal erasure'.[2] Nostalgically perhaps, I look back to the
School's early days when in the private, residential setting of
Bea House a prayer service took place before lunch on class
days, and when in the Milltown Park chapel a eucharist was occasionally celebrated, notably the Methodist Covenant Service
at the end of the academic year. The School, I liked to think, was
a family and the family was a domestic church and families had
a certain right to privacy. Such a simple spirituality, or at least
these particular expressions of it, had of course no real future
then: they could not hope to survive the various winds of

2. *Post-secular Philosophy*, ed Phillip Blond, Routledge, London and New
York 1998, p i; cf Fabio Petito & Pavlos Hatzopoulos, eds, *Religion in
International Affairs: The Return from Exile*, Palgrave Macmillan New
York, 2003; Ulf Jonsson SJ, 'Religion in Sweden', *Studies* 96 (September
2007) pp 193-202.

change, favourable and unfavourable, which were already blowing and which have since changed the world and the church; in the emerging post-secular society, however, the spiritual and ecumenical imaginations will surely suggest the religious forms and expressions which are appropriate in the new, more open climate.

And is a new, alternative ecumenical vision not already emerging? Or at least an alternative expression of the older? Years ago, in 1965, I was invited to be a member of a BBC television panel to discuss a book entitled: *Rome: Opponent or Partner?* It was a memorable experience[3] and in the years since, specially as inter-religious dialogue has begun to join inter-church dialogue in the ecumenical movement, the terms 'opponent' and 'partner' have become ever more meaningful for me. While retaining some form of organic union as ideal and aspiration, an ecumenical vision, it now seems to me, must mean being able here and now to see other churches and other religions no longer as opponents but as partners at all levels in the cause of promoting unity and peace everywhere; and these partnerships can surely differ in shape and scope depending on the parties involved and their circumstances. Such a vision depends, of course, on a concern about disunity and conflict, both political and religious, in the church of all the followers of Christ, in the church of all God's people and in the world at large. The Irish School of Ecumenics was born of such a concern. With its positive attitude to religion, the emerging post-secular society can only appreciate and value such a concern and give a fresh fillip to the School's whole life and work; which in turn can only help to facilitate and accelerate the emergence of a post-secular culture where it has so far been slow to develop.

It remains to say thanks: first and foremost to Linda Hogan, Head of School and those who preceded her as Heads in fact if

---

3. As a result the redoubtable, then anti-ecumenical, Presbyterian minister, Donald Gillies, a fellow panellist, and myself became friends eventually; cf my *Healing and Hope* (Columba Press, Dublin 2003), pp 62-3.

not in name and status, for agreeing to collaborate on this project and giving it priority despite other commitments; to Sláine Ó Hógáin, ISE Librarian, and Anne O'Carroll, Library Assistant at Milltown Park for their kind helpfulness, in the wonderful tradition of librarians everywhere; to Aideen Woods, ISE Administrator for being so ready in answering queries and assembling and identifying photos; to Eileen Ellis, Jesuit Community Administrator at Milltown Park for also being so ready in answering requests for help, specially with regard to computer problems; to our Rector, Caoimhín Ó Ruairc, and the whole Milltown Park Jesuit community – this year I celebrate my Golden Jubilee as a member – and to my Jesuit friends everywhere for their encouragement and patience, in particular to Bill Callanan, David Gaffney, Ray Moloney and Joe Palmisano, doctoral student at ISE, for help in proof reading; to Ann Lane and the Reception staff at Milltown Park for being so supportive, so consistently; and to Professor David F. Ford for his substantial, challenging Foreword. He follows in the footsteps of the Hanson brothers, the twins Anthony and Richard, the Church of Ireland members, TCD graduates and English academics who were so outstandingly helpful to ISE in its early years. David Ford also grew up in the Church of Ireland and graduated from TCD and is now an English academic: Regius Professor of Divinity at the University of Cambridge. The Foreword which he has generously contributed to this book is a welcome encouragement to ISE as it approaches its forties, a decade which can be difficult for institutions as well as individuals. And finally my sincere thanks and the thanks of all of us to Seán O Boyle and his excellent staff at Columba Press for undertaking to publish this volume and doing so with their now well-established expertise.

Foreword

David F. Ford

David F. Ford is a native of Dublin who was educated at The High School and thereafter read Classics at Trinity College. He then studied Theology at St John's College, Cambridge, first at undergraduate level and then as a doctoral student, in the course of which he conducted intensive periods of research in Yale and Tübingen. In 1976 he joined the staff of the University of Birmingham, receiving his PhD from Cambridge in the following year. Since 1991 he has been Regius Professor of Divinity at the University of Cambridge. As such he is *inter alia* founding Director of the Cambridge Inter-Faith Programme (Judaism, Christianity and Islam). In 2005 he co-edited the volume *Fields of Faith – Theology and Religious Studies for the Twenty-First Century,* and he has also co-edited with Marc Caball a study of the Irish poet Micheal Ó Siadhail, entitled *Musics of Belonging* (2006). The latest of his many publications include *Christian Wisdom: Desiring God and Learning in Love* (2007) and *Shaping Theology: Engagements in a Religious and Secular World* (2007).

This book is not just a fascinating account of the Irish School of Ecumenics, one of the most imaginative and important academic and institutional developments in Ireland in the past half century. It has the added value that it is written by those who carried the responsibility for conceiving and leading the School since before its foundation in 1970. It is not, therefore, a critical history written by a scholar who has consulted archives, interviewed the main players and set it carefully in historical context – that still remains to be done and would be a worthwhile task for a doctoral dissertation. For those of us in the business of trying to shape institutions which attempt both to be academically excellent and also engage effectively in the public sphere, the book Michael Hurley and his fellow Directors have produced is even more valuable. It gives us the chance to see from the inside how others have approached the daunting task of bringing a new institution to birth and of leading it through various stages of development. The more I have myself got involved in such matters, the more I admire and need to learn from those who exercise one of the most important but generally neglected gifts in our world: *institutional creativity in the service of the long term flourishing of societies.* That is what increasingly impressed me as I read through these chapters.

At the heart of it, as so often, is the vision of one person, Michael Hurley. But, as Linda Hogan, his current successor, writes: 'It is becoming increasingly manifest that the original vision of the founder has the capacity to become exponentially greater and will enable ISE to respond with vigour to the increasingly complex issues of today.' That is the long term test of a vision, and Michael Hurley's passes it with flying colours. He was ahead of his time in how he brought ecumenism among churches together with inter-faith dialogue and dedication to religious, political and cultural reconciliation across some of the deepest differences in our world.

It was only at the beginning of the twenty-first century that most of the world (or rather, those people whose outlook had been formed by some of the dominant ideologies and world-

FOREWORD
17

views of the twentieth century – capitalist, 'secularist scientis-
tic', communist and fascist) woke up to the fact that the four to
five billion or so of the world's population who are directly involved with the major religions are vital to shaping the future.
The twentieth century was mostly, at least as viewed by the
Western-educated elites and the media they influenced, quite a
secularised time. Michael Hurley's daring alliance of faith with
intellect and institutional creativity challenged the religious and
the non-religious to take seriously the role of religion in the contemporary world. It is striking that some of the key players in
the story, especially within Trinity College, are not themselves
religious but have yet worked hard to establish ISE on a sound
footing.

I see such alliances as vital to a peaceful future in all the
major spheres of life. We can no longer claim to live in a secular
world, but nor is it simply religious; rather, it is complexly religious and secular at the same time, with no necessary conflict
between the two on many matters, many sophisticated inter-
plays of both, and no single global direction of 'progress' –
whether towards being 'more secular' or 'more religious'. Big issues often require understanding, negotiation and collaboration
across both religious and secular divides. ISE has pioneered this
in relation to both Irish and international issues and, as Linda
Hogan's look ahead suggests, it is now well placed to serve the
needs not just of Ireland but also of other parts of the world in
the coming century. Already it has generated a great deal of intellectual and practical energy in the service of reconciliation,
and its alumni are working out its ideals around the world.

I have been encouraged to write a foreword that engages
with some of the key topics of the book, and I will do so with
two questions in mind. First, what are the lessons from its past
and from elsewhere for ISE as it enters its next phase in line with
the direction in which Linda Hogan is leading it? Second, what
are the lessons that the rest of us who are involved in analogous
enterprises might learn? I will discuss first the foundational
vision, then the shaping of an appropriate institution, and will

finally issue my own challenges based on my Christian and inter-faith experience.

The Vision of Ecumenics

The most obviously distinctive thing about ISE is its concept of 'ecumenics' that combines the inter-church, the inter-faith and the tasks of reconciliation and peacemaking in the whole of society. Even within ISE there is, as the debate about the naming of Linda Hogan's post made clear, an ongoing debate about the adequacy of the term 'ecumenics'. Can it make the transition from intra-Christian relations to the wider meaning? Since the term in origin refers to the whole inhabited world, there is no philological reason to limit it to Christians, and I would be with those who want to stick by it and explain its scope whenever possible. Ecumenics in the ISE sense goes well with ecology as two matching core concerns for our century.

There are lessons to be learned from this match. When the scientific world began to realise that its specialties could not cope adequately with the interconnectedness of the elements of the natural world and the further interconnectedness of the natural and human worlds, the response was a new range of inter-related disciplines that considered the environment in systemic terms. Developing these was, and continues to be, a massive intellectual challenge. A fundamental question for ecumenics is whether the measure of the intellectual challenge has been taken. There are of course many integrative discourses, especially in the social sciences. But what about theology? For Christians the deep connections need continually to be thought and rethought in terms of God and the purposes of God, in terms of the ways in which God is the ultimate interconnector. Now that religion is returning to the public sphere it cannot have a private theology that is not exposed to the rigours of intellectual standards across other disciplines. This does not mean that other fields dictate what may be concluded in theology but it does call theologians to be at least as intelligent, knowledgeable and constructively and critically interactive as others.

One of my main concerns for theology is whether it is up to this task. It needs to be thoroughly engaged with the best past and present thinking. This has implications for its institutional location: the integration of ISE into Trinity College Dublin, for all its problems, is obviously the right move, and will be discussed further below. It also has implications for the collaborations and networks in which ISE participates: the temptation is likely to be to relate mostly to those who are concerned with wider educational dissemination and with practical activities rather than to those who can offer greater intellectual intensity.

Yet it is not just an intellectual challenge. The integration of the intellectual with the imaginative and the practical has been an ongoing concern of ISE and part of its attraction to so many students over the years. This is also, I suspect, part of its appeal to TCD, since universities are rightly increasingly concerned about their contribution to society. I see this wider challenge as being to find a contemporary wisdom. Within Christian theology, wisdom has generally been seen as present not only within but also beyond the church, and other religions have analogous positions. Within the contemporary university, wisdom is often neglected in favour of knowledge, skills and know-how, but the pressure to take seriously the responsibilities accompanying the power of knowledge and its applications has helped to bring it back onto the agenda under various guises – often concerned with values, ethics, leadership and professional formation. The ISE vision could be seen as an appeal for 'joined-up wisdom' relating to churches, religions and society. As such it might benefit from being more self-conscious about itself as a wisdom-seeking institution.

Elements of Institutional Creativity
As Director of the Cambridge Inter-Faith Programme, which is still in its infancy and has also had the advantage of being part of the University of Cambridge since its inception in 2002, I read with a feeling of some awe the story of the founding of a completely independent institution and the complexities of integrating

it into a university. So much of the thought and work needed to build an institution is hidden; there is something heroic in the long term dedication of time and energy required to overcome the obstacles to the success of any new institution, especially one that challenges accepted ways of perceiving and acting. Three elements of this story stood out for me in particular: funding; the nature of the contemporary university; and the importance of theology and religious studies within universities.

Funding has obviously been the nightmare of each director. The dilemma is common: on the one hand, a wonderful vision, a superb team of teachers, administrators and other supporters, successful outreach activities with demands for many more, eager students from many countries; but, on the other hand, constant funding problems, sometimes to the point of threatened bankruptcy. There is a massive frustration in knowing one can do something pioneering and worthwhile on many levels and fronts but then having to devote a totally disproportionate amount of time and energy (including emotional energy handling anxiety in oneself and others, creditors, potential benefactors, and endless oral and written presentations to funding bodies) on raising money or saving money by painful cuts.

The good news in this story is that somehow ISE has survived. I savoured the moving expressions of gratitude to the people and groups who have made the donations, handled the finances and fundraising, been advocates in many quarters and remained loyal through continuing difficulties. There is nothing quite like a long term institutional project for sorting out who really does share a vision and is willing to put their money and other gifts where their mouth is. I salute those mentioned with honour in these pages.

But the other side is that the financial problems continue. One way of looking at this is: of course they do, and it is appropriate that ISE share in the precariousness that most of the rest of the world experiences. Yet there are degrees of precariousness, and for an institution to flourish it needs some stability and protection from constant financial uncertainty. The obvious way to ensure such stability is for ISE to have the right long term settlement within Trinity College Dublin (on which more below) and also (whether through TCD or, for many of the outreach activities of ISE, directly from governments, churches, foundations and individuals) short term and medium term support from other sources. There is no single answer to the funding problem. But there is a best solution: *endowment*. It is no accident that the world's top universities are well-endowed and not dependent primarily on short-term funding decisions by politicians and others. The more endowment there is, with secure income for essential expenditure, the better ISE will be able to fulfil its mission – and the better it will be able to gather funding from other sources. Clearly ISE has recognised this, and now that it is integrated within TCD there may be a new possibility to gather endowment. This will partly (perhaps even largely) depend on the level of support for ISE from within TCD. It is to this second element, that of the university, that I now turn.

On the current global situation of universities – by which I mean the sort of world class research university that TCD is – and the ways they relate to the religions (a topic on which I have found myself increasingly exercised in recent years, in print[1] as well as in practice), my broad position is as follows. Universities like TCD are faced with huge challenges, of which the main six are:

- Can it marry research with teaching across a wide range of disciplines?
- Can it offer an all-round education that forms students in ways that go beyond information, knowledge and know-how?
- Can it cultivate forms of collegiality that enable conversations and collaborations across specialties, generations and practical concerns?
- Can it contribute broadly to the common good of society,

---

1. Most recently in *Christian Wisdom: Desiring God and Learning in Love* (Cambridge University Press: Cambridge 2007) and *Shaping Theology: Engagements in a Religious and Secular World* (Blackwell: Oxford 2007).

both national and international?

- Can it be well-endowed and well-governed, accountable to many stakeholders but also with appropriate independence?
- Can it be appropriately interdisciplinary in its academic life, its contributions to society, and its discussions about its own purposes and policies?

In facing such challenges, the points made above about the simultaneously secular and religious character of our world and the need for the sort of 'joined-up wisdom' that ISE represents are relevant. If universities are to respond adequately to the twenty-first century world they need to become (or at least some of the best need to become – there is always going to be a plurality of types of university) multi-faith and secular universities in which the search for wisdom goes on across disciplines, professions, spheres of society, ethical and religious traditions and generations. The demands on universities are rightly growing: there are almost no other institutions in our world where there is any possibility of engaging with the sorts of issues and tasks that universities (at their best) can tackle. But there are also massive pressures that militate against facing those six challenges in a coherent way. ISE (at its best) is concerned with each of the six, and, while it is only one way of approaching them, it has great potential if TCD recognises the gift it has been given.

I have not tried to find out independently how the internal politics of TCD has been moving in this matter, but it does seem as if people at all levels of the university have responded positively to the ISE vision. Some chapters revealed problems in the area of religions and theology. This is entirely predictable, since ISE represents something that is bound to appear problematic to many in a field dominated by specialties and academic guilds. Nor are the problems unreal or insignificant; but one cannot help feeling that the chance to work them through is likely to be a great benefit in the long term. The sort of academic environment that might result from a genuine marriage of ISE with a strong School of Religions and Theology could be the envy of other places. Most major universities have not begun to realise the significance of the religions and associated issues and the need for high quality interdisciplinary academic engagement with them. TCD is being offered the chance to be a world leader in this. Also part of the offer is the chance to have national and international outreach of a sort which other universities will also want to emulate and with which they will want to collaborate. If ISE does the right quality work and TCD gives the right level of support, then the future is bright. And, as already suggested, the whole development would be greatly assisted and rendered irreversible if there were major endowment. Surely a wealthier Ireland can find some surplus to realise such a powerful vision?

My third point about the field of theology and religious studies follows on from this. This field is the scene of considerable controversy and conflict within and beyond schools and universities around the world. Just focusing on universities, it is clear that most do not take the study of religions very seriously. (I remember a conversation with the Vice-Chancellor of one of the newer British universities that had a secular ethos and no department of religion, in which I asked him where on his campus what are arguably the two most influential books in the world, the Bible and the Qur'an, could be studied. His reply was that he thought the Bible figured in English and Medieval Studies.) Where they do take the field seriously, the main form is 'religious studies', in the sense of the study of various aspects of the religions through a range of academic disciplines.

This is fine as far as it goes, but the main problem is that the neutral, objectivist ethos often rules out pursuing questions of truth and goodness to the point of arriving at any conclusions or practical implications. It is as if in the area of economics and business a university were to rule out academics being at all involved with governments or businesses as they try to work out how to run the economy and make money (or, even more extreme, were to insist that an economist who uses money and takes part in economic activity is no longer 'objective'!). University involvement with the religions seems to me to be similarly handicapped and arbitrarily restricted if it excludes contributions from academics of various faith commitments and none, and if it does not encompass critical and constructive relations with a wide range of religious and non-religious bodies.

Among the world's universities who do attempt to do this, there are three main approaches. One (mainly seen in the United States and in Islamic countries, but increasingly elsewhere too) is for a university itself to be confessionally tied to a religion. Another is for a confessional or ecumenical 'divinity school' to be part of a largely secular university (as, for example, in Harvard and Yale). The third is what TCD has: theology and religious studies fully integrated into a university that is secular in the sense of not being confessionally committed, but not secular in the other sense of excluding religion in various forms. This enables ongoing negotiation about the internal and external involvements of a department and does not rule out following through on questions of truth and practice. It is a way of institutionalising the subject that has evolved piecemeal in British and Irish universities during the past century and a half. I see it as an extremely valuable development and one that deserves to come into its own in our religious and secular world. Yet it is still very much a minority approach and is also in need of further development in institutionally creative ways. The integration of ISE with TCD seems to me to be an opportunity for such a creative development, and one that could be a model for many other universities.

Lessons and Challenges

What might be some of the lessons of this book? For ISE I think there must be great encouragement to continue to develop and realise the founding vision. The basic lesson, which one hopes might be learned by some who are willing to take up the institutional, academic, practical and spiritual burdens so ably carried by the authors and others mentioned in this book, is that an enterprise like this is not only massively demanding but also hugely worthwhile. If I were choosing just one further lesson it would be: seek endowment even more energetically.

The same lessons might be learnt by others who are attempting analogous things elsewhere. My own efforts with the Cambridge Inter-Faith Programme have been continually illuminated and informed as I read this story of ISE. There has been comfort in recognising familiar hopes, joys, trials, conflicts and multiple overwhelmings. The conviction that pioneering work combining many disciplines, churches, religions and problematic situations is not only possible but imperative for the future of our world has been reinforced.

I would also in conclusion issue three challenges to ISE as it faces the rest of this century in its new institutional location.

The first is to take the university seriously as one of the main institutions through which society can transcend itself. This should complement the core ISE concerns with churches, other religious communities and societies as a whole. The university is in fact a space where all those others come together, and it is also part of a global network that is vital to the world's future. Taking the university seriously means being willing to take responsibility within it, to think on its behalf, to challenge it when necessary, and to help it become more of a wisdom-seeking institution. But above all it means building up its collegiality, especially through intensive disciplined conversations and collaborations across disciplines and across generations. If ISE were to take all that on as a core responsibility, there would be not only a good outlook for it and for TCD but also for its other commitments.

The second is not to neglect or short-change the ISE intra-Christian ecumenical commitment – a further reason for keeping the term 'ecumenics'. The temptation in a university context, and also in relation to a world where the main urgencies appear to be reconciliation and peace-making in the inter-faith and various societal contexts, is to see the divisions among Christians as less important. I think it is not so much a matter of importance ratings as of the interrelation of them all, as in the core vision of ISE. One key thing I have learnt from inter-faith engagement is that, beyond the initial phase with its difficulties, novelties and excitements, it only goes really well if going deeper into the faith of others is accompanied by simultaneously going deeper into one's own faith and responding more passionately to the cries of the world. Ecumenism among Christians should be about us who are Christian being filled with the Spirit and being attracted deeper into God and God's purposes.

The third is to read and re-read scriptures, both the Christian Bible and others. The most helpful practice that I have discovered in both intra-Christian and inter-faith relations is that called Scriptural Reasoning.[2] This is simply Jews, Christians and Muslims gathering to study and discuss their scriptures together.[3] It may be that the succession of directors writing in this book took the scriptures for granted as part of what ISE is about and so neglected to pay them much attention; but I did find myself thinking that these texts, so vital to the core identities of the various communities, deserve more explicit attention. This may be all the more important in a university context where many powerful discourses bid for attention and dominance. There is something about studying intensively the long, complex traditions of interpreting and reinterpreting scriptures and tracing their ramifications into worship, theology, philosophy, ethics, literature, art, architecture, scholarship and ordinary living that, negatively, helps to resist takeovers by less God-centred and less multilayered discourses, and, positively, helps to inspire and nourish a faith that can be both intelligent and interrogative, innovative and wise.

---

2. See *Christian Wisdom op. cit.* Chapter 8.
3. This obviously invites extension to other traditions, and this has been attempted with Hindu and Buddhist scriptures.

CHAPTER ONE

The Beginnings[1]
(1960-1970)

Michael Hurley

The Irish School of Ecumenics (ISE), formally inaugurated on 9 November 1970, can, in a true sense, be said to have begun ten years earlier, on 9 March 1960. That was the date of a public lecture on 'The Ecumenical Movement' which I gave at Milltown Park, in Dublin. The lecture was one of seven given in the first session of a new initiative which was to continue very successfully twice a year in spring and winter throughout the 1960s and on into the early 1980s. As secretary of the original organising committee, I had proposed Christian unity as a topic, presuming that an acknowledged expert, Roman Catholic of course, could be found somewhere in the country to be our speaker. We failed, however, to find one, so on the basis of the very limited knowledge I had acquired during my own theological studies in Louvain, and afterwards doing doctoral work in Rome, I made the subject up from books and periodicals and duly delivered the lecture myself.

The 1960s: A Decade of Preparation

That lecture of 9 March appeared the following January as a pamphlet entitled *Towards Christian Unity* and proved to be the beginning for me of an ecumenical apostolate or ministry which continued to grow and develop all through the rest of the decade. Nothing of all this, however, was foreseen, much less planned. It happened because the winds of change had begun to blow in the church as well as the world. In particular, Vatican II, with all its perceived ecumenical possibilities, some very real,

1. This is a revised, abbreviated version of Chapter 16 in my *Christian Unity: An Ecumenical Second Spring?*, Veritas, Dublin 1998, pp 265-291

some quite exaggerated, captured the general imagination and created a brisk demand for talks and articles as well as for discussions on radio and what was then the new medium of television. It was a learning much more than a teaching experience and altogether too interesting, too fascinating for me to hold back and not get involved, insofar as my teaching commitments allowed. It led directly, it now seems clear, to the inauguration of ISE in 1970.

After the lecture and its publication, invitations multiplied. So in January of 1962 I made my first appearance on Irish television: a talk to camera about Unity Week. In May of that year I gave a lecture to the Trinity College branch of the Student Christian Movement, but to satisfy the existing regulations of the Catholic archdiocese, the session had to be held outside College in a hotel. The following August I attended the Central Committee meeting of the World Council of Churches in Paris, not of course as an official observer or visitor but only as an accredited journalist for *The Irish Press*. And in October that same year, on the very weekend Vatican II opened, I was in Belfast lecturing in the Church of Ireland chaplaincy of The Queen's University and preaching at the Catholic chaplaincy Sunday morning Mass in Aquinas Hall, run by the Dominican Sisters until 1994. In his Lenten pastoral the previous year, Bishop Mageean of Down and Connor had mentioned my pamphlet, adding 'I cordially commend it to you to read and study.' It was my first ever visit to Northern Ireland and I was made to feel very welcome; it was a foretaste of my later happy years in the Columbanus Community of Reconciliation (CCR) in Belfast, from 1983 to 1993.

During the following years of the 1960s this ecumenical apostolate intensified and expanded. It brought me all around the Dublin Catholic archdiocese, lecturing under the auspices of its then very active Adult Education Committee. It brought me all around the country. In 1964, for example, it took me to Kenmare to address the West Cork Clerical Society of the Church of Ireland, to Cork to address a public meeting organised by

Tuairim (a lay organisation with a lively interest in religion which has since become defunct), to Belfast to address the Newman Society at Queen's University and to the Benedictine Abbey in Glenstal, County Limerick for an ecumenical conference which I had helped to organise and which remains an annual event every summer. In 1965 it took me to Newry to address the Catholic clergy of the Dromore diocese; and in 1966 to Downpatrick to address a meeting of the Downe Society and to Drogheda for the first ecumenical conference at the Presentation Convent school in Greenhills. This Greenhills initiative, which I also helped to organise, was suggested by the editor of *The Furrow*, The Reverend J. G. McGarry, and designed to complement Glenstal by taking place in a northern location and in the winter, during Unity Week. It, too, continues as an annual event.

Ecumenism in the 1960s also brought me outside the country to attend meetings: of the World Alliance of Reformed Churches in Frankfurt in 1964 (as a journalist still); of the World Methodist Council in London in 1966 (as an 'Accredited Visitor') and of the World Methodist Council-Roman Catholic Church International Commission of which I was appointed a member in 1968 and which met in various places around the world in the following years. Ecumenism in this decade also took me abroad to give short courses of lectures: in Ottawa in 1967 at St Paul University, in Glasgow in 1968 for the Catholic clergy of the archdiocese, in New Orleans in 1969 at the Notre Dame Seminary and also in Rome at the Gregorian University.

All this ecumenical activity was steadily, but as yet quite unknown to me, preparing the way for the foundation of ISE in 1970: it was providing the necessary experience and contacts. The courses of lectures which I gave not only abroad but also here at home at St Patrick's College, Maynooth, and elsewhere offered a welcome opportunity to reflect on the experience, to think it all through. The slim volume entitled *Theology of Ecumenism*, which was published by the Mercier Press Cork in 1969, shows how I was attempting to analyse and understand the new horizons which were opening up for me. It may have been and was indeed exciting work but it was also disturbing. It created tensions with church authorities, both Catholic and Protestant. Archbishop McQuaid expressed doubts to my superiors about the desirability of my continuing to work in the archdiocese of Dublin. The Principal of Assembly's (Presbyterian) College, Belfast , Professor J. L. M. Haire, was severely criticised for inviting me to lecture his theology students on 'The Catholic Doctrine of Baptism' in February 1968. A motion censuring the college authorities was proposed and debated at the June General Assembly in Church House, with Dr Ian Paisley and his followers protesting angrily outside. Happily the motion was defeated but unhappily the opponents of ecumenism within the Presbyterian Church in Ireland, so far from declining, went on growing in number during the following years.

Irish Anglicanism 1869-1969
The 1960s came to a climax for me on 15 April 1970 with the publication that year (by Allen Figgis, Dublin) of *Irish Anglicanism 1869-1969*, a volume of essays which I had edited for the centenary of the disestablishment of the Church of Ireland and which was launched and presented to the Primate, Archbishop Simms, during an interdenominational service, televised live by RTÉ, in the chapel of Gonzaga College, Dublin. It was in the course of this project, which had begun in the summer of 1968, that the ideas which later took shape as ISE and CCR (Columbanus Community of Reconciliation) first emerged and crystallised in my mind. And it was the successful completion of the project and the widespread appreciation it evoked at a critical moment in Irish history, in North-South relations in particular, which gave me the credibility required to attempt their realisation. But whereas it was to be years, thirteen in fact, before CCR became a reality in 1983, only six weeks were to pass before the opening of ISE was announced at a press conference in Dublin on 28 May 1970 and only six months before it came into operation in October and was formally inaugurated on 9 November. Indeed, the launching of *Irish Anglicanism* in April and the launching of

ISE in November were so closely linked (and not only in time) that they became confused. The compiler of 'Some Notable Events in the Catholic Life of Ireland in 1970' for the 1971 *Irish Catholic Directory* conflated the two. There is no entry for 9 November but that for 15 April reads misleadingly as follows:

> An Ecumenical Service was held in Gonzaga College, Dublin, today to launch the new school of Ecumenics ...
>
> A specially bound volume of essays, edited by Father Hurley, commemorating the disestablishment of the Church of Ireland was presented to the Church of Ireland Archbishop of Armagh, Most Reverend Dr Simms.

1969/70 proved to be a very full, very busy academic year. As soon as the typescript of *Irish Anglicanism* was in the hands of the publisher in early September 1969, my first move with regard to what was eventually to become ISE was to share the idea with my Jesuit superiors and try to persuade them to support it, to own it. It could have no future, I knew, certainly no long-term future, as a mere personal initiative of my own. Providentially, my Provincial then (1968-75) was Cecil McGarry. He was not only a former Rector and former student of mine at Milltown Park but also a former lecturer in ecclesiology who, for his doctorate in Rome, had made a special study of modern Anglican ecclesiology, and read a paper on the subject at the 1965 Glenstal Ecumenical Conference. Significantly, too, at this very time he was preparing a special Province Delegate Meeting to take place in early January 1970 to discuss the future of Irish Jesuit ministry and was inviting submissions. A letter of his to me dated 4 November shows that I had already made such a submission about ISE (no copy, however, survives), but in his view not in sufficient detail: 'I would fear for the ideas [he wrote] unless they are developed: they may be taken to be impractical hopes or dreams, whereas they could be made attractive needs.'

Ecumenics: What and Why?
For most of that first term I had teaching commitments outside

the country and this letter reached me at the Gregorian University in Rome. The result was the paper 'Ecumenics: What and Why?' which attempted to meet the Provincial's request for more detail and which I finished on 7 December 1969. The first part of the paper outlined in some detail a two-year programme for those who had already completed their basic theological studies. With some modifications this was the programme followed in the early years of ISE.

My answer to the question 'Why?' in this paper provides an echo of the debate which had begun in the mid-1960s as to whether ecumenism in religious and theological education should be a dimension or a discipline: a dimension of all disciplines or a special discipline by itself. In June of the following year, 1970, the Vatican Secretariat for Promoting Christian Unity published its views on the question in Part II of its *Directory* and declared that 'Even though all theological training has an ecumenical aspect, courses on ecumenism are not therefore superfluous.' It was not until 1993 that the Vatican made such courses obligatory instead of optional for BD students. My view in 1969, as a result of my experience during the previous years, was that the special discipline was necessary for the sake of the dimension and that an institute such as ISE was necessary for the sake of both. It would meet 'the present need for ecumenically competent personnel'; it would educate and train those who would teach the discipline and who by so doing would help to create the dimension. Like the Johann-Adam-Moehler-Institut für Ökumenik at Paderborn and the Institute for Ecumenical Research at Strasbourg, ISE would be 'a centre of research which houses a community of scholars' but, unlike them, it was to have its own systematic teaching programme and would not merely sponsor occasional seminars or simply engage in service teaching for other institutes.

This paper was subsequently published in the following July number of *The Furrow*. More significantly, however, at least in the immediate instance, it arrived in good time for the Irish Jesuit Delegate meeting held at Manresa House, Dublin, from 5-

7 January 1970 and was approved by this meeting as 'very reasonable':

> It involves only one man [manpower was a crucial criterion of
> the delegates], who has had the freedom to establish himself as
> a worldwide expert in this field, recognised formally by the
> Bishops [at the previous October meeting of the Irish Bishops I
> had been appointed a member of their Advisory Committee
> on Ecumenism], with the contacts among all the Christian de-
> nominations which offer the opportunity of financial and staff
> support, and may make an Institute possible.

Financial and Church Support

This approval was not only 'very reasonable' but very generous because the paper, although addressing fairly thoroughly the questions 'What?' and 'Why?' and in an appendix the question 'Who
[will teach]?', failed to address the question 'How?', i.e. the crucial
problems of structure and finance and recruitment of students.
These, along with the immediate preparations for the launch of
Irish Anglicanism on 15 April, came to absorb my attention from the
New Year on. During these months of 1970 I sometimes referred to
ISE as 'in process of formation' – a phrase borrowed, of course,
from the history of the World Council of Churches.

Strange as it may seem to those who know something of the
subsequent history of ISE, finance was the least of our problems
in the beginning: the Irish Flour Millers' Association (IFMA)
seemed happy to be our benefactors. Their energetic Public
Relations Officer, Dan Mullane, had taken a professional interest in both ecumenical projects (*Irish Anglicanism* and ISE). He
saw them as having 'considerable national importance' and succeeded in persuading Peter Desmond Odlum to give them not
only his own support but that also of the Association in which
the Odlum Group of companies played a prominent part. At Mr
Mullane's suggestion I wrote formally to Peter Desmond
Odlum about the two projects on 1 October 1969 and, on my
return to Ireland, had an encouraging meeting with him in his
office on the afternoon of 28 January 1970.

Feeling assured of financial support, my next priority was to meet with the Provincial's solicitor and on an informal, unofficial basis with members of the other churches to inform them about the proposed initiative and to seek their advice, support and patronage. Scribbles in my diary remind me that I discussed it with the Archdeacon of Dublin, The Venerable Raymond Jenkins, a close Church of Ireland friend, on 20 January on the occasion of a meeting to launch an appeal for the rebuilding of Damer Court which took place at the Four Courts Hotel in Dublin; with the Principal of Edgehill (the Methodist Theological) College, Belfast, Rev Richard Greenwood, on 23 February; with the Secretary of the Dublin Council of Churches, Rev R. W. J. MacDermott, on 24 February and with the Secretary of the Irish Council of Churches, Rev W. J. Arlow, on 13 May. There will, of course, have been other meetings, but contact with the Roman Catholic authorities and in particular with Archbishop McQuaid was reserved to the Provincial. Without the permission or at least the acquiescence of the Catholic archbishop in whose jurisdiction the School was to be based it would have been impossible for the Provincial to go ahead with ISE.

Archbishop McQuaid had already acquiesced in the arrangements for an ecumenical service on 15 April on the occasion of the launch of *Irish Anglicanism*. Would he acquiesce again? On the margins of a meeting of provincials and bishops on 23 April Father McGarry raised the question with him and wrote to me as follows from Limerick the day after:

We finished so late that I only saw the A. B. [Archbishop] for a moment. He is not at the moment sympathetic to things ecumenical. He does not want you to read a lesson at St Patrick's [Dublin, on 12 May, at the special service for the centenary of Disestablishment]; of course there is no problem about presence. Seeing the way things were and the lateness of the hour, I just said to him that I would be coming to see him on my return to Dublin about the School of Ecumenics, 'when he would, I hoped, be feeling more ecumenically benign'. I don't know what will happen, but it is too important to prejudice in any way while there is any hope of acquiescence on his part. Keep smiling, hoping and praying.

Eventually the attitude of the Archbishop became less negative and more sympathetic. Just a month later, on 22 May, the Provincial felt able to write to the President of the Episcopal Conference, Cardinal Conway, and to the Secretary of the Episcopal Commission on Ecumenism, Bishop Ahern of Cloyne, informing them about 'the proposed opening of a small school of ecumenical studies in Dublin'. In his letter to the Secretary he added: 'Approval of the School and its commendation by your Episcopal Commission would be something I would greatly appreciate.' A week later, on 28 May 1970, a press conference organised largely by Dan Mullane was held in a Dublin hotel.

Public announcement

The press statement issued for this conference puts the proposed school in the context of the frustration which even then was becoming increasingly widespread in ecumenical circles:

> Ireland is not alone today in having an acute ecumenical problem. All over the world there is a growing suspicion if not conviction that ecumenism has reached a dead-end. The scandal of disunity has become the scandal of ecumenism.
>
> Education in ecumenism has unfortunately not kept pace with progress in ecumenism. Ecumenics is the subject which teaches ecumenism but ecumenics scarcely exists in religious education or theology programmes at any level in any country. If there are no teachers of ecumenics the reason is that there are no Schools of Ecumenics. The Irish School of Ecumenics proposes, among other things, to fill this gap and so to help to remedy, at its real source, the present worldwide ecumenical malaise.

The press statement went on to make quite clear what 'Ecumenics: What and Why?' had left unclear: ISE would be an independent, unofficial, interdenominational institute, 'confident that its courses will be immediately recognised by other theological institutions as fulfilling certain requirements for degrees conferred by them.' It would not be associated with the Milltown Institute, a possibility originally envisaged but which would have placed it under Roman Catholic auspices. As an interdenominational initiative ISE would be unlike the ecumenical institute at Paderborn which is under the auspices of the Roman Catholic archdiocese and unlike the ecumenical institute at Strasbourg which is under the auspices of the Lutheran World Federation. It would be more like the World Council of Churches' institute at Bossey near Geneva, except that Bossey is official and non-Roman Catholic and less systematic in its whole approach. It would also be more like the Tantur Ecumenical Institute for Theological Studies in Jerusalem which, when it opened the following year, would be governed by an ecumenical board – its members serving only in a personal capacity – but remain Vatican property.

The Irish School of Ecumenics, it was stated, is not an official institution of the Irish churches but its authentic interdenominational ecumenical character is guaranteed by its five patrons and by its teaching staff as well as by its students who in principle will be half Roman Catholic, half non-Roman Catholic.

The five patrons were named in alphabetical order: Bishop John W. Armstrong (Church of Ireland), Reverend Professor John M. Barkley (Presbyterian), Reverend Cecil McGarry SJ (Roman Catholic), Reverend Robert A. Nelson (Methodist) and Mr Peter Desmond Odlum. The latter was not denominationally or otherwise identified in the press statement which had been typed in the offices of the IFMA. Although a member of the Church of Ireland and of Quaker background, it was not on behalf of either of these connections but rather on behalf of the IFMA that he saw himself acting as ISE patron. When, through unforeseen circumstances, he found himself unable to be present at the press conference he arranged for his place to be taken by Mr Norman Odlum, a brother and business associate. The other four patrons were all present in person. The various teachers were also named in the press release. Representing the different Christian traditions, they were very generously taking time off from their ordinary duties, academic or pastoral, to offer short courses at ISE in the areas of their competence. These courses, it was announced, would be taught in a classroom made available by the College of Industrial Relations which was very conveniently situated near Milltown Park in Dublin and was then under Jesuit auspices with Fr John Brady, a former student of mine, as Director.

The weeks following the 28 May press conference were spent making the existence of ISE more generally known and preparing for its opening and formal inauguration. A letter of mine to Peter Desmond Odlum of 10 August summarises the results of all this activity: so far, apart from one crisis, all had gone well and I had 'solid expectations for at least eight' students for the first academic year. A four-page prospectus was printed (no copy seems to have survived) and widely distributed: the July issues of *The Furrow* and *Theology* carried it as an insert. Contact was made with some of the people prominent in the theological world of Scotland, England and the USA with a view to recruiting students. In the course of a two-week visit across the water in late June, I visited Edinburgh where I met Professor Tom Torrance; Birmingham where I met Principal John Habgood of Queen's College (a joint Anglican-Methodist initiative) – he was later to be Archbishop of York – and London where I met Professor G. R. Dunstan of King's College. All were very encouraging and so, in a letter, was Dr Walter Wagoner, Director of the Boston Theological Institute (a federation of seven theological schools), who wrote of his 'enthusiasm for your Ecumenical Institute and its related programs. There is nothing quite as comprehensive and thorough – your plan differs from Bossey.'

The Rector of Milltown Park, Fr Jack Brennan, was also approached about the possibility of a site in the grounds for an ISE building. With the approval of the Jesuit Provincial such a site was allocated (that now occupied by Cherryfield Lodge), meetings were held with Andy Devane of the architectural firm, Robinson, Keefe & Devane, and with officers of the Planning

Department of Dublin Corporation, and sketch plans were drawn up not only for a permanent building but also for a temporary prefabricated structure which would be ready by the end of September. The cost of this building, approximately £16,000, and the running expenses of the School for the first year, approximately £14,000, would be underwritten by the IFMA. A formal letter to this effect was sent to the Provincial on 10 September.

The World Council of Churches
Contact was also made with the World Council of Churches (WCC) in the hope that the General Secretary, the Reverend Dr Eugene Carson Blake, would accept an invitation to give the inaugural lecture; the arrangements for this were finalised on 24 July when I passed through Geneva on my way to Rome on other business. Granted my own background, a Protestant seemed necessary to inaugurate the School in order to emphasise its inter-Church character, and nobody seemed more appropriate than the General Secretary of the leading non-Roman Catholic ecumenical body. This invitation, however, turned out to be controversial. In the mid-1970s, in the aftermath of the School's International Consultation on Mixed Marriage, it would be adduced by Roman Catholic critics, who included Archbishop Dermot Ryan of Dublin, as an argument to suggest that ISE was more Protestant than Catholic in its ecumenical sympathies and theological thinking. At the time a number of Northern Presbyterians considered the invitation inopportune, insensitive to the depth of anti-ecumenical feeling which was growing among Northern Protestants and the main target of which was the WCC. There was a suggestion that the invitation be withdrawn.

Mutual ignorance continues to characterise relations in Ireland between North and South, with the additional features of indifference in the South and antipathy in the North. It was, of course, more prevalent in 1970 than it is now, but even then many of us did know from experience something of the depth of

Protestant anti-ecumenical feeling in the North. One of the leaders of the anti-ecumenical wing of Irish Protestantism at that time was the Minister of Agnes Street Presbyterian Church in Belfast, the Reverend Donald Gillies. His *Unity in the Dark* had appeared in 1964, arguing that the ecumenical movement 'bids to become the greatest menace to the truth of the gospel since the time of the Reformation'. In late November 1965 Donald Gillies and I had appeared together on a BBC Northern Ireland television programme as members of a panel to discuss a recently published book entitled *Rome: Opponent or Partner?* During that programme Mr Gillies had not hesitated to make clear that because of my Roman Catholicism his evangelical convictions and conscience would not allow him to consider me to be a Christian. Until the end of the decade the main argument of the opponents of ecumenism and of the WCC in particular was theological: its 'Romeward trend', its unfaithfulness to 'the historic evangelical Protestant faith' which prescribed scripture alone, grace alone, faith alone. In the 1970s, however, an additional argument began to surface: the WCC was allegedly supporting terrorists in Africa and, if in Africa, perhaps also in Northern Ireland.

> Grants from the Special Fund of the WCC's 'Programme to Combat Racism' were causing misgivings in many countries. Naturally the misgiving was even greater in a country subjected to terrorism by the Provisional IRA. This greatly strengthened an opposition already growing on theological grounds.[2]

This was the situation which some Northern Presbyterians saw developing in the summer of 1970. Their church's membership of the World Council was at risk and they wanted above all to protect this. There was every reason therefore why an official such as the Moderator of General Assembly should absent himself from the General Secretary's lecture. The current Moderator

---

2. Eric Gallagher & Stanley Worrall, *Christians in Ulster, 1968-1980* (OUP,1982), p 143.

was none other than Principal J. L. M. Haire who had hosted my lecture on baptism two years previously, had taken a prominent part in the ecumenical service for the presentation of *Irish Anglicanism* on 15 April and, two months previously, had invited me as one of his special guests to his installation as Moderator. The situation now, however, was so serious that Principal Haire did decide to absent himself. It is a well-known fact that the constraints of office often oblige authorities, both civil and religious, to follow the prevailing rather than their personal views.

On the other hand, there seemed to be no compelling reason why the School should withdraw the invitation. On the contrary there seemed to be every reason for leaving it stand. Many felt that 'we cannot have another Ripon case on our conscience'. In 1967 Paisleyite threats had led the Church of Ireland authorities to cancel a lecture on Vatican II by the Church of England Bishop of Ripon. In retrospect this was seen to have been unwise: it had only served to strengthen the hands of the anti-ecumenical extremists.

So the invitation to Dr Eugene Carson Blake was not withdrawn. It led the following year to an ill-fated if not ill-advised intervention in Northern Ireland on the part of Sodepax (Joint Committee on Society, Development and Peace), itself a short-lived ecumenical experiment between the Vatican and the WCC. Otherwise the visit was highly successful. It helped that the General Secretary was himself a Presbyterian and that he was accompanied on his visit by a Northern Irish Methodist, the Reverend Wilbert Forker, who was then on the WCC staff in Geneva.

The negative repercussions of the visit affected ISE in the first instance; they were mainly financial and the financial crisis they caused was to erupt in September. Whether there were negative repercussions for the Presbyterian Church in Ireland is arguable. It did terminate its membership of the WCC in 1980 but the part played in this by the ISE invitation of 1970 was negligible and, once freed the following year from the constraints of the Moderatorial office, Principal Haire resumed his ecumenical activities. For the rest of his life he was a faithful supporter of ISE and continued to support it with the help of an endowment fund set up by his family and friends for this purpose.

Northern Ireland Conflict Analysis

Another of my concerns during that July and August of 1970 was, as I told Peter Desmond Odlum in my letter, a project due to begin in the early autumn under the joint auspices of ISE and the Centre for the Analysis of Conflict (CAC) in London. It was to be a 'controlled communication' involving representatives of the opposing traditions in Northern Ireland. This project was, in fact, carried out: a first session at least took place. Because it was an early attempt – though of a particular kind – at the cross-community exercises which have since become common in Northern Ireland, because it was the first academic exercise to take place under the auspices of ISE, because it introduced to Northern Ireland the influential Australian expert in conflict resolution, Dr John Burton, and because it anticipated in some way the place which Peace Studies has since come to acquire in ISE, this 'controlled communication' deserves some mention here. After so many years, however, it is not easy to reconstruct what happened and how it came to happen.

It was Professor G. R. Dunstan who introduced ISE and the CAC to each other. He had lectured at the School's International Consultation on Mixed Marriage and spoke of the Centre's work when he gave me lunch at King's College, London on Thursday, 2 July. He duly reported my positive reactions to his friend Tony de Reuck, an associate of the Centre, who lost no time in passing them on to the Director, Dr John Burton, at University College, London. He in turn wrote to me without further delay the following Wednesday, 8 July, offering to sponsor an initial session in London and explaining the nature of the exercise: 'a face-to-face situation presided over by a group of social and political scientists who would contribute their knowledge about the nature of conflict and help the parties to a conflict to make accurate assessments of the motivations of each other'.

CAC's interest in opportunities for research, but also an urgency deriving from the deteriorating political situation, will explain the speed of these reactions. Spurred on by this I immediately contacted Mr G. B. Newe of the Northern Ireland Council of Social Service and Mr – later Dr – Maurice Hayes of the Community Relations Commission, both of whom were encouraging and helpful. I met them in Belfast on 15 July and again on 7 August, and with the co-operation of Mr Billy Blease, Northern Ireland Officer of the Irish Congress of Trades Unions, arrangements were in place by mid-August for a group of six shop stewards to participate in a 'controlled communication', to take place in London from 13 to 19 September, all expenses to be borne by CAC. Tony de Reuck's letter to me (14 August) begins effusively:

> We owe you our delighted congratulations and warmest thanks – your proposed group for the Northern Ireland controlled communication is as good as could have been hoped for, most appropriate and acceptable.

In the event nothing went wrong; everything went smoothly. Two of the shop stewards who had participated and whom I have succeeded in identifying and meeting were quite positive in their recollections, one of them saying that it was 'a truly wonderful experience'. Also participating was Dr Maurice Hayes, who finds space for a mention of the event in his published memoirs and who, in a lengthy conversation, referred to it as 'an exciting thing and influential'. All six shop stewards, he felt, would have had Northern Ireland Labour Party links and been anti-sectarian in outlook. Though divided politically and religiously they were more united on socio-economic issues – and also 'in vilification of the referee' at a soccer match they attended together!

Dr Hayes gave me to understand that what made this 'controlled communication' particularly influential in his view, was the fact that it introduced Dr Burton to Northern Ireland. His background and his approach impressed Dr Hayes. He had

been head of the Australian Department of Foreign Affairs before becoming an academic, researching conflict in various parts
of the world, including Cyprus. And his approach as well as his
experience was impressive: it was gradualist – 'foothills before
heights':

> He had developed a model of conflict resolution that encour-
> aged people to work together on functional matters in which
> they had a common interest, until they built up enough trust
> to deal with the more divisive issues.

Further sessions of the 'controlled communication' had been
envisaged and tentative arrangements been made for a preparatory visit to Belfast by Dr Burton and Mr de Reuck sometime
between 20 September and 17 October. These further sessions
did not take place but Dr Burton and two of his assistants did become involved in Northern Ireland affairs and prepared a report
for the Community Relations Commission in 1971. An investigation and assessment of all these activities would seem to be a
worthwhile project remaining to be undertaken.

Financial Crisis

A decision by the IFMA to withdraw support from ISE because
of its links with the WCC was the financial crisis which hit the
School in September. Hard on the heels of the Association's letter of 10 September undertaking to fund ISE, which the
Provincial had acknowledged on the 11th, thanking them 'for
the munificence of their gesture', the following arrived on his
desk:

> Dear Father Provincial,
> In connection with the setting up of an Irish School of
> Ecumenics, my Committee have given this matter further
> consideration, and I am to ask that no action be taken on foot
> of the contents of our letter of even date, pending a Meeting
> on the subject between my Committee, yourself and Fr
> Hurley.

I had already the previous day received a telephone warning about this development from the Public Relations Officer and wrote to him as follows on the 10th:

> I feel it may be helpful, especially to avoid misunderstanding, to put on paper what I take to be the meaning and result of our telephone conversations yesterday. Since your Association's letter to the Provincial dated 10 September the circumstances have changed: the World Council of Churches has taken an action which your Association cannot approve of or be associated with and which in the Association's judgement, would make it impossible to obtain funds from other sources to ensure the future of the Irish School of Ecumenics. In these changed circumstances your Association could make financial assistance available only to a School of Ecumenics which concerned itself exclusively with Ireland: with the promotion of better relations between Catholics and Protestants, between North and South, in Ireland, and which – to accomplish this – did not involve any non-Irish personnel either as students or teachers. Because the Irish School of Ecumenics does at present include non-Irish students and teachers, your Association has no choice but to withdraw its letter of 10 September to the Jesuit Provincial, in order that it may be seen to have no connection whatever with the World Council of Churches.

The reference is, of course, once again to the WCC's 'Programme to Combat Racism' and its alleged support for 'terrorist' organisations. My letter went on to explain away ISE's links with the WCC and concluded: 'If, as you said, today's decision [by the IFMA Executive Committee] is bound to be negative I shall make an effort to enlist financial support from others. I must at least try.' I had just returned from a meeting of the Methodist-Roman Catholic International Commission at Lake Junaluska in the USA and was due to attend a congress in Brussels from 12 to 17 September. I cancelled my attendance at this latter, staying at home instead to write begging letters and make begging telephone calls – with some encouraging results, notably a cheque for £1,000 from the Carmelite Provincial at Whitefriars Street, Father J. Linus Ryan, O Carm. The immediate crisis was averted and, everything else being in readiness – teachers, students, a library (courtesy of Milltown Park) and a classroom (courtesy of the College of Industrial Relations) – the ecumenical feast, like the marriage feast of Cana, went on. Building plans had to be abandoned and the name of Peter Desmond Odlum had to disappear from the list of patrons, but the academic year opened as intended on 19 October. ISE's basic financial situation has, however, remained precarious ever since.

The official meeting envisaged in the second letter of 10 September from the IFMA was delayed because of the Provincial's absence from the country. When it took place on 30 November the position as conveyed to me by the Public Relations Officer remained unchanged. The following day, however, the President, Secretary and another member of the Executive called on the Provincial to present ISE with a £5,000 cheque which was to receive 'no publicity or public acknowledgement' and to express their 'extreme embarrassment' at the situation which had arisen – but also their interest in and hopes for ISE. In his letter of acknowledgement to the President the Provincial wrote:

> I would ask you to thank your Association for me, for their generosity in this matter, and to tell them that I appreciate very much the complications which arose in this very difficult situation. I regret any embarrassment which they may have felt and hope that they will be able to allow all of this to fade into the past.

In preparing this memoir on 'The Beginnings of ISE' it seemed appropriate to try to renew contact with IFMA. What I found was that the Association itself had gone out of existence in 1989 and that those most immediately involved in 1970 were either deceased or too ill to be interviewed. I did, however, have

the good fortune of a long informative meeting on 25 October
1994 with A. W. Dickson Spence (Dickie Spence), a well-known
cricketer and umpire who was on the staff of IFMA in 1970, and
who was its last Secretary. (He died suddenly in May 1996.) As a
result of this meeting and of other contacts, I have come to see
that in 1970 the flour-milling industry was already in steep decline owing to the removal of tariff restrictions and a decline in
consumption, that on economic grounds alone the generous
offer of support for ISE coming mainly from Peter Desmond
Odlum, a former President, and from the Public Relations
Officer, Mr Dan Mullane, would have been difficult to sell to the
shareholders in the first instance or to maintain subsequently. I
now understand and accept that the decision to withdraw support was, therefore, a business one, that the WCC angle was an
excuse rather than the real reason. The discovery that IFMA was
a twenty-six county organisation and hence less vulnerable to
anti-ecumenical attitudes, has made this new understanding of
what happened in 1970 all the more credible. Some puzzlement
must remain but in retrospect it is difficult not to feel relief as
well as gratitude: gratitude for the invaluable encouragement
which ISE 'in process of formation' received in its early stages,
but relief also that it was saved at birth from becoming dependent on a failing financial resource.

University Recognition
When ISE's first academic year opened on 19 October, there
were seven, not eight students. They came from a wide variety
of backgrounds and when the year was over, one of them, Rev
Austin Masters, SSM, was to become Assistant Secretary of the
Board for Mission and Unity of the Church of England.
However none of these first students obtained a degree at the
end. The hope expressed at the May Press Conference that the
School's courses 'will be immediately recognised by other theological institutions as fulfilling certain requirements for degrees
conferred by them' was premature and indeed naïve insofar as it
failed to realise that academic institutions are just as slow to

move as the churches. But before the academic year even began, during the summer of 1970, sure and firm grounds for our hope of university recognition emerged in the person of the Reverend Professor Anthony Hanson of Hull University who, when he visited me during the vacation, offered any help he could as Head of the Hull Department of Theology. Before the year had ended that hope had in fact been realised.

But first of all an approach was made locally, to Trinity College Dublin (TCD). The interdenominational character of ISE and my own Roman Catholic background seemed to suggest that a link with a Protestant or non-denominational department of theology would be more appropriate than with a Catholic one, such as St Patrick's College, Maynooth. TCD, I found, would be happy to equiparate ISE students with those from the Institute for Advanced Studies and thus allow them, if suitably qualified academically, to register for an MLitt or PhD degree. But it could not see its way to granting a postgraduate award for the successful completion of ISE's own course. Because of Hull's readiness to help, no serious effort was made at this time to overcome TCD's reservations, expressed in meetings with the Deans of Graduate Studies and of Arts. So I travelled to Hull in early January and again in late February. Professor Hanson himself visited ISE in late March and satisfied himself that the syllabus provided adequate material for a one-year postgraduate course such as Hull's own B Phil. On his return, therefore, he proposed ISE's affiliation with the University and steered a proposal to this effect through Department, Faculty and Senate with consummate skill and characteristic speed.

In his submission, Professor Hanson had added one non-academic consideration: 'If we can accommodate this course within our B Phil arrangement, we shall be making a very practical contribution to the improvement of the embittered situation in Ireland.' There is an added significance, therefore, in the fact – however coincidental – that the Vice-Chancellor of Hull, Sir Brynmor Jones, chose the week of 12 July to come to Dublin and hold a press conference to announce the good news. The follow-

ing month, August 1971, was to see the introduction of intern-
ment without trial. Just six months later, on 30 January 1972,
came Bloody Sunday. The need for what ISE was offering was
becoming ever more glaring. It may also be noted that ISE's affiliation with Hull is the clearest sign of the link already suggested
between *Irish Anglicanism* and ISE. Anthony Hanson's twin
brother Richard was then Bishop of Clogher and was present at
the 15 April ceremonies. It was he who must have commended
ISE to Anthony. They both became ardent supporters of ISE and
in 1987 dedicated to me their joint work, *The Identity of the
Church.*

Floreat ut Pereat

According to the only surviving account, that in the *Irish
Christian Advocate*, I had, in my speech at the July press conference, thanked the University of Hull 'for bringing it [ISE] closer
to the death demanded by its motto: "May it flourish in order to
perish".' This motto in its Latin original, *floreat ut pereat*, had occurred to me one morning during the early summer of 1970. It
gives lapidary expression to the insight I had expressed in
'Ecumenics: What and Why?'

In conclusion it must be noted that schools of ecumenics, like
all the institutions of the ecumenical movement, are not only
born to die but are born to put themselves to death, to commit
suicide; that they live to die as soon as ever possible, as soon as
the task is completed of reconciling the churches in the unity
which is God's will for his people.

This motto and the eucharistic nature of the church suggested
to Mr Gerard Slevin who was then Chief Herald that an ear of
wheat would be an appropriate emblem for ISE: the ear of wheat
which in the fourth gospel dies to yield a rich harvest and which
in the eucharist becomes for us the Body of Christ. The logo
combining emblem and motto was designed by Myra Maguire
of the National College of Art who was a member of the
Presbyterian Church in Ireland.

The idea of dying and rising was also emphasised that summer by the gift of a crucifix from an unusual source. Protestants prefer crosses to crucifixes but this crucifix had belonged to the Very Reverend Andrew Gibson, MC, DD a former Moderator of the General Assembly of the Presbyterian Church in Ireland. As a chaplain in World War I he had found it in the mud and rubble of an unidentified French village and, having failed to find the owner, brought it back to Ireland and gave it a place of honour in the study of his Cork manse for twenty-one years. This crucifix was presented to the School by Dr Gibson's son and the minister of Rathgar Presbyerian Church, the Very Reverend T. A. B. Smyth. The Dublin sculptor, the late Garry Trimble, was commissioned to carve a new cross of Irish oak for the figure and to design and execute an accompanying commemorative plaque cast in bronze. Both were ready for the School's inauguration in November and in my concluding address I referred to the crucifix as the School's 'most cherished possession'. With the plaque it continues to be displayed in the foyer of the School's Dublin premises, Bea House.

CHAPTER TWO

The First Decade
(1970-1980)

Michael Hurley

The inauguration of the Irish School of Ecumenics took place
with great éclat on 9 November 1970. The inauguration address
was given by the General Secretary of the World Council of
Churches, the Rev Dr Eugene Carson Blake. Attendance was by
invitation; the invited audience of some 350 guests represented
the academic and ecclesiastical worlds. By contrast, however,
the School in actual fact had at first no resources of its own: no
home, no staff, academic or secretarial, no assurance of eventual
university recognition and no financial security. But it did have
Patrons from the four main churches. And it did have friends.
Together we survived and this was surely our greatest achieve-
ment in the first decade. We survived despite all that we lacked
at the start and despite all the difficulties, which were mainly
twofold: ecclesiastical and financial.

The Basics
As noted in the opening chapter, some of the facilities we lacked
– office space and a classroom and access to a library – were
made available to us by the Jesuit communities at Milltown Park
and the nearby College of Industrial Relations; and university
recognition came to us the following summer. A bequest made
to a Jesuit friend, John Mulligan, enabled us to acquire a premises
of our own with residential accommodation at 20 Pembroke
Park in Dublin 4. It was named Bea House after the Jesuit
Cardinal who as President of the Vatican Secretariat for
Promoting Christian Unity had done so much at the Vatican
Council to launch the Roman Catholic Church into the ecumenical movement. Unfortunately work to prepare the house for

occupation could not begin until the late summer of 1971 but it was ready by October, for the beginning of our second year. This would have impossible were it not for the generous help of a number of friends, both lay (Eileen Kennedy, Angela and Elizabeth Russelle) and Jesuit (Derek Cassidy, Jim Hayes and Des O'Grady).[1]

In January of our first year a part-time secretary was engaged, Ruth Moran, and, as funds became available, a Research Lecturer in Systematic Theology in 1972, Rev Dr Alasdair Heron, a Presbyterian from Scotland; a Research Lecturer in the Sociology of Religion, Mr John Fulton, a Roman Catholic from England, the following year; and in 1980 a Lecturer in Continuing Education, Rev Declan Deane SJ.[2] Seven of the eight students who had registered in the months since May 1970, when we had begun to do some marketing, were present for the opening. And they were an encouraging group, interdenominational and international: two Anglicans, five Catholics; one Maltese, one Scottish and one from the US, two each from England and Ireland; they included one woman.

First Syllabus

The syllabus which these students followed in that first year consisted of courses in methodology, history, comparative Christianity, sociology, ecumenical theology, pastoral problems and interchurch relations. All the teachers, except for myself, were visiting lecturers volunteering their services: one from Scotland, two from England, one of these an American Lutheran. The three-fold division into Interchurch Relations, Interfaith Relations and Religion and Society did not emerge until after the International Consultation on Mixed Marriage in 1974. Field Education was already included but not only at home during term time to become acquainted with a religious

---

1. An extension to this property was refused planning permission a few years later.
2. He was unavailable for a year and Rev Brian Lennon SJ substituted for him.

denomination other than one's own but also abroad for six weeks of the summer vacation to become acquainted with ecumenical centres and interchurch activities. This latter proved too ambitious and never became a reality.

Academic Council

In June 1971, the Patrons established the School's Academic Council for Research. Originally the Jesuit Provincial was the only one of the Patrons to serve in his official capacity; the others served in their personal capacities. They were invited to do so by the Provincial in order to guarantee that the life and work of the School were genuinely ecumenical – and not just, as unsympathetic Protestants might have suspected, a Jesuitical front for old-fashioned convert-making. Initially it was in order to meet the requirements of the Revenue Commissioners that the Patrons established the Academic Council for Research. It was a condition for allowing the School to have charitable status, to receive covenanted subscriptions which would qualify for tax relief. The following year Council, which had a large international membership, established a smaller Executive Board, composed exclusively of its own members, to carry out its policies and decisions and in general to administer the School's affairs with the help of committees. But Council reserved to itself the appointment of permanent staff and such major matters of policy as a change of its Constitution. Council became the School's Governing Body.

Finances and Trustees

Soon after the School's inauguration the Provincial associated with himself as its Trustees four members of 'International Christian Leadership-Ireland'. A Geneva colleague had alerted them to the visit of Dr Carson Blake and, having heard about the School's aims and needs, they expressed an interest in helping. They were Mr F. C. Combe a retired Dublin businessman, Dr J. F. Dempsey, formerly General Manager of Aer Lingus and at the time a Director of the Bank of Ireland, Mr Frederick Jeffery, Vice-

Principal, Methodist College, Belfast and Ms Margaret Hamilton Reid, Chairman of Switzers, the department store in Grafton St, Dublin; they were respectively Church of Ireland, Catholic, Methodist and Presbyterian.[3] As Trustees, one of their first actions was to address press conferences in Belfast and Dublin on 15 January 1971.

Fundraising

This fundraising effort received considerable publicity but there were no plans, no staff for a follow-up. It made clear the need for a professional approach and arrangements for this were speedily made. The services of an English firm were engaged and an appeal for a 'Foundation and Research Fund' was launched in January 1973, again with press conferences in Belfast and Dublin. In the meantime a secretary had begun work the previous January, a Campaign Director in May, a Sponsoring Committee had been formed and a brochure was available in time for the launch. A target of £200,000 had been agreed but when the Campaign Director came to retire in July 1973, barely half of this had been reached. Considerable disappointment and dissatisfaction were expressed but there was no question of the School closing down. To carry on the work of fundraising and, in the words of the Finance Committee (Minutes 22 June 1973), to 'halt a certain growing defeatist attitude', it was decided to appoint a Development Officer. He subsequently became a regular member of staff, and from 1974 for two years the post was held by a Jesuit priest, Derek Cassidy, who was made available to the School by the Jesuit Provincial.

Approaches to Government

Fundraising included approaches to the churches and to government. These were now intensified, but bore fruit only much later. Already in January 1972 as Director I had meetings with

---

3. Originally, as mentioned in the opening chapter, there was a fifth Trustee, a representative of the Irish Flour Millers' Association (IFMA) Peter Desmond Odlum, in recognition of their financial involvement.

the Taoiseach, Dr Jack Lynch (10 January) and with the Minister for Education, Mr Pádraig Faulkner (26 January); and a request had been made that the School become a designated institution under the Higher Education Authority (HEA) Act 1971. The following year there was a new government and in May 1973 further approaches were made by correspondence with the Ministers in the Departments of Education, Mr Richard Burke, Finance, Mr Richie Ryan and Foreign Affairs, Dr Garret FitzGerald; sympathetic replies were received and a meeting took place with the Minister for Finance. But as late as 1979 the Minister for Education, Mr John Wilson (as quoted in the Director's Report to the November 1979 meeting of Academic Council) was still maintaining:

> I find that the position as outlined to you in September 1972 is unchanged—I would be precluded from making any financial assistance available to the Irish School of Ecumenics unless and until the State is empowered to provide financial assistance for third-level institutions generally in respect of theological studies.

However, at the 1975 meeting of Academic Council the President of Ireland, Cearbhall Ó Dálaigh had reiterated the view, taken by the Commission on Higher Education over which he had presided as Chief Justice, that 'theology is a proper subject of academic study and should be allowed to take its place in our university system'. He had gone on to speak of the importance of ecumenics and returned to this in a subsequent letter to *The Irish Times* (24 November 1975). Eventually therefore in 2000, by virtue of its association with Trinity College Dublin (TCD), the School did receive designated status under the HEA Act 1971.

Approaches to the Churches
Approaches to the churches were in the short run no more successful than those to government. In May 1973 a request was made to the Irish Council of Churches and to the Irish Episcopal

Conference of the Catholic Church that they arrange for a national collection in aid of the School to be made in churches on the Sunday of Unity Week in January 1974. A delegation of influential Catholic laymen met Cardinal Conway. In the immediate nothing positive resulted from these approaches. News of the forthcoming International Consultation on Mixed Marriage was beginning to worry the Catholic hierarchy but eventually Unity Week collections in aid of the School did become common in parishes and congregations around the country.

What was possibly and hopefully a financially significant event took place on the weekend of 23 March 1975. An inter-denominational delegation from the churches of the Rhineland, a party of nine led by the Catholic Bishop of Essen and the Praeses of the Evangelical Church in the Rhineland were guests of the School. The weekend culminated in a meeting in Bea House where speeches were made by, among others, the President of Academic Council, Fr Paddy Doyle, and the Minister for Foreign Affairs, then Dr Garret FitzGerald, and where a substantial cheque was handed over. The follow-up from the event was however disappointing; it was not as significant as we had hoped. Monies subsequently received from the Rhineland were exclusively from the Evangelical Church. The International Consultation on Mixed Marriage had already taken place and, when the delegation visited Armagh, Cardinal Conway may have managed to convey to the Bishop of Essen something of the anxiety which the hierarchy felt about the School.

Major Research Projects
Financial problems continued to dog the life and work of the School and at the end of the decade another fundraising campaign was being prepared. But the precariousness of its financial situation was not as inhibiting as it might have been. Thanks to the vision, courage and devotion of its Patrons, Trustees, Council members, staff and those volunteers, notably Mollie and Nancy Reidy, who helped around Bea House, especially in

the library, the School went from strength to strength. Its student body was slow to grow; at the end of the decade it counted only eighty past students, over half of whom, fifty, were Catholic and over half of whom, forty six, were Irish (Summer 1960 issue of *Unity: Newsletter of the Irish School of Ecumenics*). As Research Lecturer in the Sociology of Religion, Mr John Fulton undertook an education project entitled 'The Effects of Denominational and Multi-denominational Schooling on Young Adults in Ireland: A Contribution to the Debate on Shared Schools'. But due to ill-health and his departure to a post in England he never completed the project.[4] Two other research projects were however successfully undertaken and an adult education programme was inaugurated in Northern Ireland under the auspices of the New University of Ulster.

International Consultation on Mixed Marriage

The first of these two other research projects was on Mixed Marriage. My own experience of interchurch relations in Ireland and elsewhere since the early 60s was more than enough to convince me that mixed marriage was an ecumenical problem that needed attention urgently. And this was no mere personal conviction. Some Catholics would disagree, notably Archbishop Dermot Ryan of Dublin. In 1964, however, the Second Vatican Council had passed its *Decree on Ecumenism*, had made recommendations, if no decision, on the subject of mixed marriage, and in 1965 had passed its *Declaration on Religious Freedom*. These actions had profound implications for mixed marriages and the following years were to see documents issuing from the Vatican giving some, if not full, effect to these implications.

The Irish hierarchy, however, was less than enthusiastic in its response to these Vatican documents and the angry complaints of the other churches, especially the Church of Ireland, probably only aggravated their reluctance. As a result the official

---

4. His subsequent work *The Tragedy of Belief: Division, Politics, and Religion in Ireland* (Oxford, Clarendon Press 1991) owes much to his years in ISE, 1973-9.

Ballymascanlon talks, begun in September 1973, concentrated on the ultimate issues – such as 'Church, Scripture, Authority' – of a remote, eventual church union rather than on the immediate issues – such as mixed marriages – of peaceful co-existence, of Christian unity here and now.[5] The consequent tensions, especially against the background of the worsening Northern troubles, only highlighted the urgent need for the dialogue on mixed marriage which the School was about to meet. Our own research lecturers, now three,[6] set themselves to work on theological, ethical and sociological aspects of the problem; papers were commissioned from other scholars, Anglican, Methodist and Lutheran, and an international consultation was arranged to meet in Dublin from 2-5 September 1974. Here our fifteen specialists were joined by some one hundred others, half of whom were Catholic, half Protestant, and one-third of whom were from outside Ireland.

Two of the fifteen specialists were to become particularly committed to the ISE and deserve special mention. The first, Rev Professor G. R. Dunstan, whose name has already occurred in the preceding chapter, became the sponsor and host of the School's annual London Lecture at King's College. For many years this was given by distinguished Irish scholars such as F. S. L. Lyons and Margaret MacCurtain and took place at King's College; it contributed greatly to our academic reputation. The second of these fifteen, Rev John Coventry SJ of Heythrop College, London and co-founder of the Association of Inter-church Families (England) came regularly after the Consultation to do some teaching and to encourage the fledgling mixed marriage associations in both parts of the country.

The Proceedings

The publication of the proceedings of the Consultation on Mixed

5. Cahal Daly / Stanley Worrall, *Ballymascanlon. An Irish Venture in Inter-Church Dialogue,* Belfast: Christian Journals Limited, Dublin: Veritas Publications 1978.
6. Rev Dr John Hayes was given a temporary appointment for one year to help as a Research Lecturer in Social Ethics.

Marriage followed in due course.[7] The Consultation included
four sessions on the nature of marriage on the grounds that the
churches' disunity on the issue of mixed marriage played its
part in putting the institution of marriage itself at risk. It also included four (one public) sessions on interchurch marriage. A
significant number of couples involved in a mixed marriage
were beginning to see themselves as belonging to both of the
churches represented in their persons and to wish their children
like themselves to belong to both these churches. Pastoral approaches to mixed marriage was another subject. It had a particular relevance arising from the fact that the Irish hierarchy in its
directives was alleged to be out of step with other hierarchies.
By way of clarification experts from Australia, Britain, France,
Germany and Switzerland examined 'positions and trends' in
their respective countries. The concluding address was given by
Dr Garret FitzGerald (then, as mentioned earlier, Minister for
Foreign Affairs). He remarked that 'As one of the progeny of a
mixed marriage … it would be hard for me to assent to a propos-
ition that asserted that such marriages are inherently undesir-
able, for by doing so I should, in a sense, be negating my own existence.'

Interfaith Marriage
But the highlight of the whole proceedings was undoubtedly the
opening session on interfaith marriage. The suggestion that we
should not limit ourselves to a consideration of inter-Christian
marriage had come from Mr Sean McBride, Nobel Peace
Laureate and then a Board member. My initial reaction was
somewhat negative: we already had more than enough on our
hands; the two international commissions then at work in the
field (in one of which the Catholic Church had the Anglican
communion as partner and in the other the World Alliance of
Reformed Churches and the World Lutheran Federation) did
not have interfaith marriage in their remit. In the event the paper

7. *Beyond Tolerance: The Challenge of Mixed Marriage*, ed Michael Hurley,
Geoffrey Chapman, London, 1975.

by Adrian Hastings on marriage as exogamous, as an alliance between two groups or societies as well as two individuals, and that by Kenneth Cragg on the problems and possibilities of Christian-Muslim marriage, simply blew our minds. As a result the School adopted Interfaith Relations as a main section of its ecumenical curriculum.

In its review of the book of the Consultation, *The Church of England Newspaper* did very pointedly ask 'What unconscious arrogance determined that all sixteen contributors ... should be men?' On the other hand, *Biblical Theology* welcomed the book with lavish praise as 'an impressive and massively documented scholarly and practical treatment of a vexed subject'. More soberly *Doctrine and Life* stated: 'It remains matter for legitimate pride that an Irish institution should have stimulated so much thoughtful and constructive perception within the area of greatest tension between committed Christians.' Despite the gender imbalance, participants were generally happy. But the Irish hierarchy were not happy.

Catholic Hierarchy Opposition
The ecclesiastical difficulties which, as remarked in the opening paragraph of this chapter, the School had to face in its first decade did not really surface until the occasion of the International Consultation on Mixed Marriage. Insofar as they were positive and meant more than a lack of support, they involved mainly the Roman Catholic hierarchy. Three of the members of the Episcopal Commission on Ecumenism had been present at the formal inauguration. This was promising, especially because they had been conspicuously absent earlier in the year at the ceremonies connected with the publication of *Irish Anglicanism*, the volume of essays which I had edited to mark the centenary of the disestablishment of the Church of Ireland. The secretary of the Commission, Bishop Cahal Daly, had also accepted membership of the Council and Board of the School but very soon excused himself from membership on the grounds of numerous other commitments. When he was in-

formed in July 1973 about the Consultation to take place in
September 1974 he misread the letter. He presumed the
Consultation was scheduled to happen in 1973 and wrote up-
braiding the Director for not having consulted his Ecumenical
Commission.

The situation got worse when Archbishop Dermot Ryan of
Dublin, who in the beginning had been a friend and supporter
of the School, became negatively critical. In early January 1974
he did not hesitate to write:

> I must therefore require that your programme be re-arranged
> to make places in both the private and public sessions for the
> presentation of the viewpoints of persons with a genuine
> pastoral experience in this country.

After the Consultation he wrote 'to register my strong disap-
proval' of the way he presumed – without previous enquiry
from the organizers – eucharistic hospitality had been encouraged during the proceedings. In the following years he more
than once complained that the School was a Protestant rather
than an ecumenical institute.

Relations between the School and the Catholic hierarchy
reached a nadir on 13 February 1975 when the Secretary of the
Episcopal Commission put a very negative resolution before a
meeting of the Advisory Committee on Ecumenism of which I
was a member. Some twenty or more priests would have been in
attendance; three bishops, members of the Episcopal commission, were also present. The resolution concerned a report just
published on the Consultation (not 'of' as the resolution mistak-
enly stated); it included the following crucial sentence:

> Since the question is of great ecumenical and pastoral
> importance, the Advisory Committee states that, for its part,
> it regards the paragraph in question [about the religious up-
> bringing of the children of a mixed marriage] as quite unten-
> able as an interpretation of 'the Catholic's obligation in divine
> law to do all he can to hand on his faith to his children and to
> have them brought up in the church'.

During the discussion Professor (later Bishop) Kevin McNamara proposed as an amendment that 'gravely misleading' replace 'quite untenable'. This highlighted the controversial, extreme character of the resolution and would surely have affected any vote. But eventually no voting took place. When the chairman of the afternoon session, who was Canon Pádraig Murphy of Belfast, attempted to put the unamended resolution to a vote, Professor Corish intervened to raise a point of order: unfinished business, the tabled amendments, remained to be dealt with; and the meeting broke up in confusion.

The School managed to survive these ecclesiastical difficulties for two main reasons. Firstly because as Director I was no mere individual but, to the surprise of some of the hierarchy, was fully supported by my Jesuit superiors. Indeed, were it not for the robust support of the Jesuit Provincial, Fr Cecil McGarry, in his correspondence with the Secretary of the Episcopal Commission on Ecumenism, the School could hardly have survived, without at least a change of Director. And it managed to survive secondly because the School itself was no denominational Roman Catholic institution but interdenominational and ecumenical, to oppose which in those years of the sectarian troubles in the North would have been decidedly impolitic, inopportune. But knowing how worried and defensive the hierarchy were about the issue of mixed marriage, we should (as I acknowledged in *Healing and Hope*, Columba Press, Dublin 2003, pp 84-6) have been more sensitive to their concerns and fears.

International Consultation on Human Rights
The Rev Alan Falconer from the Church of Scotland, who became our Research Lecturer in Systematic Theology in 1974, brought with him a special interest in Orthodoxy and in social ethics, thus anticipating the later ecumenical emphasis on combining more closely the Faith and Order and the Life and Work aspects of the movement. Looking ahead, he saw that 1978 would be the thirtieth anniversary of the UN Declaration of Human Rights. He proposed that the School, because of its inter-

est in Religion and Society issues, prepare for this anniversary
and sponsor another international consultation at the time. The
Board welcomed this proposal. The Chairman had a particular
interest. He was an expert on Vatican II's *Declaration on Religious
Freedom* and on the Catholic liberalism of Daniel O'Connell and
other nineteenth-century thinkers. This, he was writing at the
time, had been 'scrubbed from the race-memory of the Irish by
an Ultramontane clergy, a parochial nationalism and a bigoted
unionism'.[8]

'Understanding Human Rights: An Interdisciplinary and
Interfaith Study' emerged in due course as the title of the project.
The dates 30 November to 4 December 1978 were chosen for the
proposed consultation. Contacts were made and contributions
commissioned from interested scholars. Mr Falconer himself
prepared a survey report on 'The Churches and Human Rights'
which *One in Christ* published in October 1977. In March of that
year information about the project with a request for suggestions was sent to all the Irish church leaders. The following
month people involved in human rights activities in both parts
of Ireland participated in a preparatory seminar. And in
November the School issued a press release giving information
about the topics being researched in preparation for the
Consultation to take place the following year and the names of
the scholars engaged in this research.

The law, philosophy and politics figured prominently among
the disciplines represented in the programme of the Consultation
– as deserved by their major role in the history of human rights,
in the American Declaration of 1776, for instance, and in the
French Declaration of 1789. The Christian and the other religions
may not have played such a positive role in that history but
today they are very much involved in the philosophical and
theological understanding of human rights as well as in their
implementation, in the promotion of justice. So the different

8. Louis McRedmond, 'Not to be coerced', *Studies* 67 (1978) p 33;
'Northern Ireland: A Challenge to the Churches in Ireland?' *One in
Christ* 12 (1976) pp 90-8.

churches, Anglican, Catholic, Lutheran, Methodist and Presbyterian, also figured prominently in the programme of the Consultation and with them there was a Muslim scholar from Pakistan, a former Director of the Islamic Research Institute in Islamabad[9] and a Marxist scholar, a Hungarian from the University of Essex. Notable too (by contrast with our previous international consultation) was the fact that one of the addresses of welcome at the opening of the Consultation was given by a member of the Irish Episcopal Conference. By contrast also with the Consultation on mixed marriages, the gender balance had improved, however slightly: two of the chairpersons and one of the speakers were women.

The geographical distribution of the research scholars is also significant. Notable among the countries represented are Argentina, Canada, Finland, and Israel. If we include leaders of Consultation workshops, The Czech Republic, Switzerland, Tanzania and Zimbabwe should also be added. And, if we include the countries of origin of the participants in the Consultation, Guyana, the Philippines and Russia must be added. Three Russians participated: the Secretary of the Department of Interchurch Relations of the Moscow Patriarchate Dr Alexy S. Buevskiy, his interpreter, and the General Secretary of the Baptist Union in the USSR, Rev Alexei Bickhov. Their presence added Baptist, Orthodox – and Communist – dimensions to the proceedings. It had been facilitated by Mr Sean McBride who had received the Lenin as well as the Nobel Peace Prize and who at the Consultation gave an opening address on 'The UN Declaration Thirty Years After'. On his return to Moscow Alexy Buevskiy (who during the Consultation, my diary remarks, had charmed and hugged everyone) sent the following telegram:

9. Dr Rashid Ahmad Jullundhri. Three other Muslims participated in the Consultation: Dr A Ah Kinany, Director of the Paris Office of the Muslim World League; Dr Muhammad Iqbal, Lecturer in the Huddersfield Polytechnic and Mr Mohammad Akram Khan from Liverpool, Assistant Secretary of the Union of Muslim Organizations of UK and Eire who on his return sent a kind letter of appreciation and thanks.

Dear Father Michael comma cordially grateful for concern and hospitality stop very happy that you and your colleges [sic] labours on International Consultation have [been] crowned by considerable success stop sending you english text of my presentation stop asking prayers Alexy Buevskiy.

Consultation Final Statement

The issues which received particular attention during the Consultation are listed as follows in its final Statement:

The interdependence and inseparability of civil, political, social, cultural and economic rights;

The right of women to equal participation and leadership in both the civil and religious structures of society;

The involvement of First World Christians and churches in political and economic structures which oppress Third World peoples, e.g. investment policies;

The rights of prisoners and the treatment of prisoners throughout the world;

The rights of minorities in an increasingly pluralistic world.

The Statement urged the participants 'to promote study and action' on these rights and expressed 'the fervent hope that humankind would not have to wait much longer for the full implementation of the rights enunciated in that [UN] Declaration'. The Statement is printed in the proceedings of the Consultation published in 1980[10] with a recommendation from a Judge of the Supreme Court who was President of the Law Reform Commission, The Hon Mr Justice Brian Walsh. He recommended the book as 'an invaluable collection for the law-student and law-maker'.

10. *Understanding Human Rights: An Interdisciplinary and Interfaith Study*, Dublin: Irish School of Ecumenics, 1980, ed Alan D. Falconer, p 237. For reasons of space the book omits a number of contributions including the opening address by the exiled Bishop of Umtali, Most Rev Donal Lamont, the closing address by the General Secretary of the World Council of Churches, Rev Dr Philip Potter and the presentation made by the representative of the Moscow Patriarchate, Dr Alexy Buevskiy.

But how was the Consultation financed? A paragraph in the May 1979 issue of *Unity: Newsletter of the Irish School of Ecumenics* gives the answer as follows:

> The cost of the Consultation was about £26,000. Of this some £4,500 was recovered in fees. The rest was specially contributed as follows: £14,000 from Germany, £2,500 from USA, £1,000 from Holland and £4,000 from the Irish Catholic agency for World Development, Trócaire.

Adult Education Certificate in Ecumenics

The buoyancy of the School during the last years of its first decade is further illustrated by its establishment of a course leading to an Adult Education Certificate in Ecumenics. It was a Northern Ireland project, inaugurated at Benburb, Co Tyrone, on 14 September 1979. The first mention of this initiative that I find is in the minutes of Executive Board for 13 March 1978. Here it is stated that I had discussed the project with Professor Anthony Hanson of Hull on the occasion of a meeting of the Academic Council for Research in November 1977.

The date is significant. It was that year that the Peace People received the Nobel Peace Prize. In retrospect it would seem clear to me that the immediate background for the inauguration of the Certificate course in Northern Ireland was the emergence of the Peace People. 'Nothing', write Gallagher and Worrall, 'in all the years of violence did more to focus attention on Ulster.'[11] However, the Peace People created an embarrassment for the School. The great Peace Marches sponsored by them, culminating in the Boyne march in Drogheda on 4 December 1976, led our friends in the US and elsewhere to ask what we in ISE were doing for Peace in Northern Ireland. We ourselves were in no doubt that our commitment to an improvement of interchurch relations, for instance to the ecumenical education of clergy and teachers and to the easing of tensions with regard to mixed marriages, was a significant contribution to peace, to an improve-

11. Eric Gallagher & Stanley Worrall, *Christians in Ulster 1968-1980*, Oxford University Press, 1982, p 177.

ment of community relations in the North. But this failed to impress. We are not mentioned in Gallagher and Worrall's chapter on 'The Peace Movements'. Members of staff did have occasional engagements in the North. In the first term of the academic year 1977-78, I myself was in Belfast twice to lecture in the extramural series on ecumenical questions at Queen's University. The fact remained that the School as such did not exist in the North and for many non-Irish, especially Americans, the North was another country, another church. Church partition, they knew, must follow political partition and the example of post-World War II Germany seemed to prove it. This was damaging for the image and interests of the School, not least for its prospects of support, financial and other, from abroad, from other churches and other countries, especially the US and Germany. So what would probably have happened anyway in due course was precipitated by events in Northern Ireland in the late 70s. We established an institutional presence in the North: the Certificate in Ecumenics. The contrast with the beginning of the School in 1970 is interesting. The establishment of the School itself was not so much a result of the Northern Ireland situation in particular but of Vatican II and its concern for Christian unity in general.

Hull

Anthony Hanson was aware that in ISE we were already thinking seriously of making a fresh effort to establish a link with Trinity College, Dublin, that the link with Hull would end before too long. But he knew that this was not for lack of appreciation and gratitude for Hull's initial readiness to take us under its wings. In response to my mention of our proposed Northern Ireland project he again acted with typical speed. The Board minutes for 13 March 1978 tell us that an Adult Education Certificate award has recently been established by Hull. My own diary tells me that Bernard Jennings, Hull Professor of Adult Education, was here to discuss relevant matters with us during the Summer of 1978 and again in the Summer of 1979.

At an early stage the Certificate was variously envisaged as a reading course with some weekend seminars and lasting three years; as involving six weekend seminars a year over two years; and as involving one weekend and one Saturday each term for the six terms of two years. To satisfy the required number of contact hours, it eventually came to involve two Saturdays as well as the one weekend each term. Three of the terms were to be spent on Interchurch Relations, one on Interfaith Relations with two on Religion and Society issues. A fieldwork exercise – some participation in the life of another church – was required between meetings. And the award would be granted on the basis of a written examination.

According to my diary there was originally some question of the course being taught in two centres, one in the North and one in the South. The idea may have been an attempt to forestall the criticism that once again the School was showing itself to be too concerned with Northern Ireland. The Board minutes for 8 November 1976 note another letter from Archbishop Dermot Ryan reminding us once again that 'there are more fundamental problems in the field of ecumenism than mixed marriages and N. Ireland'. The possibility of a Southern centre featured in our conversations with Queen's University Belfast. We were hoping that they would succeed Hull as the awarding body, but it emerged that they would have found themselves unable to grant an award to students in a Southern centre as distinct from those in a centre in the North. Eventually the Certificate course was in fact taught in two centres but the second was also in Northern Ireland, in Magee University College in Derry.

Benburb

Why choose Benburb as the location for the course? Residential facilities would be required for the weekends and Benburb provided these at a reasonable cost. It was, still is, a retreat and conference centre run by the Servite Fathers, a Roman Catholic religious congregation. In the academic year, 1977-1978 Dermot MacNeice, one of our students, was a member of this

Congregation and he assured us in advance of the welcome we would receive. Besides, Benburb was not so far removed from Belfast and though in the county of Tyrone it was in the diocese of Armagh where Archbishop Ó Fiaich also assured us of a warm welcome. The teaching on single Saturdays would later move to Belfast, to St Anne's Cathedral. This was at the suggestion of the Rev William Arlow, a canon of the Cathedral and then executive secretary of the Irish Council of Churches; he wished our work to be associated with the cathedral's study centre.

Queen's University Belfast (QUB)
In our search for funding for the new initiative we approached Stormont. The Board minutes for 12 March 1979 tell us that Lord Melchett, Northern Ireland Minister of State for Education, had advised that we should approach one of the higher education establishments. We had already in March 1978 made an approach to the Minister and in September of that year had an interview with officials of his department. The advice to approach one of the higher education establishments came in January 1979 in a letter from the Minister's Private Secretary. As a result I had a meeting on 1 February with the Head of the Extra-Mural Studies department at Queen's University. Our request was that QUB would validate the Certificate and this request came before the Board of Extra-mural Studies at a meeting on 20 April. I was present by invitation at this meeting to make a presentation but the Board's decision was negative.

On 24 April the Chairman of the Board, Professor H. M. Knox Professor of Education at QUB wrote to convey the decision. His letter is quoted in full in the Minutes of ISE Board for 14 May. The decision was reached only 'after an exceptionally long and searching discussion'. They would not want to be involved 'in a merely nominal way'; they would want a 'high degree of involvement', 'full involvement in planning and organizing courses' would be 'essential' but this was 'beyond our capacities'. Besides, another awarding body besides QUB would be necessary for centres in the Republic.

This latter difficulty was unforeseen but we had never seriously considered a Southern centre and quite obviously it was
not QUB's main reason for being negative. Very unusually they
wanted full control: much more than Hull and eventually the
New University of Ulster (NUU) wanted. They wanted more
than some significant role in appointing staff, approving the
courses and in assessing the candidates. They wanted 'full involvement in planning and organizing the courses'. This re-
quirement, I now gather,[12] was an expression of what was
University policy at that time: not to get involved in anything
that might cause religious controversy; the Department itself
had been positive about our request.

New University of Ulster (NUU)

As recalled in the previous chapter, TCD at the beginning of the
decade had not seen its way to validating our course for a postgraduate award. Now at the end of the decade this rejection by
TCD was being repeated at the hands of QUB. But as in the beginning we had gone more successfully from Dublin to Hull, so
now we went from Belfast to Derry and with similar success. We
approached the other Northern Ireland establishment of higher
education, then entitled the New University of Ulster. We established contact with its Institute of Continuing Education based
in Derry. This was made easier by the fact that a fellow Jesuit, Fr
Sean O'Connor, already worked with the Institute. Various visits to Derry followed, in September and November 1979 and in
February 1980. Professor Alan Rogers of the Institute proved
very co-operative. It was agreed that, beginning in the academic
year 1980-1981, the Certificate course would be taught in Derry
as well as Benburb and that the School would appoint its own
Lecturer in Continuing Education. This was done in February
1980. Meantime on 14 September 1979 the Certificate course had
been inaugurated at Benburb with sixteen students and on 15

12. From Ms Pat Patten who in 1979 was a member of the Extra-Mural
Studies Department in QUB, in a conversation in Belfast on 9 February
2006.

November 1979 Academic Council had appointed my successor as Director. 1979, it will be recalled, was the year of the Mounbatten and Warrenpoint assassinations and of Pope John Paul's appeal for peace on the occasion of his visit to Ireland.

Retirement

The idea of retiring as Director of ISE came into my head for the first time on 15 January 1977 during evening prayer in the Jesuit community of Marquette University in the USA. I had stopped off there on my way to St Paul-Minneapolis where I was to fulfil a number of Unity Week engagements. Where did I get the idea? My Jesuit superiors did not put it into my head. Was it because of the precariousness of the School's finances and its poor relationship with the Irish Catholic hierarchy? Academically and ecumenically the School was buoyant but not so financially and ecclesiastically. Our financial failure was a bitter disappointment and a severe handicap but I did not see it as a resignation matter. Our ecclesiastical failure, our failure to enjoy a good relationship with the Catholic hierarchy did weigh heavily on me. In retrospect I think it played a larger part in my decision than I was willing to admit at the time. There is no mention of that factor in the following extract from the July 1978 meeting of Board:

> The Director's idea of resigning in 1980 was discussed at length … In reply to questions and to suggestions that he might delay his departure, the Director explained that, while he greatly appreciated the confidence of Board, his main reason for considering resignation was the welfare of the School which, as he saw it, could not develop properly and flourish if it continued to be dependent on the person who was largely responsible for its beginnings and early years. After ten years (1970-80) the time, he felt, would have come for the School to acquire this measure of independence. But the change, whenever it came, would be critical – it could make or break the School – and it seemed best, therefore, to ensure its success by careful and early planning.

Why was I silent about the negativity of the Catholic hierarchy as a factor in my decision to retire? It is true that in the late 70s our problematic relationship with the hierarchy was improving. Bishop Cahal Daly paid us a formal, friendly visit in April 1977; the following year six members of the hierarchy paid individual visits to the International Consultation on Human Rights and one of them, as recalled above, gave an address of welcome. Again on the occasion of the Papal visit, Cardinal Willebrands of the Vatican Secretariat for Promoting Christian Unity came to visit us. Speaking at the end of a luncheon in his honour, after addresses by the Jesuit Provincial, Archbishop McAdoo (Church of Ireland) and Rev Ernest Gallagher (Methodist), the Cardinal expressed the wish that 'you may continue and flourish in your research and study'.[13]

Archbishop Dermot Ryan of Dublin, however, continued to view us unfavourably and would not move to Rome until 1984. He was a very forceful personality who wished to dominate the ecumenical scene. He duly assumed the position of co-Chairman of the Interchurch Ballymascanlon Talks when it became vacant on the death of Cardinal Conway. But when the vacancy was filled and Professor Tomás Ó Fiaich became Archbishop of Armagh and President of the Episcopal Conference, Archbishop Ryan failed to hand the chair back and held on to it until his move to Rome in 1984. It was not easy to forget the authoritarian tone of his letters, especially on the occasion of the International Consultation on Mixed Marriage. No doubt the basic problem was ecumenism and the reluctance of the hierarchy to share power. However, I did hope, I think, that my going would ease relationships, but seemingly I did not want to emphasise the problem.

---

13. *Healing and Hope* (p 87) is mistaken when it states that Cardinal Willebrands visited the School in May 1978.
14. Cardinal Ó Fiaich found this very hurtful especially as Ballymascanlon was in his own diocese, cf *Healing and Hope*, p 86 note 1.

A Protestant Successor?

Board addressed the problem very seriously and very honestly. Granted the negative attitude of the Catholic hierarchy and of the Archbishop of Dublin in particular, could my successor be a Protestant? The July 1978 Board meeting agonised over the question and, especially in view of what was to happen, the minutes are worth recording. Board agreed that 'in principle the denominational allegiance of the Director is a matter of indifference because of the interdenominational character of the School'. But it also agreed, and unanimously – so the minutes add – that 'for no reason of principle, but granted all the actual circumstances of the concrete situation, the next Director would, most appropriately, be a Roman Catholic'. Academic Council, meeting the following November 1978, urged that 'this conclusion be kept absolutely confidential as its disclosure would be damaging to the School', and stressed that the advertisement to appear in January 1979 be an open one, which Board of course intended it to be.

The Rev Dr R. H. S. Boyd

The rest is history. Board appointed a selection committee with as external assessor the Rev Professor Ronald Preston of Manchester University. Eleven replied to the advertisement: one woman, ten men; one Methodist, one Orthodox, two Presbyterians and seven Roman Catholics. One of the five short-listed candidates was the Rev Dr R. H. S. Boyd, an Ulster Presbyterian, born in Belfast in 1924, a graduate in classics of TCD and in theology of Edinburgh University, formerly Theological Colleges' Secretary of the Student Christian Movement of Great Britain and Ireland (1951-3), lecturer in Gujarat United School of Theology, Ahmadabad, India (1961-74), author of many publications in the areas of inter-religious dialogue and of Christian unity, since 1974 living and working in Melbourne as a parish minister with many commitments in the field of ecumenism.

The Selection Committee unanimously recommended Robin

Boyd for the post of Director and this recommendation was unanimously accepted by Council who, as stated above, made the appointment at their meeting on 15 November 1979. Not surprisingly, a hundred thousand welcomes awaited Robin and his gifted, gracious Australian wife, Frances, when the following year they arrived to take the School forward into the 80s.

The opening chapter recalled that one of the first gifts which the School received was a crucifix from an unusual – Presbyterian – source. The following defiant paragraph, which was part of my concluding address at the formal inauguration, may not unfittingly bring this chapter to a close:

Whatever the artistic merits of the figure, this crucifix is of course of considerable ecumenical and historical significance. But for the Irish School of Ecumenics its significance is above all spiritual. Because the School is like him in his death, it will, we know for sure, be like him in his glory. In the power and providence of God which are exercised through the ministry of his people, the Irish School of Ecumenics must, before very long, rise above the ground, breaking the bonds of death, of poverty and humiliation, confounding its critics and opponents and all those of little faith who would have doubts about its future, and providing a permanent abode for its now homeless students and this homeless crucifix which will ever remain its most cherished possession.

CHAPTER THREE

On the Way[1]
(1980-1987)

Robin Boyd

Robin Boyd grew up in Belfast, and was ordained in the Irish Presbyterian Church in 1951. He served on the staff of the Student Christian Movement of Great Britain and Ireland in the 1950s, and later taught theology in India and wrote *An Introduction to Indian Christian Theology* (CLS, Madras, 1969 and 1975), *India and the Latin Captivity of the Church* (Cambridge, 1974) and *A Church History of Gujarat* (CLS, Madras, 1981). Director of the Irish School of Ecumenics from 1980-87, he wrote *Ireland: Christianity discredited or Pilgrims' Progress?* (WCC, Geneva, 1988). He has served as a parish minister in Melbourne, and as chairperson of the Uniting Church in Australia's Christian Unity Working Group, and recently published *The Witness of the Student Christian Movement: Church ahead of the Church* (SPCK, 2007).

1. An extended version of this chapter is available in the ISE Library.

Arrival

When the question of a successor to Michael Hurley first arose it
was assumed by many people that the second director would, as
a matter of course, be a Catholic. But in fact the position was advertised: a friend of mine from student days, Tom Lyle, sent a
copy of the advertisement to me in Australia; I applied, travelled
to Dublin for an interview, and while still in the Milltown Park
building, was told that I had been appointed.

I was a minister of the Uniting Church in Australia who had
begun life as a Presbyterian in Belfast, had been ordained in the
Irish Presbyterian Church in 1951, had gone to India as a mis-
sionary of my church to work in the then United Church of
Northern India, which in 1970 united with five other traditions,
including the Anglican, to become the Church of North India,
the widest spectrum of churches which had ever united. From
India I had gone in 1974 to Australia, the country of my wife
Frances, and had been received as a minister of the Presbyterian
Church of Australia, which in 1977 entered union with the
Methodist and Congregational churches to become the Uniting
Church. So I was deeply committed not only to the ideal of unity
but to the *actuality* of living in a united Church.

My commitment to ecumenism had been nurtured by the
Student Christian Movement (SCM), of which I had been a
member during student days in Dublin, Edinburgh, Belfast and
Basel, and on whose London headquarters staff I had served
from 1951-53. Only at the very end of my time there did we
begin to include the Roman Catholic Church within the sphere
of practical ecumenism. But this we did – memorably – in a 1953
student pilgrimage to centres of the priest-worker movement
and the liturgical renewal in France. My model of ecumenism
was based on the SCM; for we were aware that the modern ecumenical movement was the child of the missionary movement
as mediated through the SCM. It was a model which the SCM
passed on to the World Council of Churches (WCC).

The ISE Heritage

Michael Hurley has told the story of the genesis of the ISE, of which I had now become director. Following the vision of Vatican II he had planted this ecumenical grain of wheat which had now become a flourishing plant, with the motto *Floreat ut Pereat*, based on John 12:24. It was flourishing so that some day, its work of unity accomplished, it might perish.

Michael was determined that the School should operate at the highest level of academic integrity, and he had succeeded – through his friend Anthony Hanson – in securing its academic affiliation with Hull University. There was the hope that it would some day be possible to create an organic link with an Irish University; and meantime a link had been forged – at certificate level – with the New University of Ulster. Michael had created a great deal of goodwill for the School in the Irish churches, and also internationally. There was, however, especially in the North of Ireland, a strong latent antagonism to any ecumenical enterprise.

'The Troubles'

Although the foundation of the School had been related to the ecumenical awakening stimulated by Vatican II rather than to the Irish political situation, it so happened that it coincided with the beginning of the 'Troubles' which were to continue for almost forty years. There had been a hardening of the traditional Protestant/Catholic division, demonstrated firmly – and for me embarrassingly – by the withdrawal of the Presbyterian Church from the WCC at its 1980 Assembly, just two months before my arrival, the specific occasion for withdrawal being the supposed encouragement to terrorism given by the WCC's Programme to Combat Racism (PCR). My years at the ISE were to be politically turbulent ones, witnessing the H Block hunger strike of 1980-81 and the 1985 Anglo-Irish Agreement.

The Staff

The School staff was very small. The Rev Alan Falconer of the

Church of Scotland had been lecturer in ecumenical theology
since 1974, and had established a fine reputation in Ireland,
Britain and the wider *oikoumene* through his writing, lecturing
and bibliographical contributions to ecumenical journals. Bill
McSweeney had recently taken up his position as lecturer in social
ethics. A former Catholic priest, he was deeply committed to the
idea of the compassionate society, and was beginning to work
out his plan for a department of peace studies. Fr Declan Deane
SJ had been appointed to head the programme in Northern
Ireland, but was not available for another year, so the programme was being looked after by Fr Brian Lennon SJ, soon to
take up residence in Portadown – that traditional stronghold of
Protestantism. The remaining teaching was done by distinguished part-time, visiting lecturers, including Frs Gabriel Daly,
Enda McDonagh, Redmond Fitzmaurice and Dermot Lane, Sr
Carmel Niland, and others. The fact that these were all Catholics
was balanced by the fact that two thirds of the full time staff –
Alan and myself – were Protestants!

Fr Raymond Kennedy of the Holy Ghost Fathers had just
been appointed executive secretary of the Foundation and
Research Fund, with responsibility for raising finance for the
School. Mrs Ruth Moran was the director's secretary; by the time
she retired she would have worked with five directors. Mrs
Barbara Duncan was the accountant, who had the gift of keeping us all cheerful. We were soon joined by Miss Dympna Ryan,
who would efficiently resource the School for many years to
come. They were based, like me, at Milltown Park, where most
of the lecturing took place. The academic staff, and the library,
were at Bea House in Pembroke Park, about a mile away, where
the library was looked after by Sr Alice Walsh, under the librari-
anship of Alan Falconer, while the housekeeping was in the
charge of Mrs Mary Hogg.

Objectives
I was immediately faced by three tasks of development. First, it
was essential to increase the number of students. Secondly, it

was important to do everything possible to build up the School's presence in Northern Ireland. And thirdly it was vital to complete the process of affiliation with Trinity. The fact that I was a TCD graduate made this a congenial task, if not always a simple one.

There was also the question of my own church. Strangely enough, despite its withdrawal from the WCC, the Presbyterian Church had for years taken a leading part in ecumenical enterprises in Ireland – like the Corrymeela community – and was still involved in many interchurch projects. I was delighted when I was received once more into the church as a minister, and officially inducted into my job as director by the Dublin Presbytery. I knew that I could rely on the wisdom and ecumenical experience of many friends in my own church, especially my former teacher Prof Jimmie Haire, a wise and experienced ecumenist with an impeccable background in classical Reformed theology.

And finally there was our own ISE community. Michael had spoken to me of the community as a family – a family like all others with its high points, its low points, its secrets, its triumphs. I hoped that we would continue to develop as a true Christian *koinonia*, a place of inquiry, study, prayer, music, joy and peace; a community which prepared its members for intentional ecumenical living, witness and action.

A Director's Wife?

Michael Hurley is a Jesuit. So where did a director's wife fit into the life of the School? When Frances arrived from Australia in November 1980 this was the question we had to try to answer. Like me, she came from a missionary and SCM background, and in Melbourne had been fully engaged with teaching religious education at a large school for girls. Suddenly she found herself in a new country, and it took time to find an appropriate sphere of activity; but with the encouragement of Alan Falconer and Alice Walsh she found her place as a volunteer in the library, and in helping to build up the Bea House *koinonia*. The strain of being separated from our two daughters and their families was perhaps the most difficult part of our time at the School, and the role of prodigal parents in a far country was not an easy one.

Structures

The structures of management at ISE were inherited from Michael Hurley, who kindly left me to 'direct' things in my own way. I must admit that I wasn't very happy with the idea of 'direction', as my tradition was more one of achieving consensus with colleagues, and making decisions in that way. But I was glad to have Michael's workable structure, and in its main outlines it continued unaltered in my time.

The four *Patrons* were the guarantors of our ecumenical authenticity. My contacts with Archbishop Armstrong in Armagh and Prof John Barkley in Belfast were naturally limited, though very cordial. But both Joe Dargan and Robert Nelson lived near Milltown Park, and there were many occasions when I dropped in on them for a cup of coffee and wise advice.[2]

The Academic Council was a large body of about fifty members, which met twice a year, once in formal session and once for more informal discussion. This highly qualified group enabled me to get to know people whom I could consult if any problem arose in which one of them happened to be an expert, in practical matters like salary structures as well as for more theological issues.

The Executive Board of approximately ten members met each month and was the forum in which the day to day work of the school was scrutinised, and major policy decisions made, if necessary for recommendation to the academic council. Fr Austin Flannery was a very helpful, wise and sensitive chairman.

Academic Staff Meetings were held fairly frequently, mostly at Bea House, and usually consisting simply of Alan, Bill and my-

2. Joe Dargan's term as Jesuit Provincial ended on 31 August 1986 and he was succeeded as Patron by Fr Philip Harnett. Archbishop Armstrong died in mid 1987, and Archbishop Robin Eames accepted our invitation to succeed him as Patron.

self, with occasional participation by Brian Lennon or Declan Deane from the Northern programme, as well as part-time lecturers. They were informal, and at most we noted decisions, rather than keeping formal minutes.

The Foundation and Research Fund had a large *Sponsoring Committee*, consisting mostly of influential people in public and business life in Ireland, the UK and the USA, and it was reassuring to have as joint chairmen Robin Lewis-Crosby, an experienced banker, and Donal O'Sullivan, until recently Irish ambassador in London.

The Students

The students in the main graduate programme came from a steadily increasing number of backgrounds: Ireland, Britain, Europe – eventually including East as well as West Germany – the United States, Canada, Latin America, Australia, New Zealand, the Philippines, many parts of Africa, India, Sri Lanka, Burma. The number of churches represented was also very large, and included people from all the main traditions, Roman Catholic, Orthodox, Anglican and Protestant.

Many of the students went on to take positions of high responsibility in their churches, in the countries of their birth or choice. Joe Seremane, who came from the South African Council of Churches for a short period of study, had already spent years in prison; and when he returned to a South Africa still in the grip of apartheid he continued the struggle for justice; Peter Schuttke (Scherle), who graduated in 1987, became Professor of Cybernetics and Church Theory in Herborn, Germany; Vinodkumar Malaviya (1987) became Bishop of Gujarat in the Church of North India, and Paul Colton (1987) Bishop of Cork, Cloyne and Ross in the Church of Ireland; Esther Mambo (1986) became Academic Dean of St Paul's United Theological College, Limuru, Kenya; Sr Margaret Kelly OP (1986) became Regional Prioress of the South African Province of Dominican Sisters; Oliver Rafferty (1983) became Professor of Church History at Maynooth. I think of them as lights shining in many scattered places on the dark globe of the earth.

Ecumenism – the World and Ireland

In September 1980, less than a month after my arrival, Alan
Falconer encouraged me to go to a meeting of the *Societas
Oecumenica* in Münster, Germany. It is a matter of regret that in
the following years I rarely found the time, or the financial resources, to take part in such international conferences.
Fortunately we were able to attract leading ecumenical figures
to Ireland, or – mindful of our meagre budget – take advantage
of the fact that churches or other organisations had invited them
and would let us share their wisdom.

I gradually built up a network of friends and advisers, like
Archbishop George Simms, by then retired and living in Dublin,
whom I had known when he was dean of residence in Trinity in
the 40s; Theo Moody, historian, Quaker, and once my tutor in
Trinity; Ray Davey, founder of the Corrymeela community, and
his successor John Morrow; Alan Martin, who had been a colleague in India; Ruth Patterson, already deeply involved in
crossing the frontier between Catholic and Protestant; Jack Weir,
Clerk of Assembly of the Presbyterian Church; Eric and Ernest
Gallagher of the Methodist Church; Bill Arlow, Eric Elliott and
Edgar Turner of the Church of Ireland.

It was a pleasant surprise when, on the day I began work, I
found my name already inscribed on the door of my office in
Milltown Park; and among new Catholic friends were members
of the Milltown Jesuit community like Jim McPolin and Ray
Moloney and – through links with Glencree and Corrymeela –
Una O'Higgins O'Malley.

Michael had warned me that I would need to become familiar with the media people, and I found them most helpful. RTÉ's
Kevin O'Kelly was always wise and encouraging. And I think of
the support and stimulus given by Louis McRedmond and Seán
MacRéamoinn; of Pat Nowlan and Patrick Comerford at the
Irish Times, and 'Ginnie Kenneally' of the *Irish Independent*, who
was later, as Virginia Kennerley, to become a student at the ISE,
then editor of our journal *Unity*, and eventually one of the first

women ordained as priest in the Church of Ireland. In the North too there was a group of interesting media people looking after religious affairs – Ernest Rea, Trevor Williams and Bert Tosh, for a start. The Irish media saw ecumenism as a promise rather than a threat or a bore.

At the political level too there was informed interest in ecumenism. The leader of the Fine Gael opposition, Garret FitzGerald, and his wife Joan, were deeply committed to Christian unity, and frequently took part in theological and ecumenical events. And it was a gift of grace that two successive British ambassadors, Nicholas Fenn and Alan Goodison, were similarly committed.

Our study programme followed the triple model familiar from the history of the WCC – Faith and Order, Life and Work (eventually to become 'justice, peace and the integrity of creation') and Mission (already closely linked with interfaith dialogue). The Dublin M Phil programme, of which the Northern Ireland certificate programme was a miniature replica, required students to take courses in all three of these areas of study – and then to select one area for specialisation, including the writing of a dissertation. We were still in the era of written examinations, and were fortunate in our extern examiners, including Anthony Hanson of Hull, Duncan Forrester of Edinburgh, and Liam Ryan of Maynooth.

Ecumenical Theology
The ecumenics programme, dealing with issues like eucharist, ministry, authority and the Petrine office, was in the hands of Alan Falconer, assisted by Gabriel Daly and others. I shared their conviction that this was central to our teaching activity; it was essential to lay a biblical and theological foundation for all ecumenical activity, for churches had never been known to unite unless someone had worked hard and accurately on drawing up theological documents through whose mediation the parties could unite with integrity.

Peace Studies

Soon after my arrival, Bill McSweeney proposed a research programme on 'Technology for Development and Peace', which
was soon modified into a three-year project entitled 'Towards a
compassionate Society: Ireland in a technical and nuclear Age'.
Deeply committed as he was to the Irish government's policy of
neutrality, which was under pressure from NATO and from the
European Community, he planned to initiate a separate department of peace studies. This aroused considerable discussion on
the Board as to whether or not the School should devote its slen-
der resources to issues of peace and neutrality, rather than con-
centrating on Christian unity. It was decided that the department should function as 'the Religion and Society section of the
present Ecumenical qualification' and that it should at first offer
a certificate, to be followed later by M Phil and Diploma courses.
Des Dinan was appointed as occasional lecturer in Peace Studies.

Interfaith Dialogue

Cross-cultural mission was still a central concern for Irish
Catholics and Protestants, but the nature of Christian relationships with people of other faiths had become problematical, and
'dialogue' had become the favoured term. By 1974 Michael
Hurley had included interfaith relations in the teaching pro-
gramme, with Fr Redmond Fitzmaurice teaching a course on
Islam. Since then Jewish-Christian dialogue had become part of
the syllabus, under the direction of Sr Carmel Niland of the
Sisters of Sion, and with the co-operation of Dr David Rosen,
Chief Rabbi of Ireland. I taught a course on interfaith dialogue,
and later one on 'Reality and Realisation in Christianity and
Hinduism'.

Northern Ireland

The Northern Ireland programme, begun in 1979, was now in
charge of Brian Lennon with courses in both Belfast (with occasional weekends at the Servite Priory, Benburb), and Derry. The
students were very highly motivated; some of them, especially

on the Catholic side, had come to ecumenism through the charismatic movement, in which they had become friendly with Protestant Christians, and now wanted to find out more about the theological and sociological factors separating the churches, and ways of overcoming them.

The Dublin graduate ecumenical course included a week's 'fieldwork' in Northern Ireland, usually over the New Year period. Catholic students had placements in Protestant environments (often with clergy families), while Protestants stayed in Catholic homes or communities. We were greatly helped in making these arrangements by Ruth Patterson, Fergal Brennan, and – after the establishment of the Columbanus community – Michael Hurley.

Worship and koinonia
As I look back at the School's life in the 1980s I confess that the worship of our community fell short of what it might have been. Alan Falconer was concerned and innovative, was in touch with ecumenical liturgical developments, and good at using visual symbols and recorded music. But we were working under difficult conditions, with no chapel at Bea House, and no room for creating one. At Milltown Park we were free to use both the large, basilica-like chapel and the smaller oratory. And indeed we did use them, especially for our annual Unity Day valedictory service in the chapel, and for occasional services of intercession in the oratory. But in Bea House, worship had to take place in the lounge, where we were vulnerable to every ring of the door-bell. Even singing was a problem, for there was no piano.

Of course we encouraged the students to worship in local churches, and especially to go to churches other than those of their own tradition. And there were wonderful annual occasions when we prepared for, and celebrated a service of ecumenical worship on RTÉ national television. But when I think of the centrality of worship in the great tent at WCC assemblies, or in the Croí chapel at Corrymeela, I realise that we did less than we could have done.

Another lack at Bea House was a staff common room. It was

of course possible to spill over from the lounge into the dining room, and conversations were often held in the hallway, or on the staircase – or in the kitchen. Alan and Bill were based at Bea. So was the company of volunteers including Sr Alice Walsh, Sláine Ó Hogáin, the Reidy sisters, Nesta Whiteside, Euphan Stephenson, Sr Helen Butterworth, my wife Frances, and others. And soon, in the kitchen, there was Maureen Donohoe – cooking, listening, counselling, and helping to create the warm, friendly atmosphere which was characteristic of Bea House, that holy place.

Public Outreach

On the staff we were aware of being on a mission – a pilgrimage towards God's reign of unity, reconciliation and justice. Of course, as a university-linked institute, we were committed to academic integrity, and so to a certain academic neutrality. But we could not simply sit and wait for people to come to us: so our work was highly intentional: it was our hope and our intention that every student who came to us would become an ambassador for unity, justice and reconciliation.

That meant involvement in a never-ending stream of public meetings, conferences and seminars. Speakers who came to us over those years included Dr Bill Lazareth of the WCC's Faith and Order Commission, Prof J. K. S. Reid of Scotland, Prof John Zizioulas and Bishop Kallistos Ware from the Greek and Russian Orthodox traditions, Dr Kenneth Greet from the British Methodist Church, Bishop Alistair Haggart of the Scottish Episcopal Church, Fr Tom Stransky, closely associated with the Paulist Press in the US, Bishop (later Cardinal) Cormac Murphy O'Connor and Bishop Mark Santer, representing the two sides of the Anglican Roman Catholic International Consultation (ARCIC), Dr Mary Tanner of the Church of England, Prof James Torrance of the Church of Scotland, Dr (later Bishop) Sam Amirtham of the Church of South India and of the WCC's Board of Theological Education, Dr Davis McCaughey, one of the chief architects of the Uniting Church in Australia, Methodist Prof

Geoffrey Wainwright, Lutheran Dr Bill Rusch, Churches of Christ Dr Paul Crow, evangelical theologian Richard Lovelace, Prof (later Archbishop) Rowan Williams. Among those who led Bible study at various conferences were Bishop Lesslie Newbigin of the Church of South India, and Hans-Ruedi Weber of the WCC.

These were years when the divisions between East and West, Marxist and non-Marxist were acute, and contacts few; but we had speakers who crossed the divide, like Bishop K. H. Ting from China, Metropolitan Philaret from the Soviet Union, Bishop Gunter Krusche from East Berlin and Prof Jan Lochman from Czechoslovakia. There were others with experience in the areas of social ethics, peace, and reconciliation, both in Ireland and in the wider world, like Bishop (later Cardinal) Cahal Daly, Presbyterian ministers Ruth Patterson, John Morrow and John Dunlop, Prof Jean Luis Segundo, Prof Ronald Preston, Dr Alan Kreider, Prof Haddon Wilmer, Prof John Barnaby, Canon Paul Oestreicher, the Rev (later Bishop) Richard Harries, Dr Sydney Bailey, Dr Frank Wright, Fr André Lascaris.

The interfaith area concentrated to some extent on Jewish-Christian relations, and we heard Sir Immanuel Jakobovitz, Dr Eugene Fisher, Dr Pinchas Peli, Rabbi Norman Solomon, Prof John Pawlikowski, as well as our own Rabbis David Rosen and Ephraim Mirvis. On more general interfaith issues we had Kenneth Cracknell of the BCC, with whom I paid a visit to a Hare Krishna settlement on an island in Lough Erne. And Fr Richard De Smet SJ led a seminar on Hinduism.

The complete Ireland

Apart from Dublin, our courses, seminars and conferences were held all over Ireland: first in Belfast, Benburb and Derry in the North; and then in Limerick, Cork, Galway, Ballina, Carrick-on-Shannon, Cavan. We were invited to a variety of institutions – Trinity College Dublin, University College Dublin, the People's College, the Church of Ireland Theological College, Milltown Institute, Kimmage Manor, Mater Dei, Marianella, All Hallows,

Maynooth, Kiltegan. And not just in Ireland: in London, for an annual lecture and occasional seminars; later at Selly Oak, Birmingham; with the Sacred Heart Sisters in both Dublin and Edinburgh; at English ecumenical conferences at Ampleforth and Scargill.

It was easier to find venues for our work –'holy places' – in the South than in the North. But there were the glorious exceptions, like Ballycastle's Corrymeela community, with whom we soon started to hold an annual clergy conference, and Benburb Priory, and Magee College Derry, and St Anne's Church of Ireland cathedral in Belfast, and eventually Michael Hurley's new Columbanus community. These were places where voices were sometimes raised and tears shed; but where the Holy Spirit, the Spirit of reconciliation, was at work.

Networking

The ISE was only one element in Irish ecumenism, part of a surprisingly large and lively network. The Irish Council of Churches (ICC) gave the School official 'recognition' in 1984, and I was given 'consultant observer' status. Our links with the British Council of Churches (BCC) were also strong, especially through participation by Alan Falconer and Bill McSweeney in the BCC forums for human rights and peace respectively. The Roman Catholic Church was not a member of the ICC, but all four main Irish churches were linked in the annual Ballymascanlon Interchurch Conference, of whose theological committee the ISE became part in 1985. There were also the annual Glenstal ecumenical and liturgical conferences, and the Greenhills (Drogheda) annual conference. We had a particularly close relationship with the Corrymeela community, in a reciprocal sharing of gifts and resources. We frequently co-operated with the Glencree Community of Reconciliation, especially through Una O'Higgins O'Malley and Alan Martin. Important too were the twin organisations of the Irish Interchurch Families Association (AIF) in the Republic and the Northern Ireland Mixed Marriages Association (NIMMA).

We also kept in close touch with international ecumenism, especially through the WCC and the Conference of European Churches (CEC), as well as the then Vatican Secretariat for Christian Unity. We had significant links also with the *Societas Oecumenica*, with the WCC's Programme for Theological Education, and with international bilateral dialogues like those between the Roman Catholic and the Reformed Churches, and the Roman Catholic Church and the Churches of Christ. We constantly acted as an Irish information exchange for all these organisations, especially through Alan Falconer.

DEVELOPMENTS 1980-87

Rather than giving a chronological list of events at the School in my time, I would point to a number of achievements, on which I look back with gratitude.

Growth

The Dublin ecumenical programme had eight students in 1980. This number rose rapidly until it reached thirty, and thereafter remained around or just under that figure, which we felt was the maximum we could handle. A vital factor in the numerical increase was the adoption of a policy allowing the course to become a two year part-time as well as a one year full-time one. *The Northern programme* also grew, and eventually settled down at just under twenty students in each of the Belfast and Derry programmes. Peace Studies began – not yet under that title – in 1980, and grew rapidly, eventually achieving numbers somewhat greater than the ecumenical course. In addition large numbers of students attended the extramural courses which we ran in a great many places. Already when I arrived, Alan Falconer was running a highly successful ecumenical course at University College, Dublin which attracted up to 100 students for a twenty lecture course. The venues increased in number each year.

The Place of Women - in the School and in the Church
By 1980 both the Methodist and Presbyterian Churches in
Ireland already had ordained women ministers – Ruth Patterson
(Presbyterian, 1976) and Ellen Whalley (Methodist, 1977). But
the Church of Ireland, like the Church of England, did not yet
have women priests, so that the ministry of women was very
much a subject of debate, a debate which – at least informally –
could not exclude Catholic staff and students. My own position
was clear: I was totally in favour of women's ordination. Having
worked alongside women ministers, I knew by experience that
their ministry was as effective, and as blessed by God as that of
their male colleagues, and I was prepared to defend women's
ordination both biblically and theologically. Having said that, I
must confess that the ISE was slow to grapple with the challenge
of women's ministry as energetically as it might have done. We
had very effective women on the academic council and the executive board – Sr Margaret MacCurtain and Sr Carmel Niland
(both lecturers), Miss Margaret Hamilton-Reid, Senator
Catherine McGuinness, Mrs Elizabeth Lovatt-Dolan, Sr Dorothy
McLuskey, Mrs Bet Aalen and Mrs Clare O'Mahony. Our library
depended on the work of dedicated women volunteers. Our
administrative, financial and hospitality activities depended on
our female staff. Yet the school was still heavily male-dominated.

I am particularly grateful to the women students who gradually reversed this situation. I know that my own awareness was
sensitised – as it needed to be – especially to the use of inclusive
language, and the need to work towards parity of opportunity
in all areas of life, including the church. I think of Daphne
Gilmour and Alison Williams from the North, Clare Sealy from
England, Pilar Telos and Sr Cathleen Coyle from the Philippines,
San San Myint from Burma, Gillian Kingston from Dublin. I
think of the witness of Delma Sheridan and Janet Barcroft, who,
with many others, were eager to make radical feminist voices
like those of Elizabeth Radford Ruether and Katherine Zappone
heard in Ireland. I remember the seminar on 'Men, Women and
the Ministry' in October 1984 when Margaret Webster, secretary

of the Movement for the Ordination of Women (MOW) in the
Church of England led a seminar for us. And so I must confess
my failure to press for the appointment of women to significant
positions in the School. Admittedly finance was partly to blame,
and indeed very few academic appointments – men or women –
were made in my time. But we could certainly have increased
women's representation on the board and academic council.
When, in 1995, Dr Geraldine Smyth became director of the school,
and I met her for the first time, it was a moving experience.

Affiliation with Trinity College Dublin
Already in 1980 the changing of our university affiliation from
Hull to Dublin had been decided upon, but the detailed negotiation had still to be done. Trinity met us with warmth and helpfulness, and I mention with gratitude the names of Seán Freyne,
head of the Department of Hebrew, Biblical and Theological
Studies, Provost Bill Watts, Registrar Eda Sagarra, Academic
Secretary Salters Sterling, Dean of the Arts Faculty Kader Asmal
(later a minister in the South African government), as well as
other sympathetic friends like Theo Moody and Wesley Cocker
(both members of our academic council) and Terence McCaughey.
Much work had to be done by – and for – the Joint Negotiating
Committee including the drafting of a document entitled 'ISE,
Nature and Function'. Finally, in 1982, all the hurdles were sur-
mounted, and we approved the agreement which sealed this
new 'inter-institutional relationship' which in the event proved
to be only the first 'platform' of our developing association with
Trinity. We were deeply grateful to Hull University for providing us with our essential first academic affiliation; and it was
good to know that Anthony Hanson, who had been instrumental
in forming this link, was as pleased as we were in the new con-
nection formed with his own *alma mater*.

The catalytic function
Many of the enterprises on which the School embarked were
done in collaboration with other institutions or groups. We liked

to think that we were stimulating catalytic reactions, even if eventually the School itself withdrew from a project, leaving it to carry on independently. Let me give some examples of this catalytic function.

The Faith and Politics Group began at a meeting of the annual Greenhills conference (just outside Drogheda) in 1983. Brian Lennon, in charge of our Northern programme, suggested the creation of 'a Christian centre for political development'. This did not materialise, and the ISE Board was at first rather cool, affirming that 'we are academic not political'. But the project went ahead and became 'an Interchurch Group on Faith and Politics', and the School became one of its sponsors, together with the Glencree Reconciliation Community and Corrymeela. The result was the publication, over many years, of a challenging series of booklets, beginning with *Breaking down the Enmity* (1985).

Irish Ecumenical News started publication because a number of people felt that the churches in Ireland needed a journal which would give regular news of fresh ecumenical initiatives, especially in Ireland, but also overseas. So a group came together including members of the Irish Council of Churches, the Faith and Politics group, and the ISE, and we persuaded Donald Kennedy, retired Bishop of Bombay and one of the architects of Church union in North India, to act as editor of what from early 1982 became *Irish Ecumenical News*. The ISE underwrote the cost of the first issue.

The third venture which we hoped would start a catalytic action, was a Regional Ecumenical Advisers' Conference. Many Catholic and Church of Ireland dioceses had ecumenical advisers, and the Presbyterian Assembly had recently asked its Presbyteries to make similar appointments. We believed that if such advisers were to be effective it was important for them to get to know their counterparts in the other churches. So we organised a successful conference in March 1982 at the hospitable house of the Sisters of Sion at Bellinter, near Navan, on the theme 'Together in Christ'. It was a significant effort towards encouraging ecumenism at an intermediate level between the local parish and the national church.

Theological Students posed a special challenge. When, after trying without success for some years, we eventually, in 1984, managed to persuade the students of Union Theological College in Belfast (Presbyterian) to join with their Methodist, Anglican and Roman Catholic colleagues in a study day in Dublin, they insisted that they would come only if it were held 'on neutral ground'. They agreed that the Church of Ireland Theological College met that criterion! However, after a day spent in good theological discussion, and in getting to know each other, when evening came and it was time to go home, the Catholic students invited everyone to come over for a bite of supper in the nearby Marianella seminary. Hours later, the Belfast students climbed wearily but happily into their cars for the long drive home. A barrier had been broken down.

'The Declaration of Commitment', 1986

In 1985 I was invited to join in the work of a group of Northern Ireland church leaders who had begun drafting a declaration on the violent political situation.[3] They were following up work on violence already done by Bishop Cahal Daly, and were influenced by the 1934 Barmen Declaration of the Confessing Church in Germany, and the 1985 Kairos document of the South African Council of Churches. Eventually, on 24 June 1986, a brief but significant document was published, entitled *A Declaration of Faith and Commitment by Christians in Northern Ireland*. Sometimes referred to as *The Belfast Declaration*, it received considerable publicity in both press and radio, and today may be seen as anticipating – on the scriptural and theological level – some of the language used on the political level in the later 'Good Friday Agreement' of 1998.

Ireland, Britain and Europe

Meantime Alan Falconer's earlier work on human rights continued and developed in work on Irish prisons, and also in the

---

3. I could not be a signatory to the declaration, as the signatories had all to be residents of Northern Ireland.

human rights forum of the British Council of Churches. Theologically also the School's influence was felt in international spheres, for example through Alan's and my participation in a WCC workshop on the teaching of ecumenics at Bossey in 1986, and in Alan's association as a consultant with the Roman Catholic/Reformed conversations which produced the report *Towards a Common Understanding of the Church* (1986). The School also assisted in the establishment (1981) of the Irish Council for Christians and Jews, especially through the work of Alan Falconer and Carmel Niland, greatly helped by the advocacy of Dr David Rosen, who was then Chief Rabbi of Ireland.

Catholic and Evangelical
One of the sad features of 'the Troubles' was that sympathy for reconciliation and Christian unity on the Protestant side was often taken to signify weakness, a surrender to IRA violence and a betrayal of the Reformation. It was at times difficult and even dangerous for Protestant ministers to express their commitment to ecumenism, and those who did so were branded as traitors. But some of us had become convinced that one of the most important dialogues in the ecumenical movement – if also one of the most difficult – was that between so-called 'ecumenicals' and so-called 'evangelicals'. Aware of the 1986 report of the international Evangelical Roman Catholic Dialogue on Mission (ERCDOM), we decided – in conjunction with our Corrymeela colleagues John Morrow and Doug Baker – that our next clergy conference should make a special approach to some of the more conservative evangelical leaders of the Protestant Churches, so that evangelicals and ecumenicals on the Protestant side might together join in dialogue with a group of Catholic clergy. To facilitate the encounter we invited as speaker the well known American evangelical writer, Richard Lovelace. It was a memorable and positive meeting (May 1987).

Publications
Despite the busyness of the lives of the academic staff, they kept

writing and publishing. During my time Gabriel Daly published *Transcendence and Immanence: a Study in Catholic Modernism and Integralism* (1980), and *Creation and Redemption* (1988). Alan Falconer kept up a steady series of bibliographical features in the *Ecumenical Review, International Review of Mission*, and *Ecumenical News*, and edited *Reconciling Memories* (1988), the record of the project of that name. He also wrote *A Man alone: Meditations on the seven last Words of Jesus on the Cross* (1987). Bill McSweeney published *Ireland and the Threat of Nuclear War* (1985). Enda McDonagh continued his impressive output with *The Making of Disciples* (1985) and *Between Chaos and New Creation* (1986). Michael Hurley found time to write a 1983 article for *One in Christ* entitled 'Christian Unity by the Year 2000?' Brian Lennon drafted many of the published reports of the Faith and Politics group. Immediately after leaving the school I managed to write a book for the WCC's Risk series – *Ireland: Christianity discredited or Pilgrims' Progress?* (1988). And all the time the number of student dissertations was building up, and many of their authors were going on to make further contributions – literary as well as practical – to the work of reconciliation and unity.

The Library

Between 1980 and 1987 the library doubled in size, from about 8,000 volumes to about 16,000. Alan Falconer was an excellent selector of books: and however precarious our financial position, we ensured that the library got what it needed most. As a result it became one of the major ecumenical collections, used by researchers from all over the world. There was a cost, however, in that Bea House lost bedroom after student's bedroom to the library. If it was finally the growth of the library that forced the School to go in search of larger accommodation – then who would call that a fault?

Finance

Michael Hurley had been determined that the School should be independent of control by any of the churches; and the price of this freedom was financial insecurity. Our chief supporters in the Roman Catholic Church were the religious orders, both men's and women's, and especially the Society of Jesus, Michael Hurley's order. We were based at Milltown Park, the Jesuit headquarters, with very favourable rental arrangements, and a generous annual grant.

Other orders also helped us; and occasionally Cardinal Ó Fiaich would provide us with letters of support when we went out seeking for money, for example from Catholic sources in America or Germany. We also sought support from the Conference of European Catholic Bishops, aware that the Irish situation of conflict was a matter of deep concern to the European churches. Here it was important for us to secure backing from the Irish bishops – official backing – and this was difficult. 'Recognition' was the word we used, and sometimes it seemed an elusive goal. The nearest we came to it in my time was when the Catholic bishops made their presentation to the 1984 New Ireland Forum, and their report, in its section on inter-church relations, devoted a whole paragraph – and a very positive one – to the work of the School. That recognition certainly helped us in our appeal to Catholic sources overseas.

The Church of Ireland was always friendly to us, but stopped short of regular committed support. However, we usually received an annual grant from its Priorities Fund; and in Unity Week there was always a good response from individual parishes.

The Presbyterian Church was divided between strong supporters of the ecumenical movement and others whose attitude varied from the lukewarm to the positively antagonistic. Yet there were many congregations, in both North and South, which were enthusiastic supporters of reconciliation and Christian unity, and were prepared to give generously. The Dublin Presbytery, led by its clerk, my former fellow student William McDowell, was both supportive and imaginative when it provided a new car for the director, Michael Hurley's old red Renault twelve having finally reached the end of the road!

Relations with the Methodist Church were very cordial, especially through leaders like Robert Nelson, Eric and Ernest Gallagher, Harold Good, Norman Taggart, Chris Walpole, David Kerr and Jim Rea, and later through students like Gillian Kingston, Ken Thompson, Jim Williamson and John Nelson. Admittedly it seemed more difficult to obtain financial help from the Methodists than from the other churches, apart from local offerings during Unity Week. But in all our enterprises we could count on them for warm co-operation.

In addition to the four main Irish churches, we had very good support from the Society of Friends, especially through Theo Moody and later David Poole. While they were bemused by our concentration on issues like ministry and sacraments, they encouraged our work for peace and reconciliation. From time to time also the Salvation Army came to our assistance, especially on one memorable occasion (14 January 1983) when they provided us with a minibus and driver to ferry a distinguished church delegation from the Soviet Union around Dublin.

The global financial base
Through the good offices of the ICC and Michael Hurley we already had firm ecumenical friends in the Rhineland Westphalia area of the Evangelical Church in Germany (Lutheran and Reformed) who were much concerned over the troubles in Northern Ireland. I think especially of Eberhard Spiecker, Klaus Kremkau, Praeses (President) Immer, and Klaus von Stieglitz. Declan Deane and I visited Germany to follow up these contacts, and to make others, especially with German Catholic bishops.

We had support from several international ecumenical bodies. The Women's World Day of Prayer provided scholarships. The Ecumenical Church Loan Fund helped with the 'Towards a Compassionate Society' project. The German agency *Kirchen hilfen Kirchen* gave us £9000 as a result of our being included in the 'listing' of the Council of European Churches (CEC) – that listing being the culmination of long and complicated lobbying. I was able to secure the help of an ecumenical group of 'Australian

Friends of the ISE', who each year sent considerable sums. A fund set up in memory of Prof Jimmie Haire, brought more than £7500, to be used for an occasional lectureship. There were $5000 from the US United Presbyterian Church's 'Women's Opportunity Gift Fund', and donations from the Netherlands Reformed Church, the Raskob Foundation (US Jesuits) and from Bro John Driscoll of Iona College, New Rochelle, New York, who responded generously when Frances and I visited him one summer afternoon.

There was a substantial covenant from the Bank of Ireland, which helped us through the early years of my time at the School. Help came also from the Tudor Trust and the Cyril Squire Trust, and from agencies set up specially to promote peace and reconciliation in Ireland, like the well known Ireland Fund (USA).

There was also government funding, from the Irish and British governments, and also from what was then called the European Economic Community (EEC). Because our work was church-related we could not receive grants from the Irish Department of Education; but our reconciliation work made it possible for funding to be channelled through Foreign Affairs, and in this way we received considerable help. Eventually we also received help from the Northern Ireland Office of the British government, which paid half of the fees of students in our Northern Ireland programme. There were generous individuals and agencies – notably Christian Aid – who were prepared to lend us money in order to keep us in business. All these loans we managed to repay on time. And finally there were our Dublin-based lay friends – like Maureen Brazil, Maeda O'Sullivan and Peg Lewis-Crosby – who were willing to organise fund-raising events for us, including sales of work, art exhibitions, and even a cookery demonstration by a famous chef.

CREATIVE TENSIONS

One cannot live through seven years of the life of an organisation whose purpose is reconciliation and the promotion of
unity without experiencing tensions. I shall try to indicate the
nature of some of these tensions, and the ways in which we
sought to resolve them.

With the Churches

I shall mention first the relationship with my own Presbyterian
Church. I was conscious of a great deal of goodwill. I was invited
to join the Church's Overseas Board, and also the Board of
Interchurch Relations, chaired by David Nesbitt who invited me
to submit an annual report on the work of the School, which was
included in the Board's reports to the Assembly. Each year at the
Assembly there were debates on issues such as violence –
whether by paramilitary groups or by the security forces – and
relationships with the Roman Catholic community, and I frequently found myself speaking on the ecumenical side, alongside colleagues like John Morrow, John Dunlop and Ruth
Patterson. I was also conscious that there were regular opponents – Warren Porter, Harry Uprichard, Alistair Dunlop, Bertie
Dickinson and others. I tried to get to know these colleagues,
and find points of contact with them – especially in our shared
commitment to the mission of the church. It was encouraging
when the 1986 General Assembly passed a resolution commend-
ing the School to 'the interest, prayer and support of the whole
church'.

One of the questions which came up from time to time was
that of subscription – by ministers and elders – to the Westminster Confession of 1647, whose 25th chapter describes the
Pope as the antichrist. Presbyterian churches in other parts of
the world, including the Church of Scotland, had at various
times passed 'declaratory acts' which indicated that subscription to the confession could allow a certain amount of freedom
of interpretation. I doubt if any Irish Presbyterian minister believed this section of the confession to be literally true; but there

was reluctance to deal with the question, largely because any decision to modify the church's relationship to this 'subordinate standard' would be interpreted by others – and especially by Ian Paisley and his Free Presbyterian Church – as a betrayal of the Reformation. Various attempts had been made to pass some kind of declaratory act, but they had not succeeded. To our surprise, at my last Assembly, in 1987, two of the more outspoken conservative members, Warren Porter and Jim Matthews, indicated to me that they were in favour of a resolution to modify the form of subscription, and this proposal was passed by the Assembly. It was, I believe, a sign of the Spirit's working for reconciliation – and also an indication that ecumenical advocacy over the years had not been in vain.

My relationship with leaders of the Roman Catholic Church were invariably cordial, and I experienced great personal goodwill. And of course there was official support for ecumenism – from the Pope down. This did not, however, translate into inevitable support for the ISE.

An important practical question was that of intercommunion. During the 1980s, as today, intercommunion was widely, if unofficially, practised, and there was some pressure on the ISE to encourage it, as an eschatological anticipation of the unity for which we were working and which we believed would one day come. Michael Hurley had taken the firm line that the School could not adopt such a policy: we could not advertise an ISE worship service and then announce that members of all churches were welcome to communicate. We did, however, encourage students to attend each other's eucharistic services and to participate in them as far as their consciences and the rules of their church allowed them. For myself I had a threefold personal rule:

- never assume that I am invited to communicate at a service of a church where I know there is any doubt about the practice of eucharistic sharing.

- never refuse an invitation to communicate if one is given.

- when myself celebrating as a Presbyterian minister, always follow my church's practice of offering an invitation to all who communicate in their own church.

His study of the Church of Ireland had been one of the factors which led Michael Hurley to the foundation of the ISE, and his book commemorating the centenary of disestablishment had appeared in 1970. We were fortunate to have a steady stream of Anglican students at the school, from both parts of Ireland , and especially from England. For my first two years Anthony Hanson was a strong, articulate and friendly Anglican influence in the affairs of the school, whom I consulted frequently. Archbishop George Simms – who in my student days at Trinity had become a friend and helped me to appreciate the Anglican liturgical tradition – was, in his retirement, a constant source of encouragement. So also was that doyenne *éminence grise* of the Church of Ireland, Elizabeth Ferrar, who worked indefatigably as a volunteer at the School, began the arrangement of the archives, and provided a home for many overseas students. It was good to be able to contact Archbishop Henry McAdoo, then Anglican chairman of ARCIC, and his successor Archbishop Donald Caird, who had been my fellow student at Trinity. Ginnie Kennerley made a valuable contribution to the school by using her skills in the field of journalism to edit *Unity*; and Bet Aalen was an active and encouraging member of the Board. Yet there was, I think, a certain detachment between the School and the Church of Ireland. Presbyterians were either strongly pro or strongly anti. Church of Ireland support seemed more muted. Yet support was certainly there, and I think of the enthusiasm for ecumenism of Canon Bill Arlow of Belfast, David Bleakley of the ICC, Bishop Jim Mehaffey of Derry, Trevor Williams of the BBC (and later of Corrymeela), and Ian Ellis, who made a fine contribution to the documentation of Irish ecumenism. Strangely enough, the School was to be almost thirty years old before it appointed its first Anglican director; meantime there had been a regular alternation of Catholics and Presbyterians! So Kenneth Kearon's appointment in 1999 was a longed-for and significant advent.

Our relations with the Irish Council of Churches (ICC) were particularly helpful, and I could at any time seek the advice of the general secretary, David Bleakley, and his colleague, David Stevens. And it was always a particular pleasure for the School when we were able to bring together in conversation represent-atives from seemingly irreconcilable church traditions. I think of a robust but friendly encounter in Bea House between a rather conservative Presbyterian moderator, and a young English Catholic priest from Westminster; and of two young teachers from the North, one Catholic and one Protestant, who the year after they left the School brought their classes to live together for several days at Corrymeela. And I remember with pleasure the day (22 October 1986) when the four 'heads of churches'– on one of their regular Walkabouts – came together to Bea House.[4] That too was a step towards the seal of church recognition.

Within the School
From time to time, naturally enough, tensions arose within the School, though my colleagues and I were always concerned that they should not affect our common life, nor interfere with our own personal relations. I shall mention four areas where diffi-culties occasionally arose.

Peace Studies
The problem which gradually became manifest in this area was related to my conviction that the primary task of the school was to work for Christian unity, or perhaps more accurately for 'unity-towards-mission' – 'that they all may be one … so that the world may believe' (John 17:21). It seemed to me that this task was a clear consequence of the life and teaching of Jesus, and that it was important for us not only to work for unity, but to give clear biblical and theological reasons for doing so.

I became concerned lest we were failing – especially in peace studies – to give our students the necessary criteria for making

---

4. Archbishop Robin Eames, Cardinal Tomás Ó Fiaich, Dr John Thompson, the Rev Sydney Frame.

distinctively Christian judgements on political issues. Many of our visiting lecturers, like Enda McDonagh, John Ferguson, Sydney Bailey and Haddon Wilmer, had indeed made strong contributions in this area. But this did not always seem to come through in our own courses, or in the public image projected by the department of peace studies.

On one occasion, in 1985, when a peace studies publicity and fund-raising trip to America was being planned, it seemed clear to me that there was a danger of the ecumenical and theological side of the School's work being marginalised, and I felt I had to take action. The matter was discussed in the Board (15 January and 1 February 1985) and it was decided that the planned trip should not proceed. The chairman Austin Flannery and I communicated this decision to Bill, who was gracious in his acceptance of it. And I hasten to pay tribute to Bill for his insistence – despite my economy-driven reluctance – on our entering the information technology era with the purchase, in my last year, of two Amstrad computers. One other concern I had about the Dublin peace studies programme was what I felt to be the comparative neglect of the most obvious problem facing Irish Christians – conflict in Northern Ireland.

Ecumenics

This concern underlay the only real confrontation I ever had with Alan Falconer. I was totally committed to global ecumenism, and deeply grateful to Alan for keeping our eyes wide open to ecumenism at the world level (as indeed to Bill for doing the same for peace and justice issues). But my feeling was that we could do more than we were doing in making sure that our students were all encouraged – perhaps even obliged – to make some response to the situation in Northern Ireland.

I quickly realised that this criticism was unfair to Alan, who was deeply involved in work on Irish as well as global issues, for example on the reconciliation of memories, to say nothing of his work on human rights and prison reform. Fortunately our relationship was able to stand the strain I had imposed on it.

Reflecting on that incident, I realise that one of my most satisfying experiences during these years was my participation in Brian Lennon's 'Faith and Politics' group, where we were dealing with reconciliation and justice issues, but dealing with them in a biblical and theological way. When, on behalf of the School, I was involved in that sort of work, and when our documents were published as a kind of united Christian manifesto, I felt that the School was justified in having its name on the cover as a sponsoring institution.

Interfaith dialogue

My main teaching commitment within the School (though not outside it where I frequently spoke on specifically interchurch ecumenism) was in the area of interfaith dialogue. The tension here was largely a personal matter, and was the familiar one between the views which are often called exclusivism, inclusivism and pluralism. My own view at the time could probably be called a variety of inclusivism. I had written on Indian Christian theology, and was convinced that the gospel should be 'at home' in every land, and should use the language and terminology of every culture. I was all in favour of cultivating good relations between people of the different world faiths. But I was also committed to the mission on which God the Father had sent Jesus, and Jesus had sent his disciples. How did this fit in with our Jewish-Christian dialogue programme? How did it mesh, for example with the views of my friend Kenneth Cracknell of the BCC? Or with the views of my friend and eventual successor John May? These were questions with which I wrestled at the time, and which have assumed for me an even greater importance since my departure from the School.

Money!

But probably the cause of greatest tension for me – and for the School in general in my time – was money. To begin with I assumed that all was well, and left financial problems to Raymond Kennedy and the sponsoring committee. Gradually, however, I realised that all was not as it should be. Fortunately, however, the joint chairmen of the committee, Robin Lewis-Crosby and Donal O'Sullivan, did share their concerns with me – the fact that we were getting deeper and deeper into debt, and that drastic measures would have to be taken. It was a period of great strain: so much so, indeed, that Raymond Kennedy became ill, and eventually resigned in July 1983. With the good wishes of the school he departed to an ecumenical post in California. Urgent new arrangements had to be made, and Robin Lewis-Crosby suggested that we invite Gordon Buttanshaw to become our honorary financial adviser. It was an inspired suggestion. Gordon was able to present a clear picture of our precarious state, and to share it in detail with the Board. In September 1983 we appointed Ray O'Donoghue as part-time development officer, and he proceeded to do very good work – first as a volunteer and thereafter on a modest honorarium. Yet by the beginning of 1986 we had to go public with the news that the School was faced with closure; and the front page of the January issue of *Unity* made this disturbingly clear. Ray O'Donohue afterwards said that that was the move which solved the problem. The problem did not go away, but in my last two years we succeeded in making income exceed expenditure.

The strain imposed on the staff – both academic and administrative – by our constant financial difficulties was very considerable. Towards the end of 1986 some of these difficulties began to surface, and the Board appointed a salary review committee of experts from outside the School, headed by Prof David Spearman of TCD. Sadly, I was unable to resolve the situation before my departure, though I was able, I believe, to set in train the procedures which were to lead to its solution.

FAREWELL

My initial appointment to the School had been for three years, and this had been extended to six. Now I was asked if I would do a further three. I was sixty-two, our children were in Australia, grandchildren were beginning to arrive, and both

Frances and I felt that we ought to return to Australia. However, I was anxious to make sure that the School had traded its way out of debt, and that the road ahead was clear for my successor. I agreed to stay for one further year, so that he or she could take over in September 1987. And so it happened.

We acquired a great asset in John May, the new director. We were still enriched by the presence of Alan Falconer, Bill McSweeney, and – in Belfast – Michael Hurley. Unity had not yet arrived, and neither had peace. But we were on the way.

CHAPTER FOUR

Realising Our Potential
(1987-1990)

John D'Arcy May

John D'Arcy May was born in Melbourne, Australia, in 1942. After studying philosophy and theology in Canberra and Melbourne, he obtained the degrees of STL from the Gregorian University, Rome (1969); Dr Theol in Ecumenical Theology from the University of Münster (1975); and Dr Phil in History of Religions from the University of Frankfurt (1983). He was *wissenschaftlicher Assistent* at the Catholic Ecumenical Institute in Münster (1975-1982); Ecumenical Research Officer with the Melanesian Council of Churches, Port Moresby, and Research Associate of the Melanesian Institute, Goroka, Papua New Guinea (1983-1987); and Director of the Irish School of Ecumenics (1987-1990). He recently retired as Associate Professor of Interfaith Dialogue from Trinity College Dublin, of which he was elected a Fellow in 2004. He has been a visiting professor in Fribourg, Switzerland (1982); Frankfurt, Germany (1988); Wollongong, Australia (1994); Tilburg, The Netherlands (1996); Australian Catholic University, Sydney (2001); and the Istituto Trentino di Cultura, Italy (2006). Recent publications include: *Pluralism and the Religions: The Theological and Political Dimensions* (editor, London, 1998); *After Pluralism: Towards an Interreligious Ethic* (Münster-Hamburg-London, 2000); *Transcendence and Violence: The Encounter of Buddhist, Christian and Primal Traditions* (New York and London, 2003); and *Converging Ways? Conversion and Belonging in Buddhism and Christianity* (editor, St Ottilien, 2006).

Prologue

The little town of Goroka in the Eastern Highlands of Papua New Guinea, though its population in the mid-1980s was no more than 20,000, was distinguished by hosting twenty-two different Christian churches and a number of significant institutes, among them the Melanesian Institute for Pastoral and Socio-economic Service (MI), founded in the same year as ISE by the four largest churches (Roman Catholic, Lutheran, Anglican and United Church). Though my official position was as Ecumenical Research Officer with the (then) Melanesian Council of Churches (MCC) and my responsibilities extended to collaboration with the Melanesian Association of Theological Schools (MATS), it was at MI that I lived with my family, participating in all the Institute's activities and benefiting from the expertise of the staff and an excellent library. Here, in 1986, the news reached me, almost by accident, that ISE was looking for a new director. I had corresponded with Michael Hurley, who sent me his foundational article 'Ecumenism, Ecumenical Theology and Ecumenics' (*Irish Theological Quarterly* 45, 1978, 132-139) while I was still teaching in Germany, and I had met Alan Falconer and Robin Boyd through the Societas Oecumenica. What had impressed me was the comprehensiveness of the School's programme, which integrated the three components of any venture claiming to call itself 'ecumenical': the quest for Christian unity, the dialogue of religions, and the struggle for peace and social justice.

So I applied, thinking that would be the end of it and turning my attention once again to the endlessly fascinating but deeply troubled country I was working in. The MCC was in the slough of despond, having just discovered that it was in debt to the World Council of Churches to the tune of some $60,000 and unable to attract serious support from its member churches. The disaffected youth of the country was in a virtual civil war with the ineffectual legal, social and educational apparatus of the fledgling state (independent only since 1975). And an election was drawing near, with its increased scope for patronage, bribery and bullying in the fight to get the coveted ticket to the capital, Port Moresby. It was at this juncture that a telegram arrived asking me to appear for an interview in Dublin in November 1986.

So it was that I was whisked from ramshackle Goroka, with its warriors in *bilas* (traditional dress, including weapons) rubbing shoulders with neat bank clerks in knee socks, to a guest apartment in Trinity College Dublin overlooking the rugby pitch. At Heathrow the plane was held up while unclaimed luggage was unloaded and a nervous passenger mistook the life-jacket under an adjacent seat for a suspect package; and when I set off for a walk down O'Connell Street it was cordoned off because of a bomb scare. Welcome to Ireland! Instead of moving on to my native Australia as I had assumed, I was soon to be coming to grips with the situation in the land of my ancestors at a low point of the Troubles. I can only assume the interview panel overlooked my lack of administrative experience in the hope of continuing and developing ISE's tradition of teaching and research in the area of interreligious dialogue; when I asked about the financial situation, I was told: 'You won't have to worry about that.' I was naïve enough to believe it.

In the course of 1987 things finally began to come together for the MCC and its AGM was attended by the church leaders themselves; there was fresh thinking and a new attempt to get the finances and the operating structures into working order. Meanwhile, the prospect of reinstating Religious Studies at the University of Papua New Guinea and Goroka Teachers' College finally opened up. Not exactly 'mission completed', but there was a certain sense of satisfaction nonetheless as my thoughts turned to 'going finish'. My inner compass was still making the 180^0 turn from south to north, from the Asia-Pacific to Europe, from familiar Australia to unknown Ireland, and despite the exhilaration of knowing I would be able to continue doing ecumenical work at a high academic level, my apprehension grew the more I found out about the Irish conflict and the role of the churches in it. Yet my experience in Melanesia had given me a point of reference: an ecumenical interface where everything

that was problematic about world Christianity came together –
the foreignness of the mission churches, their unseemly rival-
ries, their failures to come to grips with their theological differences and the ineffectualness of their social leadership. At the
same time it implanted the deep conviction that here the
Christianity of the future was being born, and it left me with a
debt of gratitude to the ecumenically committed Christians of all
traditions with whom I had had the privilege of working. As my
family and I paid a last visit to a community of Mercy sisters in
Port Moresby, a Papua New Guinean sister who had never met
us before said, as she brought us a cool drink: 'Thank you for all
you have done for my country.' It was a humbling farewell.

1. Coming to Terms with Ireland
Some time into my tenure I heard Rev Alan Martin, minister of
Abbey Presbyterian Church in central Dublin and a convinced
ecumenist who was to become a valued friend, preach on a text
which, I sensed, had a personal relevance for him as a native of
Northern Ireland working in the South: 'But seek the welfare of
the city where I have sent you into exile, and pray to the Lord on
its behalf, for in its welfare you will find your welfare' (Jer 29:7).
As an Australian in this new and unfamiliar environment, I too
felt like an exile, but Alan's words helped me to put things into
perspective, and Jeremiah's prophecy has certainly been ful-
filled for me.

It is a truism that the culture shock of living in a so-called
Third World country is nothing compared with the culture
shock of returning to the West, and in our case we were coming
to a country we knew almost nothing about and which sometimes seemed to lie somewhere in between both worlds (I found
myself using the term Third World several times as 1987 wore
on into 1988, once in a Board meeting, only to have it struck from
the record by an irate Dr Donal O'Sullivan, formerly Irish ambassador to London). It was a depressing time, and the greyness
and dilapidation of Dublin seemed all of a piece with the constant atrocities in Northern Ireland, the unemployment (17 per

cent on average) and the rising emigration (reportedly 46,000 in 1988). Yet people were kind, colleagues were welcoming, and even before I had left Papua New Guinea letters of encouragement arrived from Dr Robin Eames, Archbishop of Armagh, Rt Hon David Bleakley, General Secretary of the Irish Council of Churches, and Rev Timothy Kinahan, whose time at the Anglican seminary in Popondetta had overlapped with mine in Goroka. Within days of my arrival Robin Boyd took me to Belfast, and with a sense of incredulity I found myself drinking coffee with the Presbyterian Moderator in Church House, looking across the road to the Academical Institute, Robin's *alma mater*. As we walked around the city centre, he remarked, indicating the statues of British noblemen and generals, 'They have a different set of heroes up here.'

For Christians, facing a challenge is an opportunity to practise the virtue of hope, and that I was determined to do. Invited to write something for *Unity* prior to my arrival, I said that having been involved in formulating 'ecumenics' as a fundamental discipline integrating all areas of communication and co-operation between religious traditions during my time in Münster, I had come to regard ISE as one of the most innovative ecumenical institutions in Europe, adding that I was encouraged by the thought that I would be joining a team of true ecumenical professionals and participating in an ecumenical community which included students from both European and Third World countries (*Unity* 32, 1987, 1). In my first contribution to *Unity* as director, I wrote:

> Such is Ireland's 'image' abroad that we must confess to being taken aback by evidence of poverty, unemployment, emigration and crime even here; but by the same token, the assurance of many friends who had been to Ireland that we would find an incomparable human warmth and richness have been amply borne out,

adding:

> In my first month in Ireland I have come to appreciate that

the network of relationships established by Michael Hurley and Robin Boyd, which cuts across all the conventional barriers to understanding and reconciliation in Ireland, is indeed a precious heritage and the enduring foundation on which the Irish School of Ecumenics rests. (*Unity* 34, 1987, 1)

Such remains my conviction to this day.

Yet morale in the School was not high, and I soon began to get an inkling of the difficulties we were facing. It was not the obvious issues – the social situation, the violence in the North – so much as the daily grind of making ends meet that set people's nerves on edge. But for me it was imperative to feel my way into the unfamiliar context, the undiscovered country that lay beneath the ever-cheerful surface, and my agenda, according to my journal, became 'the sheer difficulty of making sense of Ireland'. In one of my early attempts to formulate the School's relationship to the 'narrow and constricting Irish problem' ('The Irish School of Ecumenics and the Irish Problem', *Irish Ecumenical News* Vol 7, No 1, May 1988), I noted that I regarded 'Catholic-Protestant squabbles' as 'essentially a thing of the past', being grateful, however, that 'the Irish School of Ecumenics would have attracted me no matter where it was located, because it transcends the Irish or any other situation'. I added that ISE 'must never allow itself to be defined by the Irish problem'. Though the vision of ISE and the faith that underlies it are 'infinitely bigger than denominational dead ends ... the painful fact remains that Christian faith in one of its heartlands is unable to exercise a decisive influence on the solution of a problem fraught with historical resentments, economic injustices and political complexities'. Not for the last time, the article evoked an immediate response from Michael Hurley, who had gained the impression that, in my view, ISE was defined by the Irish problem and that Catholic-Protestant differences were a thing of the past. His letter taught me one lesson I never forgot: he had not founded ISE as a response to the Troubles, but as a basis for dealing with Christian divisions at academic level, and from the beginning he had world Christianity, not just Ireland, in view.

In an interview with Barry White for the *Belfast Telegraph* ('The new man who is looking at Ireland's ecumenical problem', *Belfast Telegraph*, Wednesday, December 9, 1987, 9), arranged by Michael Hurley, I find myself 'worried about a "backlash" against the ecumenical movement among students in seminaries and colleges, in favour of denominational identity and clarity'.

> That is something I would like to broach, not just with Maynooth, but with the Presbyterians. I want to concentrate on them, because those actually engaged in ecumenism are the old faithfuls. I don't notice too many young people. I'm told they are moving in the opposite direction, and that doesn't bode well for the future. The school of ecumenics will be going out to attract young people.

This aspiration continued to be at least partially met for many years by the annual Study Days for theological students from all parts of Ireland initiated by Alan Falconer, and by the continuing education courses run by Michael Hurley, then living in Belfast, on behalf of ISE in Northern Ireland.

Though ecumenism in Papua New Guinea had its problems, to a considerable extent they could be put down to the limitations of church leaders who were already overwhelmed by the task of keeping their own denominations functioning, let alone negotiating the complexities of ecumenical relations. Ecumenism in Ireland was more baffling. I immediately inherited roles representing the School in the Department of Theological Questions of the Irish Inter-Church Meeting (IICM, known as 'Ballymascanlon' after the hotel near Dundalk at which the meetings were held and over whose doorway, as Robin Boyd pointed out to me, stood the appropriate motto *Festina lente*, 'hasten slowly'); the annual Clergy Conference at the Corrymeela Community in Co Antrim; the annual meetings of the Irish Council of Churches; and the editorial committee of the *Irish Ecumenical News*, where I enjoyed the encouraging presence of some of the grand old men of Irish ecumenism: the Methodist minister Eric Gallagher, the Presbyterian theologian John Barkley, and Donald Kennedy,

Irish Presbyterianism's only bishop thanks to his position in the
Church of North India – his impish sense of humour never
faded: he once greeted Eric Gallagher with the words, 'Delighted
to see you, Arminian though you be'!

For years I faithfully attended meetings of the IICM
Department which always seemed to have the same agenda, till
an attempt was made to give it a new direction at a residential
workshop in Bellinter House, a retreat centre outside Dublin,
which eventually resulted in the report *Freedom, Justice and
Responsibility in Ireland Today* (1997). Three of us, the Anglican
John Marsden, the Jesuit Gerry O'Hanlon and myself, tried to
press for real innovations: the renunciation of the Orange Order
by Protestants and the offer of eucharistic hospitality by
Catholics; but to no avail.[1] I had been introduced to the 'political
theology' of Johann Baptist Metz and Jürgen Moltmann during
the 1970s in Germany, and in the 1980s I was cautiously trying to
introduce 'liberation theology' to my Melanesian colleagues;
theology in Ireland seemed devoid of any trace of either. In my
frustration I remember using the phrase, 'We're fiddling with
theological niceties while Belfast burns', which needless to say
did not appear in print.

In a contribution to the journal *Protestant and Catholic
Encounter* ('The Social Side of Ecumenism', *PACE* 20/2, 1988, 6-
8), I noted that, at ecumenical gatherings, social issues always
seemed to come up last:

> The type of consumer society which our global civilisation,
> made possible by modern technology, seems to reproduce
> everywhere, also produces that state of polarisation, inequal-
> ity and institutionalised injustice which we call 'Third
> World' when it is located far enough away from us geo-
> graphically, though sociologically it has become an integral
> part of Western societies. ... It is the peculiarity of the 'Irish

1. I was eventually able to voice my convictions in a lecture at Trinity
College during the Week of Prayer for Christian Unity, entitled
'European Union, Christian Division? Christianity's Responsibility for
Europe's Past and Future', *Studies* 89 (2000) 118-129, 128.

problem' that both types of problem, doctrinal and social, are factors in it. But where do we find 'doctrine' being discussed in terms of social symbolism; and where do we find 'society' as the medium and matrix of doctrinal discussion?

In my ignorance of the immense difficulties facing church people in the oppressive intimacy of such a relatively limited context, I had not yet come to appreciate the courage shown by many Christians such as Gordon Gray in deeply Presbyterian Lisburn, Tim Kinahan in his Church of Ireland parish in Belfast, or Brian Lennon as a kind of Jesuit loose cannon in hostile territory. In the early years a group of former missionaries calling itself Mission Dialogue used to meet in Dublin, and members such as the unflappable Declan Smith of the Church Missionary Society, the ever-enthusiastic Isabelle Smyth of the Medical Missionaries of Mary, and the irrepressible Kiltegan missionary Donal Dorr gave me the reassurance that there were those for whom an 'Irish liberation theology' was a real prospect, even though, as Isabelle remarked, 'Ireland has not yet had its Medellin.'

One place where I quickly found my feet was the classroom. The pressing need to grapple theologically with the Christian ecumenical situation in Ireland and beyond tended to overshadow what had steadily been becoming both an urgent global issue and my main area of academic interest, the theology of religions as a Christian basis for engaging in the dialogue of world religions. Robin Boyd, drawing on his landmark contributions to Indian Christian theology, had established a strong tradition of interreligious studies at ISE on which I was able to build, substituting a course on Buddhist-Christian dialogue for his on the dialogue with Hinduism. Given our straitened circumstances, there was little opportunity for expanding this section of the curriculum, but it did at least allow students to specialise in the field of interreligious dialogue, and some extremely interesting dissertations were produced. In class, however, one had to be careful: I remember a religious sister from Northern Ireland being visibly shocked as the implications of the dialogue with Buddhism began to sink in, carrying her well beyond the world of Protestant *vs* Catholic to which she had been accustomed. It was a time when the notion of thoroughgoing religious pluralism, persuasively advanced by the Presbyterian philosopher-theologian John Hick, was becoming controversial, and for a while I was able to keep the students guessing as to where I stood on the spectrum of exclusivist, inclusivist and pluralist approaches. This did not prevent Professor Duncan Forrester of the University of Edinburgh, our external examiner and an old friend of Robin Boyd and the School, from remarking that a 'Hick-Knitter orthodoxy' was showing up in the students' work. As time went on I found it necessary to move beyond this tripartite schema to explore the dimensions of *praxis* and liberation developed by the American Catholic theologian Paul Knitter, who was to become a close friend, and Aloysius Pieris SJ of Sri Lanka, whom I had visited in 1979. Meanwhile, Dr Redmond Fitzmaurice, a Dominican who had spent many years in Iran, gave the students a comprehensive introduction to Islam with all its theological implications for Christians. The field was thus firmly anchored in our programme, and it was to prove crucial later on as a complement to the international relations component of Peace Studies, but given greater resources we could have ventured even further.

It was an inestimable privilege to be invited to join the Interchurch Group on Faith and Politics, a semi-official body arising out of the Greenhills Ecumenical Conference in 1982, which contained such ecumenical veterans as Dr David Stevens, then General Secretary of the Irish Council of Churches; Dr John Morrow, Presbyterian minister and always up to the minute on Northern Ireland politics, both secular and ecclesiastical; Brian Lennon, the Jesuit *enfant terrible* who once almost blew the group apart by selecting the Republican colours green, white and orange for the cover of one of our documents; Alan Martin, Presbyterian minister in Dublin; and Tim Kinahan, Church of Ireland minister in Belfast, who brought home to me just what painful dilemmas working clergy were facing. As time went on the group became evenly balanced between North and South, clergy and laity, men and women, Catholic and Protestant, the rough edge taken off its discussions by the gentle spirit of Una O'Higgins O'Malley, and though it lapsed after the Belfast Agreement was reached in 1998 it is now being revived. It was the only group I knew where people from 'both camps' could crack jokes at one another's expense. At a stage when it was possibly too early to do so responsibly, I ventured the phrase 'political ecumenism' and the suggestion that a 'reconciliation of structures' could complement the 'reconciliation of memories' so effectively pioneered in Ireland by Alan Falconer ('Political Ecumenism: Church Structures and the Political Process', *Studies* 79, 1990, 396-405, a paper read to the Irish Theological Association. David Bleakley used the term 'political ecumenism' independently when addressing the Irish Council of Churches in April 1989).

At a commemorative dinner to mark ISE's twenty-fifth anniversary, Dr David Poole, a Quaker researcher with the Agricultural Institute who was Chair of the Executive Board for most of my tenure and is still involved in the School's affairs, went through each of the directors in turn, indicating the specific contribution each had made to the School's development. Somewhat to my surprise, I found myself being credited with having helped bring the Irish churches to accept the School to the point of actively supporting it, but on reviewing my records I realise there is something in it: the apparent isolation of the School from its base in the churches preyed on my mind, and I became increasingly explicit in giving vent to my dissatisfaction. At a Board meeting, gruff and honest Tom Walsh, director of the Agricultural Institute, said with his usual directness that until the Catholic Church *as such*, through its highest institutions, gave a lead in committing itself to ecumenism and ISE, there would be no real movement and no long-term support, a view I of course endorsed. Musing on this later in my journal, I wrote:

> … you simply can't run an ecumenical institute by the collection box … For all these years the School has run after trusts

and charities and religious orders and survived by dint of the sheer generosity of the little band of converts to ecumenism in Ireland, mostly of advanced age and more or less on the outer in their own churches. But there's the rub: 'churches' – where are they? Why aren't they supporting what is in the first instance their ecumenical institute? Do they really want it, or are they simply tolerating it? Do they want unity at all? I suspect they are terrified of the very idea, and that Bally-mascanlon and all the rest of the official ecumenical façade is just one big alibi to excuse them from ever facing up to it.

There speaks frustration indeed. In more moderate tones, I put it to the AGM of the Irish Council of Churches in Limerick (7-8 April, 1989) that ISE was staring bankruptcy in the face, not because of financial mismanagement but because the demand for its services had forced ISE to grow well beyond the capacity of its traditional support base to sustain it. It was anomalous that after almost twenty years of pioneering the teaching of ecumen-ics in a responsible and innovative way, and despite the fact that it regularly received financial support from individual mem-bers, organisations and even leaders of the churches in a private capacity, ISE still had no official relationship with the churches in Ireland and received no support from their central bodies. Moreover, no one in Ireland had come forward with a substan-tial endowment which would put the School's finances on a firm footing once and for all. 'Our finances are wrong because our re-lationships are wrong', I said. At the back of my mind was the experience of ecumenical institutes elsewhere, such as MI in Papua New Guinea, with its international funding base and the explicit – if not always reliable – support of the local churches. Were such relationships with churches impossible in Ireland, I asked, without detriment to ISE's essential autonomy? 'It's not easy to be independent when you're broke', I concluded, think-ing of the comment by an African student that ISE's cherished autonomy need not imply non-accountability. I was, of course, speaking to the converted, and they spontaneously responded with a resolution to do all in their power to bring their churches on side, but it was to be a long and difficult process. In 1989 I was still writing that 'this will be the focus of all my efforts in the coming year: to achieve a breakthrough in the acceptance of ISE – in very practical and perhaps even organisational terms – by the churches throughout the island of Ireland' (*Unity* 40, 1989, 7).

If a certain desperation becomes apparent in such words, that was perhaps understandable; but it was also dangerous, because ISE could not afford to be too close to the churches in Ireland, either, especially not to any particular one of them. It could equally ill afford to be seen as a perpetual recipient of aid; at an informal Academic Council meeting the point was made that our fundamental approach should be: 'How can we be of service?' – in the whole of Ireland. My predecessors had bequeathed us an even wider network of relationships, notably in the US and Germany, and these too I set out to maintain and extend. Together with David Pyle, our new development officer, I visited the United States in mid-1988, he following up potential donors, I visiting universities in search of students and reciprocal arrangements. Though the trip was a strain on our meagre resources, it gave us the opportunity to meet representatives of the Presbyterian Church in the USA in Washington who were exploring the possibilities of a more explicit engagement with their Irish counterparts; and I was given a few minutes in which to present ISE and its work to the annual conference of the Council on Christian Unity in Indianapolis. I also visited Germany that year, where the School already had old friends, among them Klaus Kremkau, responsible for the foreign relations of the Protestant Church in Germany (EKD) at its headquarters in Hanover, and Eberhard Spiecker, a lawyer who had already taken bold initiatives on behalf of his Lutheran *Landeskirche* to mediate in Northern Ireland. These involved meetings in Germany between representatives of the UUP (Ulster Unionist Party) and the Nationalist SDLP (1985 and 1987) and on 14-15 October 1988 a secret conference involving Jack Allen (UUP), Peter Robinson (Demcratic Unionist Party), Gordon Mawhinney (Alliance) and Fr Alec Reid CSsR representing Sinn Féin at the Angerhof Hotel near Duisburg, a crucial step forward in what was to become the Northern Ireland peace process and the prelude to direct negotiations between Spiecker and Sinn Féin. Thanks to Kremkau's successor, Detlev Nonne, I was invited to attend the *Kirchentag* of the German Protestant churches in the year of *die Wende*, the great turning point in German reunification, 1989. These were loyal friends of the School who were responsible for regular substantial grants from their churches over the years.

An ongoing relationship of a different kind, though none the less valuable, I owe to my colleagues at the University of Frankfurt, who had recently inaugurated an innovative pro-gramme called *Theologie Interkulturell* ('doing theology intercul-turally'), which included an annual visiting professorship by a theologian from a cultural context outside Western Europe and an interdisciplinary symposium, often involving scholars from all continents and a wide variety of disciplines. They needed someone for 1988 to keep the series going, and they importuned me so insistently to be the 'voice of the Pacific' that I consulted the only ISE body that happened to be meeting at the time, the Academic Council. Although the timing was awkward – I had to postpone my lectures to the second term and return to Dublin in the middle of my tenure to attend the AGM of Academic Council – in retrospect I am extremely grateful for their unhesit-ating encouragement to take up the offer (Dr Margaret MacCurtain OP, University College Dublin historian, and Catherine McGuinness, barrister and future Supreme Court judge, I remember, were especially emphatic), because it not only gave exposure to the School at an international academic level, but also enabled me to reflect on the many-sided experience of working in the Pacific while memories were still fresh, resulting in the book *Christus Initiator. Theologie im Pazifik* (1990).

When I finally returned to Dublin, the atmosphere at ISE was not good. The staff were feeling the pinch of our financial con-straints, and our governing bodies were becoming impatient with the absence of new funding initiatives. It was a painful period,

but it brought to light some of the more deep-seated reasons for
ISE's difficulties.

2. Institutionalising Ecumenics

Invited by the redoubtable Elizabeth Ferrar, former school principal in India and *mulier fortis* of the Church of Ireland, to contribute an article to *Search*, the Church of Ireland journal she
edited, I took the opportunity to reflect on the difficulties which
seemed to be congenital in ecumenical organisations ('The
Economics of Ecumenics', *Search* 13/1, 1990, 32-36). I had experienced the chaotic finances of the MCC and I had seen its regional
counterpart, the Pacific Conference of Churches, forced to sus-
pend virtually all its far-flung activities until its financial affairs
were put in order. 'And now I find the Irish School of
Ecumenics, whose motto is *floreat ut pereat*, "flourishing" (academically) and "perishing" (financially) at one and the same time.'
This prompted me to ask: 'How do you institutionalise univer-
sality? And who pays for it – and how?'

> One fairly obvious reason for the penury of so many ecu-
> menical organisations is that they are 'nobody's baby'. They
> are kept going by the committed ecumenists across the de-
> nominational spectrum, but from the point of view of partic-
> ular churches and the committees that decide how they are
> going to spend their money they are not strictly 'ours'; as my
> professor in Germany used to put it, they come under 'for-
> eign affairs'. In the minds of such people, the ecumenical
> movement cuts across cherished loyalties which have a great
> deal to do with maintaining the sources of financial support
> within the denomination, while for the more theologically
> minded it smacks of tolerance, even compromise. To engage
> in it seems tantamount to an admission of weakness – it has,
> after all, been compared more than once to the tendency of
> companies under threat of takeover to merge in order to fight
> off more powerful rivals.

> In short, church leaders can find ecumenism provocative

while their congregations can find it boring. Yet both attitudes do a grave injustice to the ecumenical reality:

> Peace has always been the great practical this-worldly goal of the ecumenical movement. It has tried to lay bare the spiritual roots of conflict and injustice, whether racial, religious or economic, and to collaborate with all who are trying to devise means to overcome them. It has taken up the cause of the poor and advocated their liberation as an essential precondition of 'development'. Unity and dialogue, though values in themselves requiring no extraneous justification, come to full maturity when they bear the fruits of peace.

Hardly 'boring'! But how does one make it happen?

In May 1988, as the result of intensive discussions in Board and Finance Committee, I drew up a memo on the School's present plans and future prospects. Noting that competition for funding was steadily increasing, I saw the School's basis of predictable support becoming

> narrower and narrower. Financial crises of increasing gravity and frequency indicate that the School's traditional basis of support is slowly drying up, but even more importantly they are symptoms of a fundamental inadequacy in its relationship to the churches which are its natural constituency. The crises are not merely organisational or seasonal: they are structural.

Long term requirements include 'a substantial *endowment fund* with capital of the order of £1.3 million' and a '*building appeal* to raise at least £400,000' (the italics here and below underline the sense of urgency in the original). O innocent optimism! Yet much later both problems were eventually solved. Projects deemed essential to the School's immediate development included the appointment of lecturers in the new Peace Studies programme and in Ecumenical Studies, an appropriate salary (and a computer!) for the librarian, participation in the Education for Mutual Understanding initiative in Northern Ireland, and a scholarly journal.

The School's natural constituency is not restricted to Ireland: it is both European and ecumenical, and its regular support base should be nothing less. Establishing such a network of structured relationships to churches and ecumenical organisations would not only help to place the School's work on a firm foundation; *it would in itself contribute to the maturity of the ecumenical movement in Ireland, in the rest of Europe and beyond.*

Impatient at the apparent indifference of both churches and governments to the School's plight, I had not quite made the mental transition from the German context, at that time still awash with funding for education, and the situation in Papua New Guinea, where an institute like MI was lavishly funded – albeit from overseas – to the realities of Ireland.

In autumn 1989, after consultation with the Trustees, I announced the coming of *perestroika* to ISE, for here too 'we must contemplate structural change' (*Unity* 40, 1989). The former Finance Committee was to be broken up into its constituent parts: a twice-yearly meeting of the Trustees; a Finance Committee properly so-called, smaller than its predecessor and charged with the task of helping us to develop procedures for financial planning and control; and a Development Committee, which would provide the Development Officer with a forum for discussing fundraising strategy and tactics. There were also to be regular staff meetings of different kinds, and a Northern Ireland Committee. The aim was to complement *perestroika* with *glasnost*. Even as I wrote this, the thought was nagging at me that the proliferation of committees is one way organisations have of avoiding problems rather than tackling them. ISE's structural problems lay deeper.

One reason I had been told at interview that I wouldn't have to worry about finances was that together with me a professional development officer, David Pyle, had been appointed. A member of the Church of Ireland, he was an experienced management consultant with fresh ideas and ambitious plans for fundraising and financial management at ISE. One catch was that while such plans are necessarily long-term, our cash-flow problems were short-term. In the particular context of ISE, unable to pay commercial salaries and guided financially by retired gentlemen who could only shake their heads at the parlous state of our accounts, this new arrangement wasn't working. I sensed that this was largely because the School was unstructured to the point of disfunctionality. The director, in a sense, was responsible for everything, from course content to office equipment, but could not attend to everything equally; Barbara Duncan skilfully kept creditors at bay; Dympna Ryan maintained our precious contacts to Irish donors, particularly the religious orders, with unfailing tact and fidelity; but what exactly was the new development officer's role? Was he managing ISE? Was he its financial controller? Or was he 'merely' a fundraiser? This problem was not finally solved till the much later appointment of an administrator, an accountant, an executive secretary of the yet to be created ISE Trust and programme secretaries, but it bedevilled my entire period in office. Gordon Buttanshaw, a retired accountant who was always sympathetic to our problems, never spared the Board the harsh details of our growing overdraft and shrinking income. A finance sub-committee met for a time so that Board could be briefed on the latest developments. Tom McGrath, who filled a similar role for the Jesuits, devoted more and more of his time and expertise to analysing our problems, insisting that we needed proper control systems to keep track of our financial position.

At a meeting of the Patrons in Loyola House, the Jesuit provincial headquarters, the idea emerged of a comprehensive and independent review of our whole operation. The Patrons urged us to undertake diplomatic initiatives with church leaders, suggesting that our predicament was political rather than financial, though there was little hope of a breakthrough in the present climate. Our accounts needed to be reorganised, and the fundraising component should be reduced to 15 per cent from its present 20 per cent. Meanwhile, we had just been granted another overdraft facility of £20,000, a sum which, in later years, would have seemed like a welcome relief but which was then regarded as grave. The Jesuit provincial, Philip Harnett, always a most sympathetic and constructive discussion partner, encouraged the use of the Jesuits' own financial advisors, John Harnett and Pat Nolan, who urged us to aim high and think future, assuring us that ISE's problem was only operational and not a big one in financial terms. For people used to dealing with big profits and big deficits, this may have been so, but for me in my ignorance of both high finance and the wider Irish scene, it was frightening – a sentiment echoed not long afterwards by the Trustees. At various times I had been advised to go after the high flyers in Dublin (and even to go on RTÉ's *Late Late Show*), to seek out the Tony O'Reillys of this world and to probe members of the government, though at Academic Council a more realistic soul – especially given what we now know about the politics of the Haughey era – exclaimed: 'The Taoiseach won't save us!'

So there was to be a Task Force to prepare a round table for the autumn of 1989 as a first step to drawing up terms of reference for a thorough review. These were overseen by the Patrons, whom, it was a consolation to learn in 1990, the crisis at ISE had brought together. The terms included:

- An examination of administrative procedures.
- Provision for financial management and budgetary control.
- Identification of possible sources of income and ways of approaching them.
- A structural overhaul of Academic Council, Patrons, Board and Trustees.
- ISE's structural insertion into the Irish context.
- Clarification of the aims and functions of ISE as an institute in Ireland.
- Advice on the relocation of ISE onto a single site.
- 'Coaching' of staff (presumably in financial management) till institutional funding was secured.

An ambitious programme, which was at least partially carried out and was to have implications far into the future. Meanwhile, a special meeting of Board called for an 'intellectual assessment' of ISE's aims and internal organisation, involving

staff and the consultants, and there was mention of a building
fund. There was no time to be lost, for in June 1990 the Board
was told that our total real indebtedness including earmarked
funds was IR£190,000; some months earlier our overdraft had
climbed to IR£51,000 with a projected deficit of IR£70,000. I kept
reminding myself that the 'real' problems were not 'merely'
financial but structural. But how to deal with them without adequate resources; how to bring structural renewal, financial viability and administrative transparency – *perestroika* and *glasnost*
– together? Nevertheless, the momentum towards change had
begun and was eventually to carry us into a new phase of development.

3) *Realising our Potential*

For an academic immersed in such problems, the danger was to
lose sight of what, in the end, it was all for. Throughout this difficult period, what was sometimes called the 'vision' of ISE and
its practical implementation were evolving; we were learning to
exploit the potential of Michael Hurley's original conception of
'ecumenics'. One of the first things to land on my desk when I
arrived was the proposal, tirelessly promoted by Bill McSweeney,
to initiate a separate Master's programme in Peace Studies. He
had already forged links with the prestigious School of Peace
Studies in the University of Bradford and had ingeniously devised a curriculum that could plausibly be taught and super-
vised with the minimal resources at our disposal. One of the
strongest arguments for this was that it would not only attract
more fee-paying students, but would at one stroke make ISE
more fundable, because it would be a purely 'secular' degree. I
sensed that it was precisely this, however, that caused considerable disquiet among the church people who were our main constituency. There was also the question of how a degree with pre-
dominantly social science content would relate to our academic
point of reference in Trinity College, the (then) School of
Hebrew, Biblical and Theological Studies.

To me, the introduction of such a programme seemed inevitable. It offered the prospect of supplying the political dimension which I had always felt was missing from the School's overall approach. At the same time, in an institute hitherto entirely determined by theology and the interests of the churches, it was going to be something of a foreign body, and there was also the possibility of what Robin Boyd called the 'tail wags dog' syndrome. Nevertheless, as I remarked in my inaugural lecture before the Academic Council, referring to the conflict situations on the islands of Papua New Guinea, Sri Lanka and Ireland: 'It is only the framework constructed by the discipline of ecumenics that makes these contexts comparable at all':

> After doctrinal agreement and the experience of 'spiritual ecumenism' have prepared the ground, it is rather the techniques of the analysis and resolution of conflicts which the social sciences study under the heading of 'peace studies' that need to be explored. ('Integral Ecumenism: Sri Lanka, Papua New Guinea and Ireland', *Doctrine and Life* 38, 1988, 190-198)

Even this, however, was still taking a theological starting point for granted; what Bill McSweeney envisaged was a discipline as independent of theology as the sociology, economics and political science from which it drew its methods and data. With this, too, I had no difficulty, though I always argued for the autonomy of theology and religious studies on their own merits as commensurable with and complementary to the social sciences.

Discussion around this time revealed that the tensions were a symptom of more profound problems concerning the values espoused by the School and its ultimate viability. ISE would have to adapt to the conditions in Ireland and abroad in which it must live. The School needed to have an articulated philosophy which could explain to its ecumenical constituency the necessity and legitimacy of shifting from a position in which theology was its primary academic discipline to become truly interdisciplinary. More accurately, perhaps, we were beginning to explore what we meant by theology in relation to other disciplines such as sociology and international relations.

In the end, the issues were resolved over the years by the students themselves. After some initial friction between the two groups in the cramped circumstances of ISE (an American in the first year's Peace Studies intake referred contemptuously to the 'glorified Bible study group' she was expected to share facilities with!) they began to take an interest in one another's courses, the theologians beginning to realise the contribution the social sciences could make to the analysis of ecumenical problems (just as Michael Hurley originally envisaged), the political scientists discovering the need to inform themselves about Islam and Buddhism and the relationship between ethics and religion.

This process, too, took time, but in the meanwhile there was the question of facilities, which of course for those coming from well-endowed American or British universities were woefully inadequate. It was only later that I realised how few relevant books we had in the library, yet the students' access to the Trinity library was severely restricted (the only question I was asked when I went before the University Council to urge acceptance of the proposed Peace Studies programme was: 'Will it put pressure on the library?'). It was a combination of rumours about this and the 'ideological' doubts about Peace Studies as a discipline that fed the myth of the 'problems' at ISE; I was approached more than once by Trinity office-bearers to discuss the 'crisis' at ISE. Though we sailed close to the wind and risked a debacle, Bill's 'creative administration' (as the first external examiner, James O'Connell, Professor of Peace Studies at Bradford, called it) and the credibility given us by the unstinting support of Bradford's School of Peace Studies carried us through, and far from being a problem the Peace Studies programme put ISE on an entirely new footing, both academically and financially, laying the foundation for its future maturity as a truly multi-disciplinary institute where processes of dialogue and reconciliation could be studied in a variety of contexts using a variety of approaches. Student numbers doubled, exceeding

9 November 1970, the formal inauguration of the Irish School of Ecumenics at Milltown Park Dublin. Left to right: Rev Mícheál Mac Gréil SJ, Rev Maurice Stewart, Rev Gabriel Daly OSA, Rev Dr James Boyd, Rev Professor John Barkley, the editor, Rev Dr Carson Blake, General Secretary, World Council of Churches who gave the inaugural address, the Right Rev Richard Hanson, Bishop of Clogher, Rev David Clarke, Rev Ernest Gallagher and Rev Robert N. Brown.

In July 1971 at a press conference to announce the link between the University of Hull and the Irish School of Ecumenics. From left: Sir Brynmor Jones, Vice-Chancellor, the author, Right Rev John W. Armstrong, Church of Ireland Patron of ISE, and Rev Professor Anthony Hanson, Department of Theology, University of Hull.

At the Silver Jubilee Service of Thanksgiving, Low Sunday 1995, St Patrick's Cathedral, Dublin.
Front: Dr Konrad Raiser, Secretary General World Council of Churches, President Mary Robinson, Dean Maurice Stewart, Dean of St Patrick's Cathedral.
Back: Dr David Poole, Chair of the ISE Executive Board, Dr Geraldine Smyth OP, Director of ISE.

President Mary McAleese, Dr Geraldine Smyth OP, Director of ISE at the launch of *Reconciling Memories*, (2nd edition), ed Rev Dr Alan Falconer and Dr Joseph Liechty, held at ISE Dublin on 21 May 1998.

Pastor Paul Fritz, Lutheran Church, Farewell Lecture: 'Dietrich Bonhoeffer: Lasting Legacy and Challenging Witness'. Joint event of ISE and Dublin Council of Churches, held on 18 February 1997.

Dr David Tombs, Lecturer and Co-ordinator of the Reconciliation Studies Programme, Mr Denis Anderson, Lecturer, Education for Reconciliation Programme, Northern Ireland and the Border Counties, Dr Andrew Pierce, Lecturer and Co-ordinator of the Ecumenical Studies Programme.

Patrons' Meeting held at ISE, Dublin, 31 May 2000.
Left to Right: Dr David Poole, Chair of the ISE Executive Board, His
Eminence Desmond Cardinal Connell, Archbishop of Dublin, Rev
Canon Kenneth Kearon, Director of ISE, Rev Dr Alan V. Martin,
Presbyterian Church in Ireland, The Most Rev Dr Robert H. A. Eames,
Archbishop of Armagh, Mr Tom Kingston, Methodist Church in
Ireland (representing Rev Edmund T. I. Mawhinney, Patron), Most Rev
Dr Anthony Farquhar, Auxiliary Bishop of Down and Connor.

Signing of the ISE-TCD Agreement, 6 December 2000, at TCD.
Front: Mr Sean Hogan (ISE Trustee), Rev Canon Kenneth Kearon,
Director of ISE, Ms Margaret Hamilton-Reid (Trustee), Dr Thomas
Mitchell, (Provost TCD), Dr Christopher Gibson (Chair of the ISE
Executive Board), Rev Dr Gerard O'Hanlon, (President of the ISE
Academic Council for Research, Provincial of the Society of Jesus).
Back: Mr Michael Gleeson, Secretary to the College, Professor David
McConnell, (Vice Provost) TCD.

The Bea House library, now holding some 35,000 volumes, has since 1983 been the pride and joy of Sláine Ó Hogáin, seen here (right) with Gillian Wylie, Lecturer, International Peace Studies Programme.

Also in Bea House library, Aideen Woods, ISE Administrator, with Ian Atack, Lecturer and Coordinator, International Peace Studies Programme.

The Patrons' Dinner, held at ISE, Dublin, 23 February 2007.
Front: Ms Paulyn Marrinan Quinn SC, Lecturer & Co-ordinator, Evening Diploma, Conflict & Dispute Resolution Studies, Rev Mary Hunter, Ms Gillian Kingston, (members of ISE Trust Steering Committee), Mr Denis Anderson, Dr Geraldine Smyth OP, (ISE staff), Dr Bill McSweeney, (Research Fellow ISE). Back: Rev Dr Dermot Lane, Dr David Poole, (members of ISE Trust Steering Committee), Professor John D'Arcy May, Dr David Tombs (ISE staff), Ms Felicity McCartney (member of ISE Trust Steering Committee), Dr.Terry Duffy (ISE Staff), Dr Noel Dorr (member of ISE Trust Steering Committee).

fifty for the first time. It is no exaggeration to say that it was the Peace Studies programme that saved us.

Yet this maturing was to be a long process, and hard upon a session with our counterparts in Trinity which highlighted the absence of a course on theology and the social sciences, the inadequate use of Trinity personnel from other departments, the growing disparity between numbers of students and available staff, and the lack of a 'philosophy' or ethical perspective underlying the whole, I received a delegation of Peace Studies students complaining about the inadequate facilities, the lack of depth and focus in the courses, the disproportion between numbers of students and staff, and the Eurocentrism of the overall perspective. Significantly, they seemed to sense that even the Board was not one hundred per cent behind the venture into Peace Studies. Yet the courses on the politics of the European Union and Eastern Europe had already given us a head start in view of the dramatic events of 1989, and the next year I felt able to write:

> At ISE, we feel vindicated in having decided to go ahead with our degree programme in peace studies at a time when by no means everyone was convinced of the wisdom or appropriateness of such a move. We are now one of the very few institutes anywhere in Ireland or Britain capable of dealing with the new European developments at a scholarly level (*Unity* 41, 1990, 4).

This, and the course on the Northern Ireland conflict, was to make us more and more attractive to potential students who would otherwise never have come to us.

Our celebration of the School's twentieth anniversary in 1990, under these circumstances, was so low key as to be barely noticeable, which was perhaps just as well, because the rumblings of discontent were wider and deeper than those surrounding the introduction of Peace Studies. Our dual location, with the administration at Milltown Park and the academics and the library a mile away at Bea House, was becoming a severe handicap, engendering an attitude of 'us and them'. More ominously, a meeting to evaluate the students' questionnaires on their experience at ISE, after rehearsing the familiar criticisms about inadequate information, lack of facilities, Eurocentricity of perspective and the 'non-existent' relationship between Ecumenical and Peace Studies, yielded the comment that there was 'no "heart" to ISE'. Picking up a thesis that had been written on low intensity conflict, a student from New Zealand whose judgement I greatly respected, Bruce Keeley, remarked knowingly: 'Is ISE doing research on itself these days?'

In a special issue of *Unity* to mark the twentieth anniversary (*Unity* 42, 1990), which I introduced by inviting readers to share our sense of excitement that the school's present difficulties are those of the transition to something new, past and present students were given the opportunity to speak their minds. Bruce Keeley wrote on the gap between theory and practice in the way interfaith relations were dealt with, not least because 'the other faith communities in Ireland are tiny minorities with negligible impact on the prevailing religious climate'. Saths Moodley from South Africa praised the non-theological nature of peace studies in ISE, and Geraldine Smyth took exception to the marginal presence of women and feminist issues and the lack of an experiential process in the academic programmes. In a thought-provoking introductory article, Gabriele Scherle and Peter Schüttke-Scherle, German Lutheran theologians with a special interest in Jewish-Christian relations (which Peter had developed in his ISE dissertation), who were contributing to the teaching while Alan Falconer was on sabbatical, discerned that ISE 'has lost a sense of urgency about its direction and its end', identifying the question at the academic level as 'the relation between ecumenics, theology, inter-religious studies and peace studies'. For the latter two, 'the social sciences are the determinative discipline', and 'ISE has to make up its mind on whether it is a theology-based institute or not'.

> An alertness to this overlap [they continued] between the political, religious and theological could be a specific contribution arising from an Irish context, with its religiously

loaded conflict. … [ISE] can be (and is much more since the establishment of the Centre for Peace Studies) a learning community as a microcosm of our world.

There was something of the safety valve in all this, the release of steadily building pressure for change, and out of it was to be born a radically reconfigured School of Ecumenics which realised even more of the possibilities implicit in Michael Hurley's original conception.

Of particular concern to me was the relatively low profile of what I liked to call 'interreligious studies' at ISE. In a 1990 memo I wrote:

> Our so-called 'interfaith' section is like the planned north wing that was called for by the design of the house but never built: the logic of our evolution demands that this section be developed. This is the frontier of 'ecumenics' where the future of the discipline lies, but it also represents a constitutive dimension of Peace Studies which could give our programme a distinctive and very attractive dimension.

Noting that Religious Studies itself was in a ferment as it tried to determine its relationship to theology and 'comparative hermeneutics', I continued:

> ISE should be part of this ferment, but the study of religions here has another, more practical rationale: we may expect more and more of our potential students to be confronted by the manifold problems created by religious pluralism, in education, pastoral care, the teaching of theology, the foundations of ethics, the myriad 'new religious movements' springing up in virtually all contexts …

At the same time, I anticipated that we could be under pressure from our ecclesiastical constituency to make 'mission and evangelism' a major emphasis in our programme with a view to Northern Irish sensibilities and funding prospects. However, I argued that, within the constraints of our capabilities, both linguistic and financial, we should remain true to our original and fundamental orientation towards 'dialogue', even if this was going through a phase of unpopularity in certain Christian circles.

This was and still is the shape of things to come; in the meantime, the situation at ISE and my own role in it were coming to a head. Alongside – indeed, perhaps at the root of – our organisational and financial challenges it was becoming evident that there was an even more fundamental intellectual one to be faced. The need to give the students on both programmes the theoretical means to relate the one to the other was becoming urgent, and the consultants' advice was that I would be better suited to the latter than the former task.

Some time during my third year at ISE, it became clear to me that I would have to make a choice between the two challenges – the organisational and the intellectual – if I were to make any worthwhile contribution after such a relatively short time in this infinitely complex country. The question only needed to be formulated for the answer to become obvious to anyone who knows me: my background predisposes me to make a contribution to just that task of integrating apparently disparate elements in an ecumenical curriculum on which ISE is at present embarked.

And so it came to be – but that is another story, which will be rounded off in due course.

These first three years in Ireland were certainly not what I had bargained for. Today, both the Northern peace process and the Southern economy have made progress that was simply unimaginable in the late nineteen eighties. Then, ISE was on its own, and the whole climate in the country made people wary of committing themselves to such a struggling institute whose aims seemed to run counter to entrenched traditional assumptions in church, government and university. It was ecumenical, peace-orientated and cross-disciplinary at a time when it still seemed more prudent to maintain clear boundaries between denominations, states and academic disciplines. Now there is movement on all these fronts throughout Europe, and ISE has both contributed to and benefited from this change of attitude. Hard as it was at the time to understand the context that made so many things seem inevitable which have now passed into history, I'm glad I stayed long enough to see the convictions on which ISE was founded finally vindicated. The School has always been innovative and unconventional, and it is my hope and belief that it will remain so.

CHAPTER FIVE

Negotiating diverse cultures
(1990-1994)

Alan Falconer

Alan Falconer, a native of Edinburgh who was educated at George Heriot's School, studied at Aberdeen University and at the Ecumenical Institute in Geneva before being ordained in 1972 in the Church of Scotland. After two years as Assistant Minister at St Machar's Cathedral, Aberdeen he joined the staff of the Irish School of Ecumenics where he taught for twenty-one years and was Director for the last five. In 1995 he joined the staff of the World Council of Churches in Geneva as Director of the Faith and Order Commission. Since 2004 he has been the minister of the Cathedral Church of St Machar, Aberdeen. Dr Falconer has served on a number of international and national bilateral dialogues on behalf of the Reformed Churches, and has published widely on issues of ecclesiology, worship, interchurch dialogue, reconciliation and human rights. His current interests include theological reflection on the arts and the works of artists, poets, composers and novelists.

A telephone call late at night on 30 June 1990 from the Rev Dr
William McDowell, the Presbyterian Patron of the School, sum-
moned me to attend the meeting of the Patrons at the Jesuit
Provincialate the next morning at 9 am. For the previous three
months I had been enjoying a period of study leave and still had
the prospect of another three months ahead. All this was to
change dramatically. After a sleepless night wondering why the
Patrons, who generally only saw staff on formal occasions, were
so urgently requiring my presence I appeared at Eglinton Road.
Dr McDowell's parting words – 'There is nothing to worry
about' – had brought little comfort or relief!

At this meeting with the four Patrons (Rev Philip Harnett,
the Jesuit Provincial, Archbishop Robin Eames, Church of
Ireland Patron, Dr McDowell and the Methodist Patron, Rev Dr
Eric Gallagher) and with Dr David Poole, the Chairman of the
Executive Board who had also been invited to attend, I was informed that Dr May had indicated that he did not wish to have
his contract as Director of the School extended, and I was asked
to accept the position of Director with effect from the 1
September 1990. The Patrons then also handed me the first confidential draft of a report which had been initiated by the
Patrons at the suggestion of Dr May and I was told that this
would need to be implemented if the School was to survive. The
report, written by two businessmen commissioned by the Jesuit
Provincial, Mr John Harnett and Mr Pat Nolan, focused on the
funding structure, the pattern of governance, the relationship
with government and the churches, staffing and staff morale
and on the inner cohesion of the School.

From the outset, it became clear that the following years
would be marked by the necessity of negotiating different cultures, each with its own assumptions and pattern of organisation
– the business world with its capacity for instant decision taking,
the university world with its time cycles and standard settings,
and the churches, each with its own authority structures and different concepts of the ecumenical vision. It was also clear that
there was great urgency about taking action on a wide spectrum

of issues. Due to the sensitivity of the report it was to remain confidential – and only parts of it were shared with the staff, the Academic Council and the Executive Board.

Because of the urgency of the situation, the Patrons had assumed a role that they had hitherto not played in the School. When the Irish School of Ecumenics (ISE) was founded, Patrons from each tradition in Ireland had been approached and appointed so that they might demonstrate the interchurch authenticity of the School to their own traditions and seek to gain support for it in their church councils, and those of their tradition outside Ireland. The Patrons appointed the Academic Council, which reported to them, but they had seldom taken an active part in the decision-taking of the School. The Jesuit Provincial also had the role of being the Chairperson of the Academic Council. It was in that capacity that he had sought the advice and support of his fellow Patrons at this time. Thus instead of a symbolic role with some additional functions, the Patrons had become effective as the principal decision-taking body to whom the Academic Council and Executive Board were responsible. Since they had taken the decision that the interim and subsequent reports had to be implemented, all other councils and the staff were expected to concentrate solely on the implementation of the report's recommendations. The report itself did not offer a series of options.

The first hurdle, not anticipated by the Patrons or the writers of the Report, was my insistence that academic integrity be maintained, and that the Patrons needed to determine whether my appointment was acceptable to Trinity College, Dublin. Over the previous decade there had been a developing relationship with the University – whereby various external examiners had helped the College to see that the highest academic standards were being achieved by the students and that a great deal of this success was due to the work and commitment of the teaching staff; and it seemed important not to undermine this in any way. A pattern of decision-taking on all aspects of the academic life and work of the School, including staff appointments where Trinity College was represented, had been established through the formation of a co-ordinating committee. It was important not to undermine the integrity of this process.

Thus it was that on 1 September I assumed office . The previous two months had been spent in consultation with the School's lawyers, examining a number of the recommendations, with staff in the university, and above all with David Poole, since we needed to plan how to implement a confidential report – and not be deflected by the Executive Board or the staff by taking decisions that might run counter to the recommendations to be implemented.

Immediately preceding my assumption of office as Director, the School hosted the biennial meeting of Societas Oecumenica (the European Society for Ecumenical Research) of which I was President from 1986-1990. The leaders of the various ecumenical institutes in Europe gathered for discussion and exchange, and for a series of presentations on the Irish situation by HE Nicholas Fenn, the British Ambassador, and Dr Garret FitzGerald. Unfortunately, Dr FitzGerald was at the last minute called to a division in the Dáil, and the British Ambassador in a most gracious and exemplary manner gave his presentation, punctuated by insertions – 'at this point Dr FitzGerald would have disagreed with me – and this is what he would have said'. Both Dr FitzGerald and Sir Nicholas have proved to be very good friends to the School over the years. This event was a reminder to staff, the university and the churches of the international reputation and standing of the School.

Recommendations and their implementation
Rather than offer a rather confusing, chronological account of the implementation of the recommendations, it may be more helpful to explore the implementation of each area of the recommendations in turn, aware that each of these was interdependent with the others and that developments were taking place simultaneously.

Throughout a period of three years (1990-93), regular meetings took place between the Director, Chairman of Board and the drafters of the report. It was clear that due to the sensitivity of certain aspects of the report to the Patrons, an edited version would be presented to the various governing bodies of the School. This was done at a special unminuted meeting of Academic Council on 21 March 1991.

The report noted that the structure of the School had served it well, but now with increasing numbers of students, a developing interchurch climate, and unclear lines of authority, it was time to address organisational issues. The Report suggested that for ISE to survive it needed to have the security of four financial pillars: an ISE Foundation, student fees, annual donations and support from the churches. It was envisaged that each of these should be able to provide £100,000 each to the annual income of the School, thus providing it with a secure base and financial stability.

With increased numbers of students, the target for fee income was normally achieved over the next five years and donation income was well over budget by 1994. This latter involved dedicated work from our development office: David Pyle and Dympna Ryan. Through annual appeals, special events and persistent visits to companies and funding agencies, they sought to realise sufficient income for the life and work of the School.

However, the principal concern of the Report to the Patrons was on the ownership of the School by the churches. The drafters of the report then rightly emphasised that for credibility, and to achieve matching funds, it was essential for the churches as national bodies to be seen to be contributing substantially to the School. The relationship with the churches had always been a problematic area. While the Church of Ireland and Methodist Church were conspicuous in their support, support from both the Roman Catholic Church and the Presbyterian Church came through the vision and energy of committed individuals and religious orders rather than through the central structures. In his period of office as Director, Dr May had prompted a recognition of ISE by the Conference of European Churches and the Catholic

Conference of European Episcopal Conferences which was predicated on a recognition of the School by the Archbishop of Armagh and the Irish Episcopal Conference. This led him to seek help in securing such recognition through the Patrons. As one of his last acts before his sudden and untimely death, Archbishop Kevin MacNamara undertook an official visit to the School, thus opening up the question for both the School and the churches. The Report to the Patrons invited them to increase their own number and to involve official representation from their churches in the School's governing bodies. To do this required delicate negotiation as to what involvement would be necessary if the churches were to give official backing.

Each patron was invited to seek the best manner of approaching their church, both in respect of nominating their Patron and of contributing on a kind of *pro rata* basis to the financial support of the School. As an aspect of this, each church was invited to consider what would be necessary for them to be involved.

To implement the recommendations of the report, the Patrons established a Task Force which would undertake the negotiations with the churches, seek to put in place the appropriate structures, and oversee the implementation of the report. The Task Force was convened by Fr Patrick Crowe SJ, and included Mrs Gemma Loughran, a Roman Catholic barrister from Belfast, and Mr Philip Jacob, a member of the Society of Friends in Dublin. Along with Fr John Macken SJ they undertook these negotiations with respect to approaches to the Archbishop of Dublin, without initially consulting either the Chairman of Board or the Director.

All of this made life very difficult for the staff and the Board. Indeed on one occasion, I wrote a letter to the Provincial (21 June 1991) emphasising that it was the Executive Board which was in charge of running the School – not the Task Force. On 26 June 1991 the staff also presented a memo to the Board on their reactions to the report. In this they expressed surprise at the secrecy of the process, and at the fact that there had been no meetings with staff beyond the original interviews with the drafters in the period of Dr May's Directorship. The staff were concerned to emphasise the need for academic freedom; they felt that direct appointment to the Board by churches might inhibit this, that emphasis on research should be represented in the structures of the School, since its trust deeds and charitable status were predicated on the School being a teaching and research institute. They also stressed that the staff and Trinity College, Dublin should be represented on the Board and the committees of the School in the new structure.

The report represented a culture of decision-taking which was markedly different from that experienced in academic or church structures, and the Task Force charged with implementation had not been directly involved in the life of the School or the ecumenical movement. The situation was perhaps not helped by the imposition of yet a different decision-taking structure without reference to the then governing bodies of the School. While one can understand why it was thought necessary to put such a parallel structure in place, the lack of awareness of the work and contribution of the School, the lack of sensitivity to the different cultures of academy and church made for a tense and at times explosive situation. This is evident in some of the correspondence which passed between the Director and the Provincial during this period.

One of the pre-requisites for Roman Catholic approval of greater involvement in the School was for a course or series of lectures on the denominational identity of each tradition. In effect this would take our studies back to a comparative methodology of ecumenism, and the churches would nominate the lecturers. From its early years the School preferred the students to acquire a knowledge of the churches' different identities by means of 'field work' and some preparatory reading. In their 'field work' they would associate with a Christian tradition markedly different from their own and attend its worship. A second difficulty with this request and recommendation was that it was the function of the co-ordinating committee with

Trinity College, Dublin and not of any 'outside bodies' to determine course structure and content.

When it became clear that this proposal would be non-negotiable, I had to try to ensure that the course could take place, but as a non-examinable element of our studies. Of course this did not satisfy the churches so that in the end, I allowed that questions from these lectures appear on my Foundations of Ecumenism examination paper with students being required to address one of them. This was an uneasy academic compromise, even though the churches nominated excellent lecturers: Dr Dermot Lane (RC), Dr William Marshall (Church of Ireland), Professor John Thompson (Presbyterian Church) and Rev Kenneth Thompson (Methodist Church). During the course of 1992 and into the first quarter of 1993 discussions with the churches continued, and it became clear that from church sources the Roman Catholic Church was prepared to match funding from the Protestant churches up to a maximum of £50,000, and that the Roman Catholic Church would be represented as Patrons by the Roman Catholic Archbishop of Dublin, and by Bishop Anthony Farquhar, chairman of the Roman Catholic Church Episcopal Conference Committee on Ecumenical Relations, while the Jesuit Provincial was to remain as Trustee and President of Academic Council, though no longer as Patron. After very delicate negotiations the discussion for the support of ISE by the Roman Catholic Church took place at a meeting of the Irish Episcopal Conference. A very persuasive case for support was made by the Archbishop of Dublin, Desmond Connell, and that support was given.

In the course of 1992 the Standing Commission of the World Council of Churches Faith and Order Commission had met at All Hallows College in Dublin. I had been asked to arrange a number of meetings for the Commission so that they could get a sense of the Irish ecumenical scene. I also arranged an opening welcome session for them where they were welcomed to Ireland by senior churchmen of all the Irish churches. Archbishop Connell graciously attended. To my astonishment a large num-

ber of the members of the Commission, in their introductions of
themselves, took the opportunity to express positive and ful-
some gratitude for the work of ISE and its significance for the ecumenical movement at large, and in particular for the theological research of the work of Faith and Order itself. While I was
very gratified for this recognition of our work, I wondered how
Archbishop Connell would receive such a positive endorsement
of us from Vatican officials and officially appointed Roman
Catholic theologians as well as from bishops and representatives
of other churches. Commission members had not been briefed
beforehand!

In seeking to secure the support of the churches, a delicate
series of negotiations which sought to inform each church of the
position being developed by the others was undertaken. This
difficult process, which was pursued above all by Fr Paddy
Crowe SJ, was essential to the eventual agreements reached. Of
course not all proceeded smoothly. Discussions with the
Presbyterian Church led to the compromise that funding for the
School would come from the Presbyterian Association, a Dublin
based fund which had supported ISE regularly in the past and
from the funds of interested congregations, and that no formal
process for nominating a Presbyterian Patron would occur.

The fourth financial pillar in the schema for establishing a
secure funding base could now be initiated. While the churches
were not officially themselves supporting ISE, the task of approaching financial institutions and businesses for support was
made difficult. With the commitment of the churches it now became possible to begin the task of establishing an Endowment
Fund. To help establish this Fund, the School received the gift of
the secondment of Mr Derek Bell from ICI-Zeneka, with the
School taking over his salary costs after one year. The establishment of such a Fund proved to be a very slow process. After extensive discussion, it was decided that the Jesuit Provincial approach Mr Peter Sutherland, then chairman of Allied Irish Banks
(AIB), and a former pupil of a Jesuit school, to act as Chairperson
of the Endowment Fund sponsoring body. After a series of spe-

cial meetings he graciously accepted to undertake this , and with the help of Dr Donal O'Sullivan and Mr Lewis Crosby, Trustees of the School, drew together a team of influential business men and women to assist him in the task. Among these were T. David Kingston of *Irish Life* and Jim Fitzpatrick of *The Irish News*. Appropriate literature was developed, and a series of breakfast meetings held at AIB to push forward on this front.

Soon, however, Dr Sutherland was nominated to, and accepted, the position of Director General of the World Trade Organization, and had to resign as chairman of the ISE Endowment Fund sponsoring body. It took some time for this initiative to regain momentum. The establishment of such a fund – envisaged as £1 million , so that there would accrue to ISE annual interest of £100,000 – was dependent on the patient work of establishing the best contact to effect introductions to the principal decision takers. How often meetings were on the brink with Mr Tony O'Reilly only to be frustrated by a change of plans at the last minute! And that was only one approach! Despite extensive work, the endowment fund did not achieve its targets at that time. On being offered the post after his year's work as executive secretary of the Endowment Fund, Mr Bell decided not to accept, and from 1993, David Poole assumed this position on a half time basis. Contacts made with leaders of business during the Endowment Fund campaign were repeatedly faced with the question – where is your government funding? Indeed it was becoming abundantly clear that it was not possible to match university level salaries for academic posts and not to exceed university level fees for students without the government subsidy enjoyed by the universities and colleges. It became clear that direct support from the government would be required to sustain the School – what came to be known as the Fifth Pillar – and this had not been the identified in the Report to the Patrons, but would become central to our work during my five year period as Director.

The final aspect of the report to the Patrons concerned the structures for governing the School. To clarify lines of authority in the School and its legal status, and to provide a structure whereby it was possible to take decisions more speedily, a revised structure was necessary. This re-defined the role of the Trustees and placed greater authority for the running of the School with the Executive Board. It recommended that the Academic Council no longer be the major body for decision-taking on recommendations from the Board but become an advisory body on academic affairs, with a particular interest in research, and have a membership reflecting a diversity of interests and ecclesial traditions. The Report also recommended that the Board members be nominated directly by the churches, as a measure of their increasing involvement in and responsibility for the School. It was assumed that this would be a condition required by the churches themselves as a consequence of their new relationship with the School. However, it became clear at an early stage in discussions with Archbishop Connell, that while he might be prepared to assume a closer relationship with the School, he was not prepared to enter a situation in which, through deeds of incorporation, the churches would be held responsible financially for the School should it become unable to sustain itself. In the event this recommendation was not given effect, but the Executive Board did become the principal decision-taking body, with the Academic Council assuming an advisory role.Only a few specific areas, such as the appointment of academic staff, remained as executive functions of the Council. To take forward all the work of the School, a new Executive Board and a new Academic Council assumed office on 17 June and 18 May 1993 respectively.

The Report to the Patrons also drew attention for the need for the Trustee status of the School to be affirmed and its charitable status reinforced. Accordingly in 1993, a new group of Trustees was appointed and accepted by Council. In the Republic, the trustees became The Jesuit Provincial for the time being, Mr Christopher Gibson, Mr Sean Hogan, Mrs Catherine McGuinness and Miss Margaret Hamilton Reid, while in Northern Ireland the trustees were The Jesuit Provincial for the time being, Mr

Paul Campbell, Mr Christopher Gibson and the Right Rev Gordon McMullan, Bishop of Down and Dromore.

To put the work of the School on a firm financial and structural footing, a series of meetings was planned and initiated with officials in the Department of Education. Simultaneously with this, what Dr O'Sullivan termed 'the demarche' on the Taoiseach began, with a considerable effort being made to solicit his support and encouragement. The approach to the Department of Education was undertaken with the help of Mr Salters Stirling, Rev Dr Dermot Lane, Mrs Catherine McGuinness, Mr Tom McGrath, and Dr David Poole. Over the years we had received some funds through the Department of Foreign Affairs for specific pieces of our work in regard to reconciliation. Such funds had always been subject to an annual application and a certain amount of kindly advocacy from Dr Donal O'Sullivan. However, it was clear that for the long term viability of the School it was necessary for us to receive a grant identified in the annual government's Book of Estimates – probably through the Higher Education Authority budget. The difficulty that the Irish government had in funding the School lay in its interpretation of the 1908 Act which prohibited the government from funding denominational education. Many approaches had been made to the political authorities on previous occasions, but no matter how well disposed they were, they all felt inhibited by that Act. Of course the School's very existence was to counteract such denominationalism, and at last this seemed to have been appreciated and accepted. By 1994, the negotiations had resulted in our inclusion in the Book of Estimates, whereby it would then have become normal for our continuing inclusion, but shortly before the budget was presented to the Dáil, the government fell and ISE once again found itself in a parlous financial situation – but the account of that belongs to my successor's narrative!

Cohesion of the School

In the previous chapter Dr May has noted some of the elements of our life and work which seemed to offer challenges to the

School as it sought to maintain its integrity and cohesion. Two problems were the relationship between the different programmes or emphases in our work, and the physical location of the School on three sites – Belfast as well as two in Dublin.

Taking a cue from the business world, the Report recommended that a Mission Statement for the School be written, which would state in clear, succinct terms the nature of ISE, its tasks and how those tasks would be implemented. The statement was drafted by the staff and presented to the Executive Board and Council of the School, being discussed and approved by the Academic Council at its meeting in 1991. The statement aimed to be thirty words in length and written as one sentence. Like the Ephesian Hymn (Eph 1:3-14), the one sentence was intended to emphasise the interdependence of all the elements in the life and work of the School. While the original statement was crafted as a single sentence, it finally extended to some sixty words and is still, I believe, a very good statement of the role and ethos of ISE. It owes much to the drafting skills of Dr May and read as follows:

> The Irish School of Ecumenics is an international academic institute, Christian in its inspiration and ethos, interdenominational in structure and personnel, existing to promote through research, teaching, and extra-mural activities, the unity of Christians, dialogue between religions, and work for peace and justice in Ireland and abroad, whose resources are available to churches and other appropriate bodies committed to unity, dialogue and peace.

The Mission statement was adopted by the staff, and approved by the Executive Board and by Academic Council. The process was as important as the result in that it enabled all the staff to explore the interrelationship and interdependence of all the aspects of the School's work, and to note how the different elements contributed to our overall life. It also helped to open up discussion on the possible integration of the various programmes of teaching and research in the School.

To enhance still further this sense of common purpose and identity, we ensured that our colleagues based in Northern Ireland would attend staff meetings at least once a month. This had the effect of a greater ownership of the entire spectrum of the work of ISE by all the staff, and it led to programme connections being made where one course built upon the foundations of others and we all learned from each other's experiences. It also enabled us to be more sensitive to the perceptions of the different constituencies in Ireland. As a further minor contribution to our cohesion, it was agreed that regular staff meetings – with or without agenda – would take place over coffee at Bea House, and that all hands would be on deck for the distributing of the School's magazine *Unity*, even if that meant simply stuffing envelopes for two or three hours. This helped in some degree to overcome a sense by some of the division between academic and administrative staff, and to create a better atmosphere among us all.

The Role of Peace Studies

Throughout the 1980s the School, under Mr Bill MacSweeney's drive and direction, had been developing an extensive programme in Peace Studies. Since 1988 a degree programme and structure had been operating and, like other academic developments in Trinity College, was due to be reviewed after an initial three year period. Thus the process of review came to be initiated in 1990 – just when the Report to the Patrons was received. One of the many concerns which was identified in this Report was the danger of the School pulling in different directions, as Dr May notes in the previous chapter. Thus the three year review was timely. The process involved a number of meetings of academic staff with Professor O'Connell (Bradford University – School of Peace Studies), and the staff of Trinity College (particularly Professor Sean Freyne and Dr Alan Matthews).

The programme was reviewed in line with the criteria established by the Committee of Vice-Chancellors and Principals in their 'Academic Standards in Universities' (1989). It included reflections on the integrity and standards of the M Phil (Peace Studies), the impact of this on the Justice and Peace component of the M Phil (Ecumenics) and the relation of peace studies to the overall life, work and ethos of ISE. The review recognised that the components of the peace studies curriculum were in accordance with developments in other universities and peace institutes. It saw the inclusion of social ethics as the specific and welcome contribution which the School could make to the wider peace studies community. One of the concerns of the School of Biblical and Theological Studies in Trinity College had been that the peace studies programme did not reflect sufficiently biblical and theological insights. It was decided that a core course to be taken by all peace studies students would be 'Social Sciences and Social Ethics' and that, for the cohesion of the School, this would become a course also taken by the ecumenics students.

The review findings were welcomed by the Executive Board, and by Academic Council on 21 March 1991, and approved by the Co-ordinating Committee of Trinity College and the ISE. Two issues arose from the review: the adequacy of our own library holdings with respect to peace studies and the negotiating of access to the libraries of both Trinity College and University College, Dublin. It was also evident that there would need to be additional staff appointed. Accordingly in March 1991, Brenda Blair and Ita Sheehy were appointed to part-time positions in the peace studies programme.

To further the link between peace studies and ecumenics, it was decided to plan for a course of twenty lectures on Ecumenical Social Ethics – reflecting on the history and methodology of the Life and Work stream of the ecumenical movement – which would be taken by all the students as part of their course, and which might be opened to a wider public. The first series of lectures was given by Professor Ronald Preston of Manchester University in the 1992-93 academic year. A second series of lectures was arranged with Professor Wolfgang Huber of Heidelberg University, but on his appointment as Bishop of the Evangelical Church of Berlin-Brandenberg had to be cancelled at the last minute.

Buildings

It had become clear, as is evident in the two previous chapters, that the physical resources of the School were strained to breaking point. Throughout her period of service at the School, Sr Helen Butterworth had sought to identify more suitable premises and from time to time negotiations had been entered into with religious orders about to sell premises to see whether an agreement might be reached with them to acquire adequate accommodation for the School – but ultimately to no avail.

However, it soon emerged that the Jesuit community was intending to close Tabor House, its retreat centre at Milltown Park. The Council of Major Religious Superiors (CMRS) were willing to rent part of the building, and the Jesuit Community made the suggestion that ISE might wish to rent the rest of it. Initially we were offered the upper floors, which would have offered spacious lecture rooms and offices, but it became clear that the floors would not be able to sustain the weight of the library, and therefore we were offered the bottom two floors for rent instead. After determining that it might be possible to fit the School into the site, while using one of the main lecture theatres in Milltown Park for lectures attended by more than twenty-five students, it was agreed to take up the offer and to put Bea House up for sale.

Of course there were strong arguments that the money realised should be used to offset the bank overdraft. The staff managed to argue that part of the money should go to furnish the new premises with a compactus system for the library, and provide proper equipment for the lecture room, that a sum at least equal to the original purchase price of the building should be invested and that the remainder of the money be used to offset part of our indebtedness. The move to the new premises was used as an opportunity for re-dedication to our Mission Statement, and for inviting as many of the leaders of the churches, university , business, political and civic communities as possible. The building was blessed at a special service by Cardinal Cahal Daly, Archbishop Robin Eames of Armagh, Rev Dr Andrew Rodgers (Moderator of General Assembly, Presbyterian Church in

Ireland) and Rev Richard Taylor (President of the Methodist
Church). The School moved to its new site in time for the academic year 1993-94 , and press coverage at its opening was extensive and positive in respect of our work.

Northern Ireland Programme
One of the explosive occasions during the process of the Report
to the Patrons occurred when the drafters of the report presented
a supplementary report on our work in Northern Ireland. No
discussion had taken place with the staff of the School in Dublin,
and this initiative represented an extension to the original brief
given to the consultants. This appendix was tabled at a meeting
of the Patrons on 8 July 1991 and it was anticipated that it would
be handled with the same sense of urgency as the recommendations of the main report itself. The Northern Ireland recommendations were well intentioned, especially since they highlighted
our relevance and involvement in reconciliation in Northern
Ireland, but they would have created difficulties in our relationships in Northern Ireland and with Trinity College, Dublin. The
proposal was to establish a degree programme (M Phil) based in
Northern Ireland which would be linked to Queen's University,
Belfast (QUB). While strong links existed between the School
and QUB – at the time I was acting as external examiner for the
BD programme – the University did not have a teaching faculty
of theology. Theology was done in denominational colleges
with the university awarding the degrees; this meant there was
no natural partner for discussions. Secondly, our educational
work in Northern Ireland was conducted with the University of
Ulster and not with QUB. Thirdly, it was not appropriate to consider a link with QUB when there was no institutional link between it and Trinity College. Both David Poole and I objected to
this report , and I later wrote a very strongly worded letter to the
Provincial objecting to its contents, its manner of presentation
and its insensitivity to the staff of the School, and to our existing
partners. I also stressed that such matters had already been the
subject of discussion in Board and the decision had been taken
not to proceed in this direction at this time. Now the suggestions

were coming from a different route, and without reference to the Board or its previous discussions. When Dr Eric Gallagher realised that there had been no consultation on this with me, he also wrote a strongly worded letter to the other Patrons saying that he could not support the proposals and asking them to reject the supplementary report.

After ten years as leader of the Columbanus Community, Fr Michael Hurley decided to return to Dublin, and thus it became clear that he would not be in a position to continue as the lecturer and co-ordinator of our Northern Ireland Programme. To succeed him, the Academic Council on 19 November 1992 appointed the Rev John Morrow, who had recently relinquished office as the Director of the Corrymeela Community. However, while Fr Michael had been able to use the premises of the Columbanus Community as his base, it was necessary to find a suitable office for Mr Morrow. After a number of explorations, it became possible for the School to rent an office in the premises of the Irish Council of Churches (ICC). The School was now in an even better position to develop close links with the churches' principal ecumenical structure (ICC) and with one of the principal reconciliation groups operating in Northern Ireland (Corrymeela).

During 1991 and subsequently, a number of new centres were established where the certificate course was given, and our educational work in Northern Ireland expanded. Then during the first half of 1993, a proposal was received from the Rt Rev John Petty, the Provost of Coventry Cathedral, that a Chair in Ecumenics be established for the School to undergird our Northern Ireland work, and that Coventry Cathedral with the aid of the School would seek to raise a £1 million capital Endowment Fund . After discussion, the intention was to establish this Chair in association with Trinity College, Dublin and the University of Ulster, and involve the various theological colleges in Belfast. This ambitious scheme, subject to many proposals and refinements, while it did not lead to the establishment of a chair, was to play a crucial role in the development of a major study on sectarianism.

Having worked for a number of years on the theme 'Reconciliation of Memories', I was interested to see how the School might build on the foundations of that work, which had received a positive reception in other parts of the world. Fr Michael, as one of his last acts as our staff person in Northern Ireland, had arranged an important consultation on Reconciliation in Church and Society, which was held in Belfast, and this raised the profile of the School as engaged with issues of reconciliation. From my own work on reconciling memories I kept being exercised by the question of the acceptance of the other as other, the embrace of the other, and not simply as an acceptance insofar as the other reflects my views. A major study and report on sectarianism had recently been published for the Irish Interchurch Meeting (the ecumenical agency which includes the Roman Catholic Church as well as ICC). One of the major contributors to the study was Dr Joseph Liechty, a Mennonite historian and one of the collaborators in our work on reconciling memories. Dr Liechty also worked with us in helping international groups to realise the complexity of the issues at stake in the community conflicts in Ireland. It became clear that what was now needed to take all this work forward was an interdisciplinary study – particularly involving theology, psychotherapy and history – to explore issues involved in the addressing of sectarian attitudes.

In drawing up a research proposal for this project, it became clear that to appoint a person to undertake it was going to cost some £300,000 over three years. Given the perilous nature of the School's finances such a project would need to be funded from sources outside the normal funding base for the School itself. I therefore made an approach to three agencies – Coventry Cathedral to see whether they might commit some of their proposed endowment fund to this process, the Rowntree Trust – through the good offices of Dr David Poole – and the Community Relations Department of the Northern Ireland Office. The project needed to be presented in such a way that each of these bodies could be persuaded to fund with integrity, while being aware of the interdisciplinary nature of the project. Thus Coventry Cathedral were approached with respect to the theological aspect of the project, the Joseph Rowntree Foundation the Social Sciences, and the Northern Ireland Community Relations unit that of the provision of resources for school and community reconciliation projects .The person I had in mind to undertake this work was Sr Geraldine Smyth, a Dominican sister who had studied at ISE and been awarded a PhD by Trinity. The Executive Board welcomed these proposals for the Northern Ireland project, but rightly insisted that the money for the project needed to be definite before it was begun. This meant that Sr Geraldine was herself then in the position to enlarge and develop the project outline in a manner that she felt appropriate with the various funding bodies. In the event, with my own departure from ISE and Sr Geraldine's appointment as my successor the project was undertaken by Sr Cecelia Clegg and Dr Joseph Liechty under the title 'Moving beyond Sectarianism',the project attracting further funds from the Dominicans, the Christendom Trust and the North American Peace Institute.

Meanwhile ... the Continuing Work of the School
Placing the normal life of the School as the concluding section of this narrative is both uncharacteristic of my time as Director and runs counter to the philosophy and practice that I developed with David Poole. In my experience, because of the ever continuing financial difficulties being faced by the School, issues of finance and structure were dealt with first by the governing bodies and only then matters academic . Often this had the effect that academic matters were discussed solely in the light of fiscal rectitude. Finance determined the School's life and activity. With the approval and support of David Poole as Chairman of Board a change of procedure took place. Discussion in governing bodies began with accounts of the life and work of the School and the decisions needing to be taken to enhance that work. The governing bodies, while rightly concerned with our financial resources, were also advisors on how to enable the aca-

demic developments to take place, and this procedure encouraged them in that role

For visits of people we hoped to influence to support our life and work, and for meetings of Irish ecumenical organisations, we developed the pattern that I would present the work of the School and then David Poole would lay bare the financial implications. I did not believe that the Irish School of Ecumenics had a right to exist *per se*, but that we existed primarily to serve the churches and the community – and on that basis made appeal for support.

During all of the above developments the normal work of the School proceeded apace. To assist me in the teaching of the courses on interchurch dialogue, I was joined by Fr Brian Hearne – recently returned from the Mindolo Institute in Zambia. He taught the course on ministry and the Petrine ministry, while Dr Kieran Cronin took my place in the joint course on theology and human rights. Sr Pamela Stotter was appointed to develop our Adult Education work in the Republic of Ireland; she increased considerably the number of students taking the certificate course, and expanded the number of centres at which this course was offered. Maureen Bassett took the place of Ita Sheehy on the peace studies staff, and on her demission of the post Dr Iain Atack was appointed. With the move to Milltown Park, which we re-dedicated as 'Bea House', Ms Euphan Stephenson who had been my part-time secretary for ten years, decided to finally retire. Euphan had, on retirement from Guiness's, offered her services to the School and she had worked with and for me every morning for those ten years

On the sudden death of Rev William McDowell, the Rev Alan Martin agreed to become the Presbyterian patron of the School. During this period the death also occurred of Professor Anthony Hanson who had been so helpful in promoting the academic standing of the School and integrating it into the life of Hull University, until it became possible for Trinity College Dublin to award the degrees. In the normal cycle of the life of the Jesuit community, Fr Phil Harnett demitted office as Provincial, and Fr Laurence Murphy was appointed Provincial, and thus became Trustee of the School and Chairman of the Academic Council.

If in 1990, David Poole had characterised ISE as growing faster than inflation, this was even more true by 1994. Student numbers reached their highest levels. A great deal of this was due to the increasing reputation of the staff, and the reception of their academic work. To read the Director's report for each of the years in this period is to be humbled by the range and quality of publications by all the staff. These publications appeared in academic journals worldwide, and attracted students who wished to explore these influential ideas further. It was also gratifying that a number of students – Dr Joseph McCann, Peter Shüttke-Scherle, and Dr Geraldine Smyth had their theses accepted for publication by major publishing houses. Many other students were able to publish articles outlining their research, thus enhancing the School's reputation still further. The quality of this research and the standards of work achieved had also brought about a major development with regard to degree awards through Trinity College. When Sr Geraldine Smyth's thesis for the M Phil degree was presented to the examining Board, we recommended that she be not awarded the M Phil, but that she continue her study to present it as a PhD thesis. This she did and was awarded her PhD at Trinity College, the first person to have gone through such a procedure for the School. Many students had completed their Master's degrees at the School and then gone on to undertake PhDs in different institutions. Sr Geraldine opened the way to really engage in a discussion in the Co-ordinating Committee about the possibility of ISE students being able to transfer to the PhD register on merit.

The staff were also becoming world travellers. Bill MacSweeney , John May and I received numerous invitations to participate in *colloquia* and other events – for the most part being invited to give papers. We were also becoming involved in international bodies. Thus both John May and I attended the World Council of Churches Assembly in Canberra in 1991, and I acted as Consultant-drafter at the Fifth World Conference at Santiago de Compostela in 1993. John May received a number of invitations to lecture in Australia and in Asia and at times I feared we were in danger of losing him!

The staff continued to be involved in nearly every ecumenical initiative in Ireland There was a constant stream of distinguished visitors, from Cardinals, Archbishops and Ambassadors to distinguished academics and senior politicians – and on most of these occasions we sought to arrange meetings with the students. One memorable visitor whose experience of ISE was to have a profound long-term effect was that of the Provost of Trinity College Dublin, Professor W. A. Watts. For the first time, it appeared he recognised the potential value to TCD itself of a more integrated structure involving ISE. The range of annual seminars continued: Jewish-Christian, the occasional seminar on Orthodox Worship and Theology, and a series of important Peace Studies lectures. The James Haire Memorial Lecture was established in Belfast and Dublin, with Dr Emilio Castro and Cardinal Daly giving the first two lectures in the series. The annual series 'My Ecumenical Vision' continued during the Week of Prayer for Christian Unity with presentations by Cardinal Edward Cassidy, Dr Eric Gallagher and Dr Elizabeth Templeton amongst others.

During 1990- 1995, the principal task of the Director had been to negotiate the very diverse cultures of the worlds of business, the academy, the churches and that of the emerging Irelands. Each of these had its own discrete language, goals and structures. For the School to survive it had been essential to learn from each and simultaneously to weave together various important threads from them all to provide a more vibrant and enduring tapestry of unity, peace and reconciliation. While the process had been difficult, and at times fraught, it did leave us in a better position to carry forward our mission, as articulated in our Mission Statement.

While the Irish School of Ecumenics was negotiating diverse cultures and becoming a lively and expanding institution, I was looking towards 1998 when I could return fully to the work of teaching and research after a period directing the School. However, that was not to be. Earlier in the chapter I noted the important visit in 1992 to Dublin of the Standing Commission of Faith and Order. Later that year I received a telephone call asking me – nay, urging me – to apply for the post of Director of the Faith and Order Commission. This call was then reinforced by another. In the event I promised to send for details. I then did no more, having decided that my work and life were in Ireland. In 1993, however, when as mentioned above I acted as a Consultant to the Fifth World Conference on Faith and Order at Santiago de Compostela, I was immediately approached by Bishop Barry Rogerson of Bristol and other members of the Standing Commission – and asked why I had not applied. They really pleaded with me that I think again; and the rest is the next chapter in my life and ministry, and the next chapter in this story of ISE.

In leaving the School I was very conscious of my indebtedness to all those with whom I had worked over twenty years, and especially conscious of the immense help I received as Director from Mr Gordon Buttanshaw, our financial advisor, and from David Poole whose friendship and camaraderie eased this very difficult period in the life of the School and made it possible to move forward in the new structures. These two colleagues themselves represented also all the many people who gave of their time and their talents in service to the School both graciously and freely – and the School would not be what it is without their contribution and that of so many others.

CHAPTER SIX

Challenge and Change[1]
(1994-1999)

Geraldine Smyth OP

Geraldine Smyth OP is from Belfast and has worked, mainly in education and theology, in the north and south of Ireland. After the M Phil
in Ecumenics course (1988-1990), she completed a PhD in Theology in
Trinity College Dublin (1993), was Co-ordinator of the 'Opsahl
Commission – A Citizens' Inquiry' on a way forward for Northern
Ireland, and became ISE Director in January 1995, a post she held till
1999 when she was elected Prioress of her Dominican Congregation.
She continues in ISE as Senior Lecturer, with research interests in sect-
arianism, reconciling memories, and ecumenical ecclesiology. In 2003
Queen's University Belfast awarded her an honorary doctorate for ser-
vices to reconciliation and public life. Publications include *A Way of
Transformation: A Theological Evaluation of the Conciliar Process on Justice,
Peace and the Integrity of Creation, World Council of Churches 1983-1991*,
(Lang, Berne, 1995); she co-edited with Andrew Pierce, *The Critical
Spirit: Theology at the Crossroads of Faith and Culture* (Columba Press,
Dublin, 2003).

I stepped from plank to plank,
A slow and cautious way;
The stars about my head I felt,
About my feet the sea

I knew not but the next
Would be my final inch.
This gave me that precarious gait
Some call experience
(Emily Dickinson)[2]

Introduction

This poem of Emily Dickinson strikes a chord in me. Portraying the poet's own journey into an unknown landscape, it echoes with my own journey between 1994 and 1999. And of course, the boat, favoured symbol as it is of the ecumenical movement, is the giveaway – although, in the poem the boat is assumed rather than depicted. One is uncertain whether the poet is walking the plank or simply testing a precarious way across water, stepping plank to plank, exposed to the night elements: I find in this the same sense of 'between-ness' that characterised the period when I negotiated my way between the improbable and the impossible, operating by a kind of night vision, in the face of the swirl of impending chaos ('About my feet the sea'). It was nothing if not a precarious time, when I and those with responsibilities of governance lived by inches and by faith. But then too there were the stars.

Narrators of memoirs do well to be mindful of the pitfalls attendant on retrieving the past. Indeed, ISE itself with its research on reconciling memories has been responsible for raising debate on the complex process of retrieval of personal memories or shared cultural and religious texts, and on their hermeneutical interplay within discourses of power and historiography.

---

2. 'Poem 120', *Selected Poems of Emily Dickinson*, ed James Reeves, Heinemann, London, 1970, p 75.

Undoubtedly, these recollections will not be innocent. But we are remembering creatures, willy-nilly, and as Emily Dickinson suggests (Poem 129): 'Retrospection is prospect's half,/ Sometimes almost more.'

The First Years: The Opportunities of Crisis?

Arriving in ISE in the autumn 1994 (just weeks after the historic ceasefires halted twenty-five years of conflict in Ireland) allowed for a period to 'shadow' and work with Alan Falconer, before his departure to lead the Faith and Order Commission at the World Council of Churches (WCC) in Geneva. The fact that I had been an M Phil Ecumenics student, 1988-1990, meant that I knew the staff and had first-hand experience of the academic programmes.

I had been designated to conduct the School's new research project on Moving Beyond Sectarianism (MBS), so revising that plan became an immediate preoccupation, and I focused on securing funding for this three to five year project based in Belfast and identifying new researchers. I then had to convince funders who had backed my project proposal that, although switching horses, I would be involved in the oversight, and – with the appointment of Dr Joe Liechty and Dr Cecilia Clegg – that two researchers would now expertly fill that role. Coventry Cathedral had previously promised £30,000 towards an ISE Chair in Belfast if it could be established. Dr David Poole, Chair of Executive Board and I went there in October (I had been invited to preach) and Canon John Petty was persuaded to direct this towards MBS. It was an affecting experience to preach in the cathedral that stood adjacent to the bombed ruins of the old structure and symbolised the reaching out of its community in a ministry of global reconciliation.

The task of finding the remaining funding for MBS and for the continuing education programme in ecumenics in Northern Ireland – energetically coordinated by Dr John Morrow and later by Dr Johnston McMaster – would remain a pressing challenge. But this task simultaneously afforded opportunities to connect with the School's existing network of associate bodies, such as the Irish Council of Churches (ICC) which generously supported the project, and to expand partnerships and funding sources.

At a simple induction service in January 1995, I felt launched, and encouraged by the prayer of those present and the many who sent good wishes, and I planted two slips from a Christmas Cactus. Perhaps I sensed desert times ahead and the need for trust in the rhythms of rooting and blooming in thin conditions. Indeed, the plant took three years to bloom, when I finally discerned that it needed to be transplanted into a larger pot!

Another launch – MBS – took place on 3 April at the Old Museum in Belfast, by long-faithful friend of ISE and till lately Methodist Patron of ISE, Rev Dr Eric Gallagher. I had worked with Eric over the previous year and more when I was co-ordinator of the work of the international Opsahl Commission. Eric was the churches' face on the commission, where his rare combination of prophetic courage and ecclesiastical shrewdness was evident, regarding what was needed from the churches and from the British and Irish governments, in shaping a future free from sectarian blindness and institutionalised separation. Now, Eric welcomed the MBS project as an idea whose time had come and as already making its mark. Indeed its significance would widen and deepen, through reflection groups within and across church traditions, including the conservative evangelical constituency, via seminars within specific sectors and through interviews and conferences.

Two other projects claimed my attention in 1995: the twenty-fifth anniversary of the School and the campaign for the School's survival – indeed a bizarre combination. The first elicited an upbeat mood of gratitude, with the staging of academic, ecumenical and liturgical events, and all that this implied in hosting visitors, writing articles and giving interviews about ISE that projected a *joie de vivre*, showing that the founding vision of Dr Michael Hurley SJ was flourishing. Behind the scenes, however, another drama unfolded, presaging thoughts of end-time, and

evoking Alan Bennett's droll expression, that every silver lining
has its own jet-black cloud. At my first Board meeting, the financial statement showed the School's indebtedness as less than a
shout away from £200,000. Tough decisions were necessary: to
convey the dire news to staff and to Academic Council; assemble the Trustees; form a small emergency sub-committee of the
Board, beginning at 9 am next day; and to compute (minus computer) a strict budget that would strain life to the limits.

Precariousness on stilts. And so, unabated for the rest of that
year – financial pressure, embattled struggles for funding and
chronic anxiety about salaries and creditors. Keeping a steady
head was helped by remembering that previous Directors had
weathered such storms and the School had survived and because of the tangible determination of those perspicacious, stout
hearted people 'that a fight for the survival must be made be
made over the next few months'. Every person and structure
swung into action. A Strategic Financial Plan was formulated by
Tom McGrath, the board member with an eagle eye for financial
viability and one of the dynamos of the 'Campaign of Action'.
Gordon Buttanshaw, our accountant, who had unerringly
steered the School through stormy and tricky waters, maintained his steadying hand during his voluntary three mornings
a week oversight. All knew the *sine qua non* was that annual
funding be obtained from the Department of Education. But
against that day, expenditure must be tightly controlled, and income increased from our four key sources: 1) student fees, 2)
central church bodies, 3) independent donations (religious orders, church congregations and individuals), and 4) from the
Endowment Fund (from which in the short term we had to bor-
row).

Clearly, these combined sources would not support necessary levels of staffing, nor library and other academic resources
required by a graduate institute with a national and international
outreach, together with rent and other liabilities. Things were
set to come to a head, since by May we would be ethically bound
to draw back from 'fraudulent trading' and to inform the

prospective students whether, come October, ISE would be in business. The faces of ISE's governing officers seemed more sepulchral with each meeting but they managed to convey resurrection hope. And right then, there was a Silver Jubilee to celebrate.

A series of Jubilee lectures had been arranged. In February Dr Alain Blancy of the Ecumenical Groupe des Dombes delivered a lecture on their recent study, *For the Conversion of the Churches.* He was graciousness personified, and although in remission from serious illness, his intelligent commitment to ecumenical reconciliation radiated in the manner and content of his lecture. March brought Professor Anton Houtepen from Utrecht for a day on 'Ecumenical Hermeneutics', with its argument for 'exploration' as the most fruitful hermeneutical key to the ecumenical quest. Dr Donald Allchin's lectures on 'Orthodoxy Today' and 'Celtic Christianity' attracted and delighted 120 participants. Unfortunately, Professor Nicholas Lossky had withdrawn owing to family illness. I did have an opportunity, however, to meet him and his wife, when he spoke magisterially on 'The Present Status of Church Unity and Future Prospects'. That was at the Silver Jubilee Conference of the Tantur Ecumenical Institute in 1997, celebrated in the teeth of a different type of crisis, just metres away from the Israeli military checkpoint on the road between Jerusalem and Bethlehem.

Our main Jubilee events occurred in Easter Week and included a visit from Rev Dr Konrad Raiser, General Secretary of the WCC who gave a fine lecture on 'Ecumenical Formation' on 22 April. He welcomed the co-operation of the WCC with the Roman Catholic Church through their Joint Working Group (JWG) and the Vatican's recent *Directory on Ecumenism* – praising the chapter on ecumenical formation as a first in any church – and citing from the JWG document as a good summary of ISE's work over twenty-five years:

> It is not enough to regret that our histories have been tainted through the polemics of the past; ecumenical formation must endeavour to eliminate polemic and to further mutual un-

derstanding, reconciliation and the healing of memories. No longer shall we be strangers to one another, but members of the one household of God (#22)

He asserted that ISE 'has held a particular place among the comparable specialised institutions of ecumenical learning and research' and acknowledged how ISE provided churches with 'space for consultation ... on issues of ecumenical concern', from the start, '[translating] its ecumenical commitment into a long-term involvement in work for human rights and for reconciliation in the Irish conflict.' He also applauded the School's taught programmes and research combining 'ecumenical studies – including interchurch dialogue, interfaith dialogue and issues of justice and peace – with a special programme for peace studies aimed at the development of processes for the resolution of conflict between churches, faiths and nations.'

A Festive Dinner took place in Jury's Hotel, Dublin, and an Ecumenical Service of Thanksgiving in St Patrick's Cathedral, Dublin was hosted by Dean Maurice Stewart and graced by the presence of President Mary Robinson and her husband Mr Nick Robinson. Dr Raiser preached. He avowed that the Jubilee was 'an occasion for thanksgiving ... to God who has visibly blessed the work begun ... by Father Michael Hurley and since then continued by his successors in the same spirit and ... commitment, ... [and] an invitation to renew the commitment which has inspired the work of the Irish School of Ecumenics since its beginnings.' His words interrupted our thoughts of debt and dying.

Certainly the concatenation of celebration and doomsday scenario brought from the wings a veritable retinue of friends and colleagues from across public life – church and academy, politics, the media and non-governmental protagonists. On one hand, during the jubilee festivities and conferences, we were buoyed by the acknowledgement of ISE's national and international contribution to ecumenical life, reminded how ISE had innovatively shaped ecumenics as a unique disciplinary field. The impulses of memory and thanksgiving sustain fragile hope. Conversely, often on the same day, we found ourselves strug-

gling to keep afloat, orchestrating a campaign for direct government funding in recognition of ISE as a research institution, yet
not knowing if rescue would come in time, and ensuring that
academic programmes lost nothing of their quality and for-
ward-looking pertinence. I am reminded, as I look back, of the
swimmer in the Stevie Smith poem whose frantic hand-signals
were misread by on-lookers as gestures of enthusiasm – while
the swimmer was 'not waving but drowning'. Such was the
double bind of our double message.

And so, meeting followed meeting on finances and communications strategy, eliciting the mediation of figures of influence,
in our endeavour to secure a meeting with the Minister for
Education. We lobbied TDs who raised questions in the Dáil and
Senate, challenging government's scandalous failure to fund
ISE. Staff did radio interviews and wrote press-releases and articles. *The Sunday Independent* ran one such where the Chair of the
Irish Humanist Association and I were pictured above our respective arguments – his on why the state should not fund ISE
and mine on why it should. I had never thought my face was my
fortune, but one reader commented that on the basis of our respective countenances, I had won the argument, before he read a
word. I pointed out the irony of the situation that ISE had been
working for a quarter of a century on issues now prominent, yet
lacked state recognition 'at the very time when the state resounded with the rhetoric of reconciliation'. That one-liner
made it into the *Irish Times* quotations of the week – 'This Week
They Said'. Thus, we strove by every means to underline the
positive story of ISE and the reason so many different persons
and groups supported us – because we were a uniquely placed
academic institution, dedicated to education, dialogue and research in areas of pluralism, reconciliation, and ecumenical engagement across all boundaries. At this historic moment, the
country could not afford to let ISE sink. Rather, the government
needed ISE and should treasure us as a unique partner.

It was a high-risk strategy aiming simultaneously – in economic terms – to communicate that we were about to drown, and

worth not a heave-ho emergency rescue from a passing lifeboat, but structured resources to keep ourselves afloat. Who wants to invest in a sinking ship? So, sending out that SOS actually risked damaging our capacity of attracting high-calibre students. It was indeed a Dickensian best of times and the worst of times: '… it was the spring of hope, and it was the winter of despair.'

Niamh Breathnach, the Minister for Education, was not amused that we had so thrust her department into the glare of the media. When we finally met, she delivered a sharp rap to our collective knuckles, claiming any grant to ISE was *ipso facto* an equivalent deprivation to some disadvantaged primary school. We listened; we spoke, and parted on benign terms. Shortly after (in May), the Minister released £100,000 as 'a once-off grant'. It was not the £150,000 p.a. we needed, and the coded language was plain. The government was holding back on commitment to annual funding. Even with a further £30,000 gained from the Department of Foreign Affairs for work in the North we were short of our goal. But we had crossed a hitherto un-scaleable wall. It was an immediate reprieve which we did not fail to cele-brate, while girding our loins for the longer haul.

On 1 August, it was our turn to read in the papers Minister Breathnach's announcement that ISE would soon be assessed by the Higher Education authority (HEA) and that we would be re-ceiving EU Funding of £200,000. Again, we harboured no illus-ion, since no time-frame was mentioned. Help from the Depart-ments of Education and Finance was promised and, indeed, their officers later assisted us in securing EU support for the next two years. A further application was submitted to the Department of Education and to the EU – the latter for the Northern Ireland programmes. So far, we had met an un-en-couraging response to our requests to the Department of Education in Northern Ireland (DENI) and to the Northern Ireland Office. Our perseverance was severely tested, but we did not desist from knocking.

I reflected often on the paradoxes buried deep in the ISE motto – *Floreat ut Pereat*. I referred to it in an article later that year in *Interlink* at the invitation of editor Fr Tom Stack. I described ISE's rich diversity, with sixty current students on the Dublin campus, from India, Zambia, Uganda, Kenya, the United States, Australia, Germany, France, Greece, Romania, Hungary, Sweden, Britain and both parts of Ireland and coming from Anglican, Reformed, Methodist, Baptist, Seventh Day Adventist and Roman Catholic traditions – observing that 'for all the signs of the School's flourishing, its motto, 'is a symbolic reminder that the measure of ISE's success will be the degree to which it makes itself redundant'. The article also afforded me the opportunity of pointing to Dr Alan Falconer's 'rich inheritance' of research on Reconciling Memories and on Human Rights and also a network of country-wide ecumenical friendships. I highlighted the expansion of ISE's continuing education programmes South and North (Dublin, Belfast, Derry, Newry – with Armagh and Enniskillen soon to follow) and the MBS research. I also noted that the School now had a Belfast base at the Irish Council of Churches' building at 48 Elmwood Avenue; this was a happy abode for ISE NI, convenient to city centre stations, chaplaincies, funding agencies which I had cause to visit – often – and to Queen's (with whose Continuing Education Department John Morrow was developing a new ISE course on 'Religion and Society'). The house was always abuzz, since it housed several other interchurch bodies, including Christian Aid. Dr David Stevens, ICC Secretary, was unfailingly supportive as colleague and landlord.

In my first report to Academic Council, I correlated what was current in ISE's life and identity with events of church and world: the brokering and breaking of ceasefires in Bosnia and the Middle East, violent clashes in Sri Lanka, the fiftieth anniversary celebrations of the end of World War II, and the commemorations of the *Shoah*. 1995 also saw continued nuclear testing in the Pacific devastating ecosystems and homelands. Refugees on an unprecedented scale were being shunted between Rwanda and Tanzania as if non-persons. There were atrocious explosions in Japan and Oklahoma, and the assassination of Yitzak

Rabin in Israel, while Nigeria saw the execution of Ken Saro-Wiwa and eight companion Ogoni human rights activists. There were some more welcome events, such as the first free elections in South Africa, the return to Palestinian rule of the ancient lands of Gaza and the West Bank, and the historic United Nations conferences in Beijing and Cairo, with reform of legislation on important matters of global development and the rights and protection of women. Such events and their subtexts were patently configured into ISE's daily life in teaching and research, dissertations, staff conference papers and publications. Such analyses fructified also in collaboration with other academic institutions, from the UK to Australia, and with international bodies such as the WCC or UNESCO, World Conference on Religions and Peace. Both theoretically and practically, we grappled with themes and dilemmas of memory and hope, ethnic identity, national identity and the unity of the church, peace and forgiveness, development and justice, and the politics of women's inclusion.

It was also the year of the Downing Street Declaration, the Framework Document and the partial rehabilitation of former paramilitary groups and prisoners, accompanied by deepening impasse over de-commissioning and all-party talks in the North. The Forum for Peace and Reconciliation opened a vista, through its public recognition of the different identities in Ireland. I was a guest at Dublin Castle when the Catholic Church and some unionists made presentations. The Forum was impressively presided over by Judge Catherine McGuinness, a Trustee of ISE. Such public occasions proved interesting ways of education on areas of public life with which as a Northerner I was less familiar. Rubbing shoulders with political figures, church or civic leaders, enabled me to see the extent of established ISE connections and to form new ones. Sometimes, I threw caution to the winds and plucked by the sleeve a passing Minister or Opposition Minister. One learned to seize the moment – as I did, for example following a service at the Jewish Synagogue when Ruairi Quinn, Minister for Finance, crossed my path, and in response to my pleading, ventured some assurances. Once, at a gathering hosted at her residence by British Ambassador, Veronica Sutherland, the Swedish Ambassador after inquiring about ISE, gallantly eased me into the direct path of Prince Charles, enabling me to offer words of welcome – and, at lightning speed, yet as if casually, mention that I was representing the Irish School of Ecumenics, and instancing some of ISE's activity in 'your jurisdiction up north'. 'That is difficult work, I imagine,' the Prince responded, 'but so important. And I wish you every success.' The Swedish Ambassador beamed.

ISE later hosted Mrs Sutherland herself, as indeed several other ambassadors. We also welcomed His Grace the Archbishop of Canterbury, and representatives of the European Commission, senior ecumenical representatives and study groups from Germany, Edinburgh, USA and Tasmania. Lady Jean Mayhew, who was active in promoting cross-community and interchurch activities in NI during her husband, Sir Patrick Mayhew's term as Secretary of State, also visited and took up the invitation later to serve on Academic Council. Indeed it was through her mediating role that we obtained a Church of England scholarship for an ecumenics student from the global south, which continues still. No shortage of recognition, except from our government. I wrote in the Annual Report:

> ... the future of the school still hangs in the balance ... So much vital energy and time is being drained into prolonged crisis-management and a repeating circle of funding applications to a range of agencies each with their own criteria, ... requiring lengthy internal and external consultation, data-gathering, drafting and redrafting processes. In many cases funding seems dependent on the reinvention of ISE in novel or popular configurations ... Without formal and structured financial acknowledgement of ISE by government, our work for reconciliation is critically undermined.

And Yet it Moves!

Despite all, in these years the undercurrent of academic work swelled and flowed. The harvest of M Phil and diploma dissertations was plenteous, with research topics intriguingly varied and often prescient – on the impact of the Schengen Agreement on Irish immigration policy, on the Muslim community in Ireland, or a biblical reflection on the land issue in the Israel-Palestine dispute, or comparative approaches to marriage and divorce in different churches, or on alternative approaches to development. ISE was daily a hub of learning and exchange, with particularly bustling numbers on Mondays when part-time students arrived – sometimes four or five travelling by early bus or train from Enniskillen, Wexford, or Dungannon or Belfast. It was a long day for travellers, with an extra lunchtime seminar on Primal Traditions, perhaps, or an evening ISE-Irish Council for Christians and Jews lecture in the Mansion House. Some formed study groups as exams approached, eager to learn from one another ecumenically and intercontextually.

John D'Arcy May was busy organising a major conference, the first of its kind in Ireland. The topic was *Pluralism and the Religions* and it brought more than a hundred participants, and international scholars to ISE – including Paul Knitter, Wesley Ariarajah, Ursula King and Gavin D'Costa. In due course the edited volume was published, which made a defining contribution to the field of interreligious discourse. In the winter of 1995-1996, on the initiative of Bill McSweeney, ISE collaborated with Friends Provident Insurance and the EU Commission in Dublin on a lecture series and conference on *Moral Issues in International Affairs*. EU commission headquarters in Molesworth Street provided the impressive venue and, in the year when Ireland held the role of Presidency of the EU, these events brought salient moral issues to prominence and showcased the international and normative structure of Peace Studies programmes and scholarship, and strengthened strategic alliances. A highly praised collection of essays edited by Bill McSweeney resulted.

During these years, churches, ecumenical and public bodies like the Community Relations Council NI, or the Council for the Status of Women in Dublin, and universities – Ulster, Edinburgh,

Liverpool Hope, for example – invited me as lecturer, preacher or external assessor. I had also carried with me existing consultancy commitments with the WCC. I was also member of a Working Group to develop new guidelines on ecumenical formation at the Pontifical Council for Christian Unity. John Cooney's invitation to give the Bishop Stock Lecture at the Humbert Summer School brought me to the beautiful cathedral in Killala. I was also privileged to preach at Canterbury Cathedral, St Giles, Edinburgh, St Patrick's Cathedral Dublin and in Trinity College Chapel – to mark the 200th anniversary of its dedication. There were invitations from parish congregations – Presbyterian, Church of Ireland, Methodist, Lutheran. That none of these was a church of my own Roman Catholic tradition shows the paradox that it has been through the hospitality of other churches that I have been most enabled to express that aspect of my Dominican charism as a member of the Order of *Preachers*. There have been some exceptions, one such from a parish priest who asked me to preach in Omagh, the year following the bombing, with all its appalling death and devastation, on the more hopeful theme of Jubilee.

Restructuring of Administration and Continuing Developments
Tradition and change are necessary if reluctant bedfellows. I suspect that directors of every organisation confront challenges of restructuring. At a rational level, this turns on the need to keep pace with change and adapt accordingly. But there are nettles to be grasped – difficult conversations and hard decisions. This touches the human side of change and regard for individual persons, in their uniqueness, loyalties and capacities. Change evokes in all of us ambivalent feelings – anxiety, enthusiasm, attachment, and fresh understandings of the originating vision in light of the signs of the times.

In accord with an earlier directive from the Trustees, I had been asked to embark on a review of administration. The task was complicated by contested issues over a new Union Agreement, uneven levels of pension provision, new public service wage agreements: on one hand a none more deserving staff; on the other crippling indebtedness. The expansion of the School, diversification of job specifications, management of one-year employment access schemes and ambivalent hints about wishing to retire, contributed to our unsteady-state position. Restructuring could no longer be postponed.

Patricia Nelis Kenny, a Trinity theology graduate experienced in business development, undertook the review at affordable cost. She built upon the goodwill and professionalism of staff in their respective areas, while firmly aiming for a whole-school approach, and for a flexible system with clear lines of responsibility. Staff contributed their analysis on lines of crossover and teamwork. Changes were phased in and kept aligned to the School's vision and policy, with regular communication to and from Executive Board and various committees – Finance, Salary Review, and Computer Committee for example.

Ruth Moran, who had been PA to every successive Director, took the decision to retire at this time (1996). I wonder how this book might have been enhanced had she written a contribution from her matchless perspective. Ruth was the welcoming face of the School and could recall by name all students who passed through since 1971. Something of the Moran legacy found new expression when her daughter, Suzanne, created an evocative design of our wheat sheaf logo, prompting a new set of prospectus brochures in the School's traditional colours of blue and gold.

The simpler administrative changes related to re-ordering of space, the creation of a hub office and locating 'opposite numbers' in proximity. Relevant training needs and computer programmes were identified. Development Office staff and the Library began the changeover to more sophisticated data-base systems, undaunted by inconceivable setbacks. The urgency of all adapting to new technology was problematic, since ISE was virtually a computer-free zone. Even I, with knowledge of little 'Word', could see that we would remain hobbled without whole scale computerisation. We were long past being able to manage our financial system without computerised budget planning and control and the capacity to generate consolidated or comparative figures of income and expenditure. Dympna Ryan, the School's utterly focused and talented Development Officer, did have the one adequate computer, but saw the urgency of a more sophisticated data system. Sláine O'Hogáin, ISE Librarian, ingeniously managed the library's 26,000 volumes with an ancient Amstrad and a programme of Bill's artful design. Staff were eager in the main. And so, we braved the virtual new world of information technology. But, it was a hungry ghost, monetarily speaking. A computer committee led by Bill Mc Sweeney and John O'Grady (an ecumenics graduate and fellow techno-*aficionado*), developed a 'needs analysis', with annual budget (amounting to the princely sum of £6,000) and strategic plan for procurement and training. Students and Administrative staff took priority, with a structured hand-me-down system according to required capacity, with academic staff at the end of the queue. We shamelessly begged and borrowed, running to earth second-hand computer dens in tucked-away alleys in search of reconditioned computers. So, enormous was our hope when in late 1997, Derek Bell, a Board member, alerted me to unspent budget to be shaken loose from Department of Education coffers on the basis of capital expenditure applications. After finally establishing that ISE was eligible I worked on a proposal, helped by the new Administrator. It was Christmas Eve, but even our dedication to getting computers was outdone by that of one senior civil servant, Mr Paddy McDonagh, who was even later at his desk at the Department of Education, ready to incorporate our application into his composite one, typifying the collaboration which characterises so much of what happens in ISE. Thus, without precedent, we gained a cool £25,000, which *had* to be spent by 31 December – although, in the prudential judgement of our Finance Committee, what had been recently outlaid on second hand hardware was to be included. Undaunted, Bill and John O'Grady embarked upon the installation spree, doing battle with the

ghosts in the machine late into the night almost to the point of
turning to wraiths themselves, but succeeding in building a system and a strategy from scratch.

It was following a primary recommendation of the Review
that the role of PA to the Director was indeed restructured: the
duties of Secretary to the ecumenics programme now aligned to
the existing part-time one in peace studies. To the residual PA
duties were added responsibilities of Administrator. Aideen
Woods ably stepped into that role, and Christine Houlahan,
with equal energy began as Ecumenics Programme Secretary
(alongside Dorothy Maguire in Peace Studies) – intrepid women
all. Together with School Librarian, Sláine O'Hogáin, Aideen
and Christine have seen the School through ten years of new
complexities and changes barely anticipated then. To Aideen
over the next few years, fell the multi-tasking challenge of establishing the new systems – information technology, purchasing
and stock control, also working with the Director in sustaining
communications and PR relating on academic events, and eminent visitors, and taking a major responsibility in the shaping of
team structures and the flow of administration.

By the end of 1996, the Review could be distilled into several
paragraphs, but not disguising the comprehensiveness of
Patricia Kenny's analysis and implementation plan, and the co-
operation of staff in embracing the change. It was gratifying to
be able to report that every office was now close to being com-
puter-equipped, a clearer data-base policy was in operation and
accounts computerised. Board was particularly pleased that the
process of developing budget categories and of entering that
year and the previous year's budget on computer was virtually
complete.

Of course, it is people, not machines, who make the difference in such undertaking, and ISE has been enriched in its staff,
paid and voluntary. There is always an interplay between needs
and demands, not least in the circumstances surrounding decisions about retirements, contracts and recruitment of new staff.
In my term of office, departures, in almost all cases, happened

by the unilateral decision of individuals themselves or by a delicate process of discernment of personal and institutional timeli-
ness and mutual benefit. Other factors come into play connected
with a person's health and energy, in the face of changing job
specification or the wish to take a different turn in work or life.
At the time, I valued the efforts of all to hold together professionalism and care of the person in these decision-making
processes. Barbara Duncan who had faithfully served ISE in the
Finance Office chose to retire at this time, but not before render-
ing the books onto computer, painstakingly, running both systems in parallel, before putting the old ledgers on the shelf for
good.

Leave-takings were conducted in an atmosphere of mutual
acknowledgement, enlivened by a farewell meal provided by
Maureen Donohue, ISE's valiant housekeeper, cook extraordi-
naire, pillar of loyalty to the School and the heart of its hospitality.
(Unsurprising the fact that it is so often Maureen's name – with
Sláine's – that are mentioned first when and wherever in the
world one bumps into ISE graduates). I was grateful for the degree of integrity with which such decisions were undertaken, for
the professionalism with which the Board sought to conduct its
business in these matters, and in that leavetakings were marked
in such way that the difference made by individual staff to the
success and flourishing of ISE, together with the friendship and
colleagueship shared, were publicly appreciated and celebrated.

Throughout, Dr Christopher Gibson, Chair of Board (from
1997), ploughed in a wealth of expertise and sound judgement,
and was unfailingly encouraging and practically shrewd in negotiation towards the practicability of an alternative angle. He
was a gracious mentor, whether on the world of companies and
commerce, or on civic or church life, with that rare combination
of integrity and flexibility. I learned much from him.

Public Relations: Students and Graduates – our Best Ambassadors
David Poole, who had done so much to enhance practical provision for students – transforming a dark basement corridor with

standard lamps and computer-wired desks, having completed eight years as Chair of the Executive Board, undertook to develop ISE's Endowment Fund on a consultancy basis. He also undertook to assist with communications and in keeping this linked to fund-raising. This was furthered through the generous funding by a Belfast donor of a part-time PR graduate-trainee (Debbie O'Donnell) under the supervision of Fleischman Hilliard Saunders, taking ISE as her sole portfolio. Media exposure was already in sharp focus, given the campaign and staff's commitment to let no month pass without some featuring in the media of the School's research, educational or public contributions on matters of moment and substance (rather than 'spin' – a word then coming into vogue). The specific emphasis was to spotlight the multi-cultural student body, themselves keen to convey why they had chosen ISE with its exciting learning environment, and its correlation of rigorous analysis and ethical praxis, global and local concerns and ecumenical and ethical methodologies.

Ecumenics From Outside In and Inside Out:
Ongoing Reflection and Renewal
The enrichment of the multicultural spark of energy which students brought to the whole ISE project cannot be overstressed. Out of their rich lifeworld, intellectual capacity and intercultural exchange, they influenced the multi-levelled epistemology and theory of ecumenics, provoking staff to self-critical and renewing definitions. Student evaluations and formal staff reflection days helped keep this process and agenda before us, as the kernel of the School's ethos, and I underlined this in more than one Annual Report. Thus, in 1997:

> As the School engages with these intertwined issues of church and world, faith and politics in their global and local dimensions, we feel called to keep reflecting on our statement of vision and what its hidden potential might be for reconciliation, unity and peace.

Referring to the new logo and sub-title, 'Ireland's Centre for Reconciliation Studies' as one aspect of our continuing clarification of our vision and purpose, I observed that 'ecumenism' and 'ecumenics' do not merely defeat the spell-check capacity of the word processor, but carry their own health warning. And although sometimes 'reluctant to hand them over to disuse', or defensive about our specialised interdisciplinary field, 'such self-questioning is useful, not just about the name, but about the ways in which the whole ecumenical enterprise has been positioned and pursued.' If ISE had prevailed through weathers of change it was in great measure due to our collective capacity to hold the ecumenical memory while constantly reaching for the plenitude of unity, willing to wrestle towards more authentic ways of understanding, expressing and discovering its sources and its surplus of meaning:

> Both beyond ISE and within its walls, it is increasingly suggested that the old vision of ecumenism as one world house – one church for the sake of one world – may no longer be an adequate vision. It is not just that it is, for now, a bridge too far for the narrow denominationalism in which so many churches … are still bound. Could it be that the old model may no longer be adequate to the insistent diversity of a world 'incorrigibly plural', but also intentionally plural? … too tied to an understanding of unity that has not taken seriously enough the scale and dynamics of diversity …'

I still believe that our constructs of what unity and reconciliation comprise have often been premised on unity as unitary, rather than as the relational and dynamic way of inhabiting the divine-human field where we encounter ourselves in and through the Other. Ecumenists, I proposed, must probe more critically the non-doctrinal factors that infiltrate theology and church practice. At the time, I welcomed the current opportunities for examining these matters further through our active involvement with the World Council of Churches' study process on 'Ethnic Identity, National Identity and the Unity of the

Church'. Clearly, in our ongoing enterprise in the field of ecumenics, dialogue and interaction were germane, together with
alertness to the linguistic diversity of the field – 'reconciliation,
communion ... peace, dialogue, healing, shalom, solidarity, understanding, service,' were some words I cited. What new con-
ceptualities are now breaking in? ISE staff have continued to
pose this question.

It is often through relationship with other groups that such
new insights dawn, and it is through creative partnerships that
ISE has opened up new horizons. Thanks to an endowment es-
tablished by Dr Margaret Haire, in memory of her late husband,
Professor James Haire, and another, established by Mr Frank
O'Reilly in honour of his late wife, Moya, we held on alternate
years the James Haire Memorial Lecture and the Moya O'Reilly
Lecture. In 1995, Robin Boyd attracted an audience of 200 in
Queen's University, Belfast with the university's active collaboration, through Professor Bernard Cullen, Dean of Theology.
The lecture, 'Focus of Unity: Ultimate and Penultimate Goals of
the Christian Movement' featured also as ISE's Academic
Council Lecture (subsequently published in the *Scottish Journal
of Theology*). Dr Geiko Müller-Fahrenholz, well-known for his
writings of forgiveness and reconciliation, was the James Haire
lecturer in March 1999 on the theme, 'Healing the Wounds of the
Nations: Towards a Common Mission for the Churches'.

In June 1996, Dorothee Sölle, eminent feminist and liberation
theologian, filled theatres on successive nights in Dublin and
Belfast for the O'Reilly lecture, 'Hope Against Hope: A Woman
in Need of Names for God', as did Gerard Hughes SJ, familiar
through his theological and spiritual writings, in 1998, 'Finding
God in Conflict.' In November1997, Dr Gabriel Daly OSA, the
longest serving ISE lecturer, delivered a splendid paper, 'One
Church: Two Indispensable Principles – Protestant Principle
and Catholic Substance.'

For some years, ISE collaborated with Selly Oak Colleges,
Birmingham on an annual conference and after Professor Martin
Conway's retirement the relationship found other expressions,

via teaching, conference involvement and reciprocal examining. Corrymeela has also been a congenial and key partner. We collaborated with them on Ministry Conferences, held annually at their arrestingly beautiful North Antrim centre. Themes intimate something of our attempt to respond to current needs theologically and ecumenically. In post-ceasefire, 1995, an upbeat mood is discernible with – 'Challenge to the Churches of the New Irish Moment'. The 1996 event staged a debate on church involvement in the critically significant community sector, and included on-site community visits.

Other occasional or annual events in which ISE was significantly involved also included the Glenstal Ecumenical Conference, Irish Council of Christians and Jews conferences, the Ecumenical Society of the Blessed Virgin Mary seminars, Irish Council of Churches, Irish Interchurch Meeting, the Greenhills Conference, Council of Churches for Britain and Ireland, Community Relations Council, NI, the Dept of Foreign Affairs (Irish government), and agencies such as Christian Aid or Trócaire, always linking local to global concerns. We were particularly happy that through Dr John Morrow, ISE co-ordinated an event and lecture to mark the Church of South India's Golden Jubilee. In such events, ISE students participated and assisted, thus broadening their study, introducing them to new people and contexts, enabling them to become inserted into the ecumenism of life. So too did our students enhance proceedings with different perspectives and enthusiasm, also helpfully keeping ISE's significance to the fore. Over this period, annual student scholarships were initiated from the Glenstal Conference, Trócaire, the Department of Foreign Affairs, and the Dominican Sisters, adding to existing commitments from WCC-Christian Aid, the Franciscan Friars of the Atonement, and the Methodist Church Mission.

Students and staff worked to ensure that taught programmes were also edged by a distinctive social horizon via interrelationships and events run cooperatively with NGOs. With an eye to the Jubilee justice aspect of the millennium, in 1998, such a con-

You are cordially invited to the launch

by

The Right Rev. Dr Michael Jackson
Bishop of Clogher

of

The Irish School of Ecumenics 1970-2007

Edited by

Michael Hurley SJ

on

Date Thursday, 1 May 2008   **Time** 2.00 p.m.
Refreshments from 1.00 p.m

Venue Irish School of Ecumenics,
683 Antrim Road, Belfast BT15 4EG

Ms. Jackie Scanlan
Tel (01) 2601144 ext 105
Email isedev@tcd.ie
Fax (01) 2601158

ference was held in Dublin's Teachers' Club on 'Debt Forgiveness', in co-operation with Ireland's Debt and Development Coalition. Visiting speakers included Anne Pettifor, Rabbi Dr Norman Solomon, Dr Zaki Badawi. Dr Redmond Fitzmaurice OP also contributed and photos taken then disclose a radiantly open countenance. Immense the shock, days later – only hours after taking his ISE class – and equally, the sense of sadness and loss to hear that he had died suddenly. In these years, we also lost other esteemed colleagues and friends, among them Fr John Macken SJ a valued Board and Council Member who had taught the course, 'Justification in Ecumenical Perspective'; Dr Brian Hearne CSSp who brought to student learning rich perspectives from African theology; Fred Jeffrey, a Methodist and one of the original trustees in NI; Professor John Barkley, first Presbyterian Patron of ISE and Council member; and Frances Boyd (d 1998), former colleague, Librarian, and wife of Dr Robin Boyd.

The changing face of Ireland was reflected in Pamela Stotter's Continuing Education programmes with topics like 'Difference on our Doorstep', and a conference on 'The Value of Diversity in Learning', as early as 1996. This was opened by Senator Mary Henry, always a supporter and friend. In 1997, the now racy Temple Bar district in Dublin was a venue for seminars on racism, refugee and travellers issues; our students benefited from learning first-hand personal narratives of racism and from critical and policy reflections on such issues. This initiative was coordinated by Dr Iain Atack in collaboration with the Irish Council for Refugees (an organisation co-founded by an ISE graduate). Temple Bar's Irish Film Centre was also the inner-city location for an 'alternative' ecumenical event for the Week of Prayer for Christian Unity, over these years. This was complementary to our annual RTÉ broadcast, where students' multicultural gifts of music or drama enriched the worship and embodied solidarity links between ISE and the local church, joining musical forces with the wonderful talent of various choirs from Cabinteely, for example, or Omagh.

Forging Stronger Links with Trinity

ISE's integration into Trinity was not completed in my term, but it was a salient preoccupation, and therefore it may be useful to give some sense of the lie of the land and the mapping of the journey.

Already in January 1995, the question was raised at a Board Meeting. Dr Poole and I reported on our recent conversation with Dr Bryan McMurry, a senior academic in Trinity and a member of our Academic Council, on how best to proceed. Board made encouraging noises, but was 'wary of anything that might lead to absorption'. There was a firm foundation on which to build. Besides existing informal links, e.g. with the Staff Office who were helpful with advice, for example, relating to salary structures and contracts, TCD academics contributing lectures on both Master's programmes, and cordial personal relationships, there were also solid inter-institutional arrangements. Since the early 1980s our degrees were MPhil awards from the University of Dublin and from that there were twice yearly joint Court of Examiners meetings (formal approval of external examiner nominations), as well as twice yearly meetings of the Co-ordinating Committee – all held in the college board room with due observance of Trinity regulations, e.g. as to programme provision, acceptance of new courses, together with the protocols associated with commencements. There was also a cost to the School in that a percentage of fees was made over to the university. Early on I had to negotiate a schedule of back-payments to TCD consequent on an erroneous undercharge. Although it put me to the pin of my wimple to make good the debt, the process gave me a bracing introduction to the college system. Trinity academics from cognate departments also served on ISE interview panels for academic appointments.

Further meetings followed with Mr Michael Gleeson and Professor Andrew Mayes, Registrar, to clarify academic, administrative and financial implications, ahead of any formal joint committee. After some delays arising from an unrelated disciplinary matter, it could be reported to Board that 'TCD now seems extremely positive.' Provost Mitchell visited the School in February 1997, and explicitly expressed his desire for a successful outcome, graciously acknowledging the enhancement which ISE would bring to Trinity in terms of its well-regarded Master's programmes, its commitment to research, and its substantial cross-border profile and lifelong learning initiatives North and South.

We acknowledged that a key short-term aim was to secure our future via annual government funding, which would in turn attract a larger numbers of students (each year we saw students who had gained acceptance to ISE, then perforce defaulting elsewhere, simply because student grants were available only for HEA-linked colleges); but this was not our primary motivation. We also acknowledged that full access to the range of university activities and facilities was a desired boon, and that staff saw the desirability of being able to engage in the intellectual life of a renowned university. I prepared a report on the work and outreach of the School for Professor Mayes and Mr Michael Gleeson in July, just as the former was taking up his new role as Vice-Provost. *Inter alia*, I harnessed theologian David Tracy's model which outlines that theology has three publics – academy, church and society – but deploying it suggested something of ISE's diversity and comprehensiveness (academic research; interchurch and interfaith theology and dialogue, and socio-political analysis and normative research). For the record, one senior academic in the School of Hebrew, Biblical and Theological Studies (which was, it must be said, vocal in opposition to ISE integration), dismissed our self-description as 'purely aspirational'.

Within ISE, we teased out what needed to be dealt with, via regular staff meetings and a special working party of Board, consisting of Dr Chris Gibson (Chair), Dr Dermot Lane, Dr David Poole and Dr Salters Sterling. This amounted to an astonishing synergy of commercial, educational, administrative and intellectual acumen, as they worked with me in identifying underlying questions relating to our ecumenical vision, our inter-cultural student body, specialised library holdings, and the interplay of our plural constituencies, also keeping an eye to staff interests and aspirations, and anticipating all manner of legal implications. It was all a delicate balancing act, or a discourse-equation with such recurring phrases, on the one side, as protecting and cherishing our identity and traditional scope – without getting lost in a sense of our own preciousness and unique identity – and on the other a collective self-belief about our capacity to embrace a wider intellectual horizon with new intellectual challenges and ecumenical opportunities. By Michaelmas term 1997, Professor David McConnell, now Registrar and Dean of International Affairs, brought fresh momentum, relating to the project as 'a big idea', and agreeing that a more urgent pace was needed. I reported to Academic Council his hope 'that we can bring a clear and mutually acceptable proposal by the end of the academic year, which would have an enhancing outcome for both institutions, academically and educationally, and without prejudice to the integrity of either'.

I also noted that we needed to keep in our view current discussions on the academic future of ISE in Northern Ireland. This was another front of expansion, with new complexities requiring that major decisions could not long be postponed. But better first to complete the picture on ISE-TCD integration.

In early 1998, further meetings occurred, with Professor McConnell and me following up in our respective domains to ensure the consolidation of intent, and a basis for delineating heads of agreement, and ensuring that there would be 'no negative financial impact on TCD departments' (School of Hebrew, Biblical and Theological Studies blood was still up), and that ISE Trust and its management structure would be maintained, and dual mechanisms developed. Fr Laurence Murphy SJ, chief Trustee and President of Council, who was constant and clear in his support through crisis periods, placed himself behind developments, and undertook to inform ISE's Patrons – who were unequivocally supportive.

By April, as tends to happen when actual decision nears, anxieties about loss of autonomy resurfaced. At such times, it is

necessary, I believe, to keep one's eyes fixed on the vision and
direction that has been agreed, and in this I kept underscoring
our own agency in shaping the future we desired, reiterating
Professor McConnell's assurances on ISE's integrity. But I knew
that the prevarication had to be addressed if I was to freely press
on towards Heads of Agreement with him and with the ISE
committees working diligently towards that goal. At the April
Board meeting, therefore, I asked for a statement of intent and
commitment. Ambivalence was voiced by each person around
the table, by some in soul-searching tones, but each, to a woman
and man, were unequivocal in restating their commitment. An
unambiguous statement was articulated and dispatched to the
Registrar:

> The Board affirms that we are whole heartedly committed to
> furthering the partnership with Trinity, and that we are en-
> gaging in negotiations on integration with the full expect-
> ation of a positive and constructive outcome for both sides.

Shortly thereafter, Professor McConnell confirmed to me that
the Provost and Vice-Provost were 'fully behind the decision to
move matters forward to the more formal negotiation stage' and
that TCD 'would propose that the HEA ring-fence funding for
ISE according to the Carysfort College model, and that ISE
would maintain its integrity and have the status of a department
within TCD'. It would also be proposed that the HEA cover capital costs, were ISE to move onto or closer to college campus.

Dr Sterling, having undertaken to work further on unit-cost
factors, did so with HEA officials. I asked ISE's solicitor, Mr Tom
Bacon, to identify necessary legal revisions of the Trust
Document underpinning the School's institutional status. The
Trustees met in May, making constructive suggestions and reaf-
firming full support, and I had further meetings with Mr Paddy
McDonagh, senior official in the Department of Education.
Based on the assurance of focused discussion towards a deal
with Trinity, the Department had a few months previously re-
sponded to our application for £150,000, with another once-off

award of £100,000. The Minister for Education, Micheál Martin paid the promised visit to ISE in mid 1997. In his July visit, Dr John Hayden, Chief Executive of HEA, demonstrated his lucid comprehension of ISE's educational significance and operation. Subsequent meetings with his staff attended to finer detail in forwarding ISE's incorporation into the HEA system, holding the two institutional integrities. We set out transitional financial needs, space requirements, budget scenarios and negotiated for the optimum deal on ring-fencing of ISE's HEA allocation, to facilitate our smooth passage and orientation into the established ground of funding entitlement and opportunity within Trinity.

In late October, a meeting took place between Professor McConnell, Dr Christopher Gibson (Chair of Executive Board), Fr Paddy Crowe SJ (who had been central in developing the School's interrelated governing regulations) and myself to finalise the basis for ISE's formal proposal. Here we set out such *sine qua non* elements as the continuing role of the ISE Trust and its fund-raising activity, the continuing integrity of ISE (in respect of its constitutive programmes and its various interlocking zones of activity). All agreed on the necessity for ISE to specify the areas of autonomy and unique characteristics and contributions of the School, and which activities would fall under the academic funding umbrella, and to define the parameters and mode of its relationship. Two models – a centre outside the faculty structure, or a department within the faculty structure – were the deemed alternatives, and there was unanimity on stressing the expected mutual gain for ISE and TCD.

Dr Sterling, meanwhile, having calculated potential costs, presented a discussion paper which drew upon his unique experience of the integration of colleges into Trinity – 'Reflections on Academic Structures Organisational Arrangements and Administrative Provision for an Irish School of Ecumenics Incorporated into Trinity College Dublin.' Unsurprisingly, it provoked a humdinger of a Board meeting. Also tabled that day was the Registrar's 'Draft Heads of Agreement' document, which was assuring in expression and deemed 'helpful'. At a late January

1999 meeting, the familiar moot points were reiterated about the necessity of protecting ISE's 'national and international identity, ethos, integrity and uniqueness', the role of the Trust, and the School Patrons. Anything approaching 'absorption' was off limits, while the 'right model of integration' needed to be found. As we traversed the same ground one more time, I recalled that this 'accordion phenomenon' was a dynamic recognisable from mediation processes, as hitherto separate groups, upon clearing major obstacles to resolution of different interests, typically revert to old positions, preoccupied about what risked being lost amid the gains. Again, I alluded to Professor McConnell's indication of the strength of goodwill in Trinity towards ISE, their desire for integration. I repeated the feasibility of maintaining both separate and joint structures, the inter-disciplinary integrity of ISE programmes as an accepted non-negotiable, and the idea of 'dual belonging'. I was also clear that with 'integration', Trinity would become the employer. I recalled the Board minute with its 'whole hearted commitment to furthering the partnership with Trinity and our full expectation of a constructive outcome'. The sub-committee clearly had further work to do in constructing a more congruent model of institutional integration than any currently extant. (To sustain resolve, it behoved us to advert to our recent receipt of a further £250,000 from the Department of Education, our largest grant ever – to take us to December 1999 – a signifier of their confidence that the deal would be done.) To enable the next phase, I agreed to write a paper articulating 'The Vision of the Irish School of Ecumenics as an Academic Institute.' In my remaining months as Director, progress was achieved with Professor McConnell, culminating in developing an outline 'Memorandum of Understanding and Agreement' taking on the reiterated concerns and forming the basis for the formal negotiations. The end of 1999 was still the target date for completion and for instituting the new funding structure. And so, Dr Gibson wrote to the Provost proposing a schedule of meetings towards the concluding of negotiations. The University Senior Officers formalised this on their side, confirming the intention that ISE become an institute within Trinity College Dublin. The ISE Director-designate Canon Kenneth Kearon was a little more than a month from taking the helm and a meeting of Senior Officers in the University would shortly formalise the negotiating structure. Undoubtedly further whirlpools would require skilful negotiation, but tides were favourable. Signs were of full steam ahead into Trinity.

'The End of Exploring' or, 'Every End a Wholly New Start'?
A favoured ecumenical metaphor (first coined to urge a synergy of East and West) is that of breathing with both lungs. Thus, you might say, one lung helped us to sustain the academic life of ISE, to plan towards the move to Trinity, to refine our powers of persuasion *vis-à-vis* EU and other funders – now with some substantial success. The other lung sustained and revitalised the academic, ecclesiological and public activities. With increased legwork and web-work, student numbers increased apace, (thirty in peace studies and twenty five in ecumenics, 1997-1998). There were new courses – *inter alia* on gender and politics, ecumenical social ethics and ethics in international affairs; and three solid staff publications. Staff research seminars were initiated in these years, creating a forum of constructive critique and support. Although ISE did not have a PhD programme then, these monthly meetings enabled staff to test research findings, give conference papers a 'dry-run', and generally intensified the culture of research. An acclaimed conference in Belfast, *Boundaries and Bonds*, proved a gratifying culmination of the first phase of the MBS project and paved the way to a dissemination phase.

Professor Mary McAleese of Queen's University Belfast had, in the early 1990s, been Co-Chair of the interchurch study process on sectarianism which had been a point of departure for MBS. And so, when she came in 1998 to ISE to launch a new edition of *Reconciling Memories*, she came not alone as President of Ireland, but with unique credentials on the subject, and wishing formally to recognise the co-editors, Alan Falconer and Joe Liechty. Her comments were penetrating, and she praised ISE's contribution to ecumenism and reconciliation, North and South, and beyond. To welcome the President was a particular personal pleasure, since, in the 1960s before the mantle of Professor or President had descended upon her, we were co-students at St Dominic's, Belfast. Her words remain significant for ISE today in the tasks of making peace with our past and working for the reconciling of divisions.

This theme had also been salient at other major ecumenical events, as at the Second European Ecumenical Assembly in Graz, 1997, attended by Dr John Morrow and me. As Moderator of the ecclesiology plenary on 'Reconciling Memories', I could see the cross weave and potential for learning and interaction, in the presentations from different traditions in Northern Ireland, Romania and from other marginalised groups. Likewise at the WCC Eighth Assembly at Harare, 1998, Dr Johnston McMaster and I encountered a number of ISE graduates. I presented a case study on Ireland in the 'Overcoming Violence' forum (another on 'Ecumenical Formation'). Words of praise, peace and justice resounded during that Assembly, as did the weasel words of President Mugabe. Konrad Raiser's body language did nothing to disguise that he would rather have been anywhere on the planet than sharing a platform with a President whose policies were already provoking moral outrage. Recalling the Assembly at this remove, it is the distressed faces of the Shona people that revisit me, or the *cri de coeur* of Bishop Paride from Sudan. As a prophet in the wilderness, his words were searing, the most memorable message of the entire Assembly. I faxed an article to the *Irish Times* – 'The Heartbeat of the Ecumenical Movement is Now in Africa', by way of responding to his plea to 'tell the world of the plight of Sudan'. On his return home, revenge for his outspokenness struck swiftly, when his car was ambushed and two of his companions shot. At Harare the decision to trans-form the Programme to Overcome Violence into a Decade to Overcome Violence was unanimous.

Ireland-Boston Axis

Earlier that year, in April, just as the Good Friday Agreement was in the final stages of negotiation in Belfast, I was in Boston as a participant in the first International Consultation of the Programme to Overcome Violence, which would prove germane, I learned later, in the decision to declare the Decade. Furthermore, personal friendships and inter-institutional relationships were formed that have lasted. With the help of John Kilbride, an Irish Bostonian, I had some meetings that later proved fruitful in funding terms. One philanthropist, Dr Tom Tracy, was open to ISE but thought a reality check might be beneficial. He, therefore, proposed a survey of ISE graduates, for which I employed an independent company, and for which he provided £25,000. The ensuing 'Report on Graduates' did indeed show how ISE had equipped them to fulfil their best potential. They were shown to be active in leadership roles in inter-church projects on peacelines in Belfast, African development and human rights agencies, peacekeeping missions on the North-South Korean border, or pioneering human rights campaigns or interfaith encounters in Europe or the Pacific. Others occupied higher research positions, or leadership positions in international and ecumenical agencies. They testified about how their time in ISE had opened up new vistas and given them competence and confidence for leadership in education, churches, or civil society animated by both conviction and the capacity for critique. On 2 April 1999 I wrote in the 'Foreword':

> ISE flourishes because its vision of unity and peace is not pursued at the expense of diversity, nor in offering 'more of the same'. ISE is itself testimony to the power of diversity when it is oriented towards reconciliation, justice and an ethics of inclusion. In this study there is ample testimony that, wherever they are, ISE's graduates are making 'a world of difference'.

The Ebb and the Flow: Not Farewell but Fare Forward, Travellers

Resigning as ISE Director was not in my plan when I attended our Dominican General Chapter in June 1998. But events took an unexpected turn when I was elected Prioress of our international Dominican Congregation. I felt torn by the pull and counter-pull of my loyalties to ISE and to my Dominican sisters (in Ireland, Southern Africa, Latin America, Lisbon and New Orleans) who had elected me. Acutely aware of the bad timing (given the stage of negotiations with Trinity), I agreed to remain until another Director was in post. In those intervening nine months others rallied around: my Dominican Council, to enable me to devote continuing time to ISE, Dr Christopher Gibson and Board, and all the staff, pulling together to maintain the focus and pace on programmes and projects: integration into Trinity, the rounding off of the MBS project, and preliminary crafting of an MPhil in Belfast, building on existing cross-border involvement of staff and students, with a contextual emphasis, and integrating analysis and models from MBS. And the inevitable round of persuading funding bodies to give us money, with some happy success from the Department of Foreign Affairs who committed £100,000 for NI projects, and the assurance of further funding from the Department of Education. At Easter 1999 I cheerfully left the tiller in the capable hands of Rev Canon Kenneth Kearon.

Looking back on these five years, the prevailing sense is of a time of challenge and change, and of huge appreciation of so much goodwill on the part of my colleagues and companions on the journey, and their willingness through the peaks and troughs, to act in concert to keep ISE flourishing and reaching out. It was a time of grace and faith.

Robert Ballagh's wonderfully executed limited edition print, 'Peace through Reconciliation' and donated by the artist in support of ISE's mission, stands perhaps as an emblem of these years. In varying tones and textures of blue and grey and deeper blue and white, the whole piece is anchored in the gesture of firmly clasped hands, above which doves hover, arise and scatter, wings lifted to new horizons and further journeying and circling into peace. Whether in spring hope or winter despair, I share the hope that ISE will not cease from exploration, treasuring the multifarious blessing of remembered gifts and living faith, and that peace will descend still in its sevenfold wisdom, energy and light.

CHAPTER SEVEN

Five Fascinating Years
(1999-2004)

Kenneth Kearon

Kenneth Arthur Kearon was born in Dublin in 1953. After education at
Mountjoy School he attended Trinity College in Dublin where he studied Mental and Moral Science for a degree in Philosophy. After further
study in Cambridge and Dublin, he was ordained deacon in 1981 and
priest in 1982. He served a curacy in the parish of All Saints Raheny and
St John's Coolock in the diocese of Dublin & Glendalough and then was
appointed Dean of Residence at Trinity College. In 1991 he became
Rector of the parish of Tullow (Dublin) before becoming Director of the
Irish School of Ecumenics in 1999. He has also, since 1995, been a member of the Chapter of Christ Church Cathedral Dublin, and served as its
Chancellor 2002-2004. Kenneth was a member of the General Synod of
the Church of Ireland, Co-ordinator of Auxiliary Ministry (NSM)
Training in the church, and a member of the Irish Council for Bioethics.
He is an Honorary Canon of St Paul's Cathedral London, St George's
Cathedral Jerusalem and Canterbury Cathedral. In 2006 he was given
an honorary doctorate by General Theological Seminary, New York. He
was appointed Secretary General of the Anglican Communion in July
2004 and took up the position in January 2005. He is author of *Medical
Ethics: an Introduction* (Columba Press, 1995) and has contributed to a
number of volumes on education, family and medical ethics.

193

The agenda for the Irish School of Ecumenics for the foreseeable future had emerged from the times of crisis experienced by the School. My predecessor, Geraldine Smyth had recognised that the School's future could only be built on a secure financial future, and to that end had opened discussions with the Higher Education Authority and the Department of Education and Science in the Republic and the response had been very encouraging, provided ISE could find a mechanism whereby it could be mainstreamed into the publicly funded third level sector. Trinity College Dublin was the obvious, though not the only vehicle, and discussions there too had been positive, provided funding could be secured by ISE.

So the task was to explore a way in which ISE could be integrated into Trinity College in such a way that its distinctiveness could be maintained. As was clear, much of the exploratory work had been undertaken by Geraldine and all the signals had been very positive so far. Negotiations on behalf of Trinity College were to be led by Professor David McConnell, Registrar of the University and soon to become vice Provost of the College. David was Professor of Genetics at Trinity and in that role had shaped and led one of the most dynamic departments in the university. I had come to know him well through his role as Chairman of the Adelaide Hospital Society. His experience there was to stand him and ISE in good stead as we shaped the future of ISE within the university. The Adelaide Hospital Society was a voluntary body, closely related to the Protestant churches in Ireland, which managed the Adelaide Hospital in Dublin, one of Dublin's oldest general hospitals. Through a series of rationalisations and modernisations of the hospital service in the Republic, which involved relocation to the suburbs, amalgamation or closure for most hospitals in the country, the Adelaide Hospital found itself to be the only hospital under Protestant management, and it too was scheduled for relocation from the city centre to the suburbs and amalgamation with two other hospitals – one general and one children's.

There had always been an awareness that its association with the Protestant churches had resulted in a distinctive ethos for the hospital, and its incorporation into the new hospital in Tallaght appeared to place that under threat. The bitterly divisive abortion debates of the 1980s had only served to underline the importance of ethical diversity within the Irish Health Service. Since I taught medical ethics in the School of Nursing in the hospital during that period, I became involved in the definition of that distinctive ethos.

The preservation of ethos was again a major issue in the future of the Irish School of Ecumenics. How does a small entity like the School preserve and protect what has been distinctive to its survival and to its success when it becomes part of a much larger institution with a different focus and ethos? In that sense Trinity College was an attractive partner because it too had treasured its own distinctiveness and identity in times past, though like many universities, much of this had been lost in recent years by financial pressures and bureaucratic reorganisation.

David also had strong commitment to the role of the humanities in the university, and that breadth of vision enabled him to grasp what ISE was about and to envision what ISE's contribution might be to the wider university.

The Memorandum of Understanding and Agreement

A way forward was to be developed in a document entitled 'A Memorandum of Understanding and Agreement' (MUA), to be agreed by the College and by ISE. This envisaged an initial incorporation of ISE into the university as an academic institution, with its own governance structure. Finance from the Department of Education and Science was to be designated during this period and ring-fenced for the School. A crucial element in all of this was the creation (subsequent legal advice demonstrated that no new entity was needed) of an ISE Trust alongside the School and recognised by the university, which would continue to enable and develop traditional ISE links with churches, NGOs, voluntary bodies and individuals committed to the vision of ISE, and would also be a source and vehicle for external funding for the School within Trinity.

The first draft of the MUA arrived on my desk at the end of my first week as Director. The negotiation of the detail of that document and related issues was to occupy and absorb the energy of most of us at ISE for the next few years. A joint negotiating team was set up to work on the detail of this under the joint chairmanship of David McConnell and Chris Gibson, the Chair of the Board of ISE.

In broad terms the MUA envisaged the establishment of ISE as an academic institute within Trinity College for a limited period (originally 3 years and later lengthened to 5 years) with designated ring-fenced finance from the Higher Education Authority. There would be an ISE Executive Board at Trinity College overseeing the School and its activities during this period. By the end of this period ISE would be fully integrated into the College.

The ISE Trust would be recognised by the university as a key element in the identity of ISE, particularly in maintaining relationships and in fundraising for the distinctive additional elements which distinguished ISE and which fell outside the funding remit of the third level sector. The Trust would also enhance the life of the School by providing scholarships and prizes to students at the School.

So the negotiations began. While the joint negotiating team oversaw the whole process, much of the detail fell to the Executive Board of the School. The School was blessed with an excellent Board who rose to the task admirably. Each was a busy person in their own right, but no one complained as the meetings became more frequent and the workload increased. The members were a very diverse body with all of the skills necessary to oversee the changeover. Academics, administrators, businessmen, all with a passion for the School to succeed, managed under the skilful chairmanship of Chris Gibson. I cannot remember any of them refusing my requests for help – most volunteered without being asked. Two in particular must be mentioned – Salters Sterling and David Poole.

David had by far the longest association with the School. Through good times and through bad his commitment to the vision of ISE had been unswerving. He offered to work on the shaping of the future of the ISE Trust, and from then on the Board knew that the development and shaping of that aspect of our future was in safe hands. John McGrath, a student and long time supporter of the School, joined him in this task. We were fortunate that the legal documents from 1971 establishing ISE as a charity in both the Republic and Northern Ireland could remain unchanged in the new structure – but the Governing Regulations and Endowment Fund documentation required substantial revision. David and John spent many long evenings in the School working on this.

Salters had enormous experience of administration in the third level sector. He had also had a life-long passion for ecumenism, and now in very active retirement was prepared to give a substantial amount of his time and all of his experience and wisdom to help ISE through this period of change and development. He was always at the end of a telephone and ready to travel to Dublin at short notice throughout this period of change.

Aideen Woods, administrator and PA to the Director, must also be mentioned. At the quietest of times her job was a full-time one, but as change followed change, her work grew exponentially. It was she who controlled and managed the paperwork during this period – demonstrating exceptional adaptability in the range of processes she was called upon to handle, from supporting intense negotiations where every word had both significance and implications, to academic reviews and the design of new programmes, and all the time maintaining the everyday life of the office. Most importantly, she ensured that in the flurry of activity nothing was missed or overlooked, as employment contracts were re-negotiated, pension schemes altered, offices moved, and so on.

Moving beyond Sectarianism

The most important and substantial special project undertaken by ISE to date had been the *Moving Beyond Sectarianism* Project.

Building on previous work at the School, especially the *Reconciliation in Religion and Society* project of Fr Michael Hurley, Geraldine Smyth's conception of a major study on the dynamics of sectarianism had caught the imagination and attracted the attention of significant players in the field of reconciliation in Northern Ireland in both church and state. The day to day work of the project was in the hands of Dr Joe Liechty and Dr Cecelia Clegg, two people of exceptional vision, tenacity and application.

I came in towards the end of the project, when the writing up of the project was the major task in hand. This was more difficult than might seem, as Joe and Cecelia were constantly called upon as advisors and consultants to reconciliation work throughout Northern Ireland and, increasingly, further afield, and time to write was hard to find.

It was clear that the conclusion of a project of this scale and impact would have to be managed carefully. Any major piece of research such as this needs to end and the report to be written so that others could examine and apply its findings as a whole. However, this project was gaining a dynamic of its own and consideration had to be given as to how it might continue into the future.

Following a period of consultation both within and outside the School a number of strands emerged. The report should be written in as accessible and readable a style as possible, and appear as a paperback. The Columba Press with its excellent distribution network would publish and market it in their ever-growing catalogue. This would make it available to professionals in reconciliation, clergy, politicians and civil society leaders.

Small study groups have been the backbone of reconciliation work in Ireland, and it was planned to engage someone to write the findings of MBS into a folder of usable material suitable for such groups. Craig Sands, a person of imagination who could 'think out of the box' and write engagingly for such groups (a task most academics find impossible!), was engaged for this work.

A second strand was to develop the MBS Report into material for use in schools and the informal youth sector. Yvonne Naylor, an experienced teacher most recently working for the Corrymeela Community, undertook this task. While both Craig and Yvonne were employed initially for one year, the scope of Yvonne's work grew and grew. Initially she prepared material for older teenagers but soon pressure was on for material for a younger age group, and then into primary school age groups, so that aspect of the project turned into a multi-annual piece of work.

Much of Yvonne's work took place in schools and she had to overcome some reluctance on the part of school authorities who were, not surprisingly, reluctant to open-up issues surrounding sectarianism in their own schools. Gradually some principals agreed, and soon Education and Library Boards became involved. Few who were present will forget the launch of Yvonne's materials in the Ulster Folk Museum. Yvonne had invited some young school children to the launch as well as senior educationalists and ISE staff and supporters. With a clever arrangement of seating she enabled the adults present to become spectators as she opened up issues of social and religious division with the young people through the use of puppets. It was a deeply moving experience for all, and established beyond doubt the value of the work she was doing.

Partnership in Transformation

The commitment of the various denominations to peacemaking and reconciliation work in Northern Ireland is incontrovertible. Though occasionally criticised from outside by simplistic and ill-informed commentators who saw the situation in Northern Ireland as 'Protestants against Catholics', the reality on the ground was very different. During over thirty years of violence and terrorism, clergy and lay-people of every denomination had provided pastoral care for victims and their families, and had worked together on local initiatives to diffuse tensions; in many areas churches and parishes were the only elements of civil society on the ground capable of holding communities together.

They had also played a major role in the work of the MBS
Research Project. How could the findings of MBS be put to the
service of these Christian communities?

Thus was born another outcome of the MBS Project – *Partners
in Transformation*. For this we engaged with the Mediation
Network of Northern Ireland. Cecelia Clegg, together with the
Rev Doug Baker, a Presbyterian minister from the United States
with long experience of reconciliation work in Northern Ireland
and working with the Mediation Network, were to lead this project which aimed to work with senior leadership within the
churches to support them in enabling their traditions to become
agents of transformation in society.

The task is an enormous one, but as Northern Ireland sought
to leave its violent and divided past behind, Christians have the
potential to make a major contribution to the shaping of a new
Ireland, North and South. MBS through the Partners in
Transformation Project, could be a significant resource to the
churches in that work. As in so many other situations, respect
for ISE was such that we received a ready hearing, and Christian
leadership at the highest levels engaged with the Project.

A New Degree

Before my coming to ISE, there had been a proposal for a third
master's degree at ISE, based in Northern Ireland. The origins of
this idea were unclear to me but some of it may lie in the fact that
a significant number of Northern Ireland students enrolled each
year as part-time students in ecumenical studies. The timetable
was carefully constructed to facilitate them by timing lectures
on Mondays in such a way that students could come from and
return to Belfast by train on the same day, and also by ensuring
that sufficient options were available on Mondays to enable the
course to be completed over a two-year period. Despite this, it is
not surprising that for such students a Belfast base would make
life easier.

In addition, with the growing level of ISE activity in Northern
Ireland, the value of a degree programme there was being recog-

nised. The value of students being able to see at first hand the work of the Continuing Education Programme and to hear from its lecturers, and the ability to study under leaders in reconciliation work in Northern Ireland, could not be overestimated.

Further, the proposal that ISE develop a third master's degree, this time in reconciliation studies and based in Northern Ireland, was named in the Memorandum of Understanding and Agreement. Trinity College was thereby interested in seeing this developed, and the Higher Education Authority would consider its funding within the overall package for ISE.

While MBS did not spawn the third degree, it did provide a stimulus as an intellectual background to the proposal. Academic staff began to meet to shape a degree programme which would build on the successful models developed in ecumenical and peace studies, and which would make a distinctively 'ISE' contribution. Northern Ireland would be the base and also the context for such a degree. The Province had already enjoyed peace for a number of years but it was recognised that creating a reconciled society would take generations. At the international level the fall of the Berlin Wall in 1989 transformed global politics, but the end of the Cold War had not ended violent conflict. Regional proxy wars on behalf of the US and the Soviet Union had ceased, only to be replaced in the public mind by other conflicts, the highest profile ones being Bosnia and the Middle East. Many such conflicts involved issues of ethnicity, nationalism and religion. Most commentators and analysts tended to use religious affiliation as a label, but they failed to take religion seriously as a factor. In many ways, Northern Ireland had been just such a situation – was it now time for lessons learned in Ireland to be shared with the wider world?

So a degree proposal emerged for a Master's Degree in Reconciliation Studies, to be based in Northern Ireland, focusing on the dynamics of reconciliation in society, and taking religion seriously both as a contributor to social division and even to violence in some cases, and also as a resource for peace-building and reconciliation. Being based in Northern Ireland was important because it was there that the resources were available, and ISE was part of a vast network of experience and energy in the field of reconciliation which could be drawn on to resource the degree programme. The Report *Moving Beyond Sectarianism* would be a key textbook.

As we began to consult with others and to talk about our proposals it was clear that (once again!) ISE had struck the right note. Our proposal caught the imagination of many both in the churches and in religious communities and also amongst practitioners of reconciliation. By now we were at an advanced stage in our negotiations for integration with Trinity College, so a major question loomed – would Trinity agree? We need not have worried. Senior figures in Trinity shared the vision. Trinity had always claimed to serve the whole of Ireland – support for this initiative of ISE was a logical next step, and so with considerable support and advice especially from key administrative staff in the College, the proposal took shape.

Assembling our first group of students was easier than I had anticipated. Our plans for a new degree were never secret, so by the time the programme was published there was a list of enquiries from potential students. Lecturing staff had not yet been appointed, and so it fell to me to answer enquiries and meet many potential students. Most had been engaged in some form of reconciliation work for some time and were seeking to put their work into an academic framework.

Reconciliation work is of its nature exploratory – there are no set answers or clear stages of progress. Many potential students had been away from study for a number of years and were wary of returning to formal education, yet the wealth of experience each could bring to the programme would mean that lectures and seminars would be interactive experiences for both lecturers and students, quite unlike any previous experience of formal education.

A major pressing question was where the programme was to take place. It looked likely that ISE would acquire 683 Antrim Road, the home of the Columbanus Community, but nothing had been finalised. We turned to our good friends in the Redemptorist Community on the Antrim Road. The Community has a major commitment to reconciliation work and knew ISE and its work well. They occupied a sprawling campus in beautiful grounds overlooking Belfast Lough, and were prepared to allow us to use a wing and some other rooms for our first year.

This degree simply would not have survived its first year were it not for the academic ability and commitment of the two fulltime lecturers, Joe Liechty and David Tombs, and the organisational skills of Caroline Clarke, the practical support of people like the Redemptorists and the good humour and understanding of our first students.

Continuing Education

My steepest learning curve in ISE was getting to know the Continuing Education Programme in Northern Ireland. This was at the core of what ISE was doing there, and its influence was spreading as fast as programmes were being developed. Johnston McMaster and Cathy Higgins were clearly over-stretched as demands on their time grew, and by the time of my arrival it had already been decided to appoint a third lecturer, with particular responsibility for developing courses in the border counties. Thus Dennis Anderson joined the team.

The effect of this programme on cross-community relations was substantial. On occasions up to 800 people were enrolled on courses at any one time, at up to twenty venues around the Province. Johnston and Cathy developed the *Communities of Reconciliation* publication, which was study material for groups who wished to address deeper and more difficult issues in the field of reconciliation.

Continuing Education in the Republic was not as extensive. Pam Stotter, who had been appointed for this purpose, had been drawn of necessity into teaching and supervision on the ecumenics degree programme but still maintained strong evening courses at the Dublin campus. With the creation of a new post in Faith and Order in the ecumenics programme and consequent reorganisation of that programme, it was possible for Pam to concentrate on Continuing Education almost full time.

This gave Continuing Education in the Republic a tremendous boost and proved that there was an interest in the study of ecumenism in the Republic. I was especially impressed with courses in Ferns in Co Wexford and Bandon, Co Cork where local support and commitment was strong. Ennis, Co Clare also had a strong programme.

Buildings

One of the very tangible and practical ways in which partners supported the School was in the provision of accommodation in both Dublin and Belfast. In Dublin the Jesuit Community had provided excellent accommodation in Milltown Park, a beautiful oasis of green in suburban Dublin. In Belfast the Irish Council of Churches was equally generous with their premises in Elmwood Avenue. With expansion of programmes and the major leap forward for the School which integration into Trinity College represented, the demand for extra space for the School was becoming urgent. This was especially true in Belfast where despite the best efforts of David Stevens and the ICC, our future needs simply couldn't be accommodated in Elmwood Avenue. The new MPhil degree programme was the catalyst, with its demands for library space and permanent lecture and seminar rooms.

So the search began in Belfast. Elmwood Avenue, situated as it was in the heart of the university area, was an ideal location, and that was our first area to consider. The newly emerging ISE Trust was prepared to take the brave step of buying a property which could then be leased to the School, but property in the university area was expensive, and prices were rising rapidly. Anything we could afford was simply not big enough for our needs, and parking (important for day and evening courses) was a major headache.

We began to cast our nets wider. Eventually we identified three four-storey buildings in a terrace on Ormeau Road. Substantial refurbishment was needed, but the building could cope with our needs for the foreseeable future. After a lot of deliberation, a mortgage was arranged and we agreed to buy the building.

I had only just set off from Dublin for a 2pm close of sale when a phone call came through from the estate agent. Our building had been set on fire by vandals during the night and was now ablaze. I sat on the side of the road, wondering what to do. Coincidentally, it was the day Craig Sands was leaving and a lunch had been arranged, so I continued on, calling in first to Ormeau Road. Barriers closed off the building and firemen had extinguished the blaze, the damage was considerable. The roof and top floor was destroyed and there was other damage to the building. Hours later and it would have been ISE's problem, but we were fortunate to be able to walk away from it all.

The search began again. We looked at several properties again, some in North Belfast. In a conversation with the Rev David Kerr, a Methodist minister in Belfast, we learnt that the Columbanus Community was considering its future. David knew ISE's work in Belfast well, and as President of the Methodist Church had made a formal visit to ISE in Dublin. He was also a Trustee of the Columbanus Community, an imaginative community committed to reconciliation which had also been founded by Fr Michael Hurley. Members joined for short periods of say a year or so, but in recent times recruitment had become difficult and it was proving difficult to sustain its common life.

David proposed an exploratory meeting with the Columbanus Trustees which proved very fruitful, and soon we were discussing a proposal that the ISE Trust buy the community's building on the Antrim Road. The building was ideal. It is a large detached house on the Antrim Road with a pleasant garden. The community had redeveloped it in recent years, turning the coach house into a library and joining it to the main house with a multipurpose atrium. No significant alterations were needed to adapt it for our use, although there were long discussions as to whether the location (in a mainly residential area) was suitable for the School. We decided to go ahead and an agreement was entered into with the Community's Trustees. We had decided to fund the purchase with a complex of grants and loans and this proved far more protracted than anyone had imagined. Generously, the Community had allowed us to move in before the deal was closed, but as months went by I am sure the Trustees wondered if the sale would ever be completed! Eventually it was, and we celebrated with a lunch for the Trustees in our new Belfast campus.

Expansion in Dublin was much easier. We were clearly growing out of our premises in Milltown Park. We had been able to rent more offices in 'Plug Street', a corridor at the back of our main section of the building, but the rapidly expanding library was proving problematic, study space was inadequate, and the small lecture room was limiting the number of students we could take on any programme. As soon as we had completed the move to the new campus in Belfast, it was clear that our accommodation needs in Dublin would have to be addressed.

We had only begun to address the issue seriously when the solution came on our doorstep. We occupied the bottom floor and half of the first floor of Tabor House in Milltown Park, an imposing four-storey granite building. The upper two floors were occupied by the Conference of Religious in Ireland (CORI). They had decided to move to new premises in Donnybrook, and so the top two floors became vacant. They were offered to ISE, and we accepted. This meant that we now occupied virtually the whole of Tabor House. It's a gracious though inflexible building – offices are much too large and there are wasteful wide corridors and a sweeping staircase, but it is a lovely environment to work and study in. Crucially the additional space had two very large rooms which could be used as lecture rooms, and the old lecture room was incorporated into the library, thus easing the pressure there.

Conflict and Dispute Resolution Studies
Sometime after I arrived I was contacted by Paulyn Marrinan-

Quin who had a proposal for a new course. Paulyn is a barrister who became well known as Ombudsman for the insurance industry. Having now left that position, she had recognised that alternative dispute procedures, where those with a grievance against a major corporation or public body are encouraged to seek means of redress other than going to court, was set to take off as a field of study in Irish society. She had pioneered such work as an Ombudsman, but recognised that those involved in providing the service generally had no formal training or qualification in the area, and that no such course existed in Ireland.

She had introduced her proposal for such training and qualification to David McConnell, and he had suggested that ISE might be able to help take the idea forward. The proposal was a challenge to ISE. Those involved in Alternative Disputes Resolution (ADR) involving mediation, conflict management, conflict resolution, and so on in the business world, usually came from a legal background. Could a values-based institution like ISE have something distinctive to contribute? Could we provide the standard for training in this field? In many ways, in our existing degree programmes, MBS and the proposed new degree in Reconciliation Studies, we were already engaged in the analysis of religious, political and social tensions and disputes, and properly channelled, this dimension could provide an appropriately larger context within which the training could be set.

After careful analysis and reflection we decided to go for it. A working party was set-up to devise a curriculum with Paulyn as co-ordinator and significant contributions from various ISE's staff, together with input from practitioners in the field. It was fascinating to see the student body assemble each year for this evening diploma. Many were sponsored or supported by their employers and included senior figures in the army and Gardaí, trades unionists, teachers, and members of the legal profession. The demand was clearly there, and in hindsight I am clear that ISE was right to take this initiative.

Conclusion

In this very personal memoir of five fascinating years when I had the honour of being the Director of ISE (the last Director, as it turned out), I have avoided mentioning names except when it has been essential to the narrative. This was deliberate, for in the end of the day ISE is about people more than events, and one cannot mention one without naming them all.

Mission statements are poor substitutes for what ISE is, for it is essentially a body of people committed to a vision of a new way of being, a new way of relating, where divisions are overcome and the walls of division are broken down.

To spend five years at the centre of this was a unique privilege, a time I will always value, and for which I thank God.

CHAPTER EIGHT

Transition Year
(2005)

John D'Arcy May

My role at the helm of ISE was to have a small but significant reprise. On Kenneth Kearon's departure in 2004, it fell to me to fill the traditional directorship post for what was to be the last time. The year 2005 not only saw some important developments in the School's work in Northern Ireland but paved the way for the appointment of ISE's first full professor to the newly-created Chair in Ecumenics. After being free for so many years to pursue my own and the School's academic interests, I was asked to assume the role of acting director until such time as the new chair was filled. It was something of a shock to find myself responsible for overseeing the new structures so skilfully set up under Kenneth Kearon's stewardship, but it was also a delight to gain closer acquaintance with the workings of ISE as a properly equipped, structured, and financed School in a venerable university. ISE was now an institute of Trinity College Dublin, with its fundraising operations transformed into a Trust which met in full Council three times a year but whose business was carried on by a Steering Committee, while academic affairs were regulated by an Executive Board presided over by the Registrar of Trinity. The Trust was ultimately responsible for preserving the ethos of the School, but more immediately for our activities in Northern Ireland, and here, in the course of the year, certain arrangements began to unravel.

The Partners in Transformation project had been generously funded by various donors (what a contrast to earlier years!), but I was soon to learn that funding in Northern Ireland is a constantly changing and fiercely competitive business. An expected second tranche of funding from an American philanthropic organisation failed to materialise. The organisation concerned had readjusted its criteria, and our own personnel had moved on, so a makeshift arrangement had been reached which saw two people, Doug Baker in Belfast and Geraldine Smyth in Dublin, responsible for carrying on the project; but for a whole complex of reasons this was not working out. In the course of the year, after a number of difficult meetings with our partners in the project, Mediation Northern Ireland, and other organisations which had a consultative role, the painful decision was taken to wind the project up. There was a danger that this would look like the inevitable failure of an ill-conceived venture, but as so often the reasons lay deeper, and thanks to the patient oversight of Cecelia Clegg and the co-ordinated efforts of Geraldine and Doug, a report was produced which in fact, as David Stevens stated emphatically at its launch, contained urgent lessons for the churches in Northern Ireland about their real commitment to ecumenism and reconciliation (*Partners in Transformation: A Joint Project of the Irish School of Ecumenics and Mediation Northern Ireland, 2001-2005. Final Report*, November 2005).

My own priorities for the year, however, were twofold: to monitor ISE's position in the recently inaugurated restructuring of Trinity College, with its immediate implications for our funding channels and academic priorities, and to ensure that the procedure for appointing our new professor led to the most advantageous result possible. It soon became clear that the restructuring was really about the implementation of an Academic Resource Allocation Model (ARAM), which confronted us with the startling news that ISE, which we had been assured was cost-neutral to the college, was now substantially in deficit. In this we were by no means alone in college, and within the ARAM framework there was provision to manage this artificial deficit over time, but it meant that my role in the restructuring process was reduced to monitoring developments, while my main attention was devoted to helping Salters Sterling, a member of the Trust Council, to manoeuvre our way out of this unexpected financial difficulty.

In the meantime, another issue had to be resolved which reawakened the debates and disagreements of times past: what were we to call the new Chair? A minority initially opted for 'Ecumenics' as being more comprehensive and in line with the School's tradition, but there was serious opposition, especially from peace studies, on the grounds that the term would not be generally understood and would frighten off candidates for whom it connoted 'churchiness' and religion. Successive meetings failed to reach a compromise, and eventually the options were put to the vote (apart from Ecumenics, they were: Reconciliation Studies; Religion and Peace; Religion and Politics; Theology and Peace; Theology and Politics). By a narrow but sufficient margin, 'Ecumenics' won out and was proposed to the search committee, while the job description included the striking phrase 'at the intersection of theology, religion and politics'. If the debates had yielded nothing else, this was an insight that could be built on. The long debate in Religious Studies about its relationship to theology on the one hand and objective scholarship on the other has now been complemented by religion's 'return from exile' to play a part in the discipline of International Relations, which is foundational for Peace Studies. Thus ISE sees itself once again strategically placed at the cutting edge of developments in peacebuilding and reconciliation.

There were some thirty-five applicants from all over the world, many of outstanding quality, and after a gruelling process of shortlisting and two days of seminars and interviews, we were all overjoyed when our colleague Linda Hogan was chosen. It was time to recite my *Nunc dimittis* (Luke 2:29), because whatever problems lay ahead – which remain considerable in a globalised environment which makes higher education as competitive as any other 'market', and we must continue to find money outside our university allocation for the extensive continuing education programme in Northern Ireland – I am convinced that ISE, with almost 90 students on three MPhil programmes, with 40 research degree candidates, and with up to 1,800 participants in its Northern Ireland community theology programme, Education for Reconciliation, is now fulfilling its potential and has become the kind of institute I always believed it could be.

CHAPTER NINE

Looking to the Future
(2006 –)

Linda Hogan

Linda Hogan is Professor of Ecumenics and currently is Head of School at the Irish School of Ecumenics, Trinity College, Dublin. She is a native of Callan, Co Kilkenny where she attended school at St Brigid's College, run by the Sisters of Mercy. She completed a BTh and MTh at St. Patrick's College Maynooth, followed by a PhD in theological ethics at Trinity College. Subsequently she spent a number of years at the University of Leeds, following which, in 2001 she was appointed to a lectureship at the Irish School of Ecumenics. Specialising in Christian social ethics, intercultural ethics, and the ethics of gender, her publications include *Between Poetry and Politics: Christian Ethics in Dialogue*, co-editor, Dublin, 2003, *Ethical Relations*, co-editor, London, 2003, *Gendering Ethics/The Ethics of Gender*, co-editor, London, 2001, and *Confronting the Truth: Conscience in the Catholic Tradition*, New York, 2000. Forthcoming publications include an edited collection on Jewish, Christian and Islamic responses to political violence, and another on the role of religion in the public square, as well as essays on the significance of the arts for ethical reflection and on the appropriation of human rights language in Christian social ethics.

The motif running through John D'Arcy May's reflection on the year 2005 is that of transition. Reflecting on the period from January 2006, however, it seems as though this motif continues to express best where the ISE currently finds itself. Much change has happened in the past seven years, yet we find ourselves at a stage where there continues to be considerable change in view. The School is midway through a strategic planning process focused on the next five years, a process that has to take account of a volatile educational and political context. We are also midway through the process of reordering the nature and functioning of the ISE Trust so as to take account of the new structures created by my appointment as Professor of Ecumenics. In terms of our relationships within Trinity, we are currently engaged in a review process that seeks to assess the workings of the relationship between Trinity and the ISE Trust. Importantly too we are also involved in a negotiation that will see ISE define a new kind of relationship with the *School of Religions and Theology* within Trinity. With so much change in the air then it is difficult to anticipate the precise outcome of discussions relating to certain institutional features of ISE, though one is clear about the challenges and opportunities on the horizon.

TRUST MATTERS

When the Steering Committee made the decision, in 2004, to create a Chair in Ecumenics, it did so in the knowledge that many of the traditional duties of the Director of the ISE, especially those associated with the ISE Trust, would fall outside the remit of the professor. By the time I took up my post in January 2006, the Steering Committee had decided that the ISE Trust would seek to appoint a person who would be recognisably the Trust's director, who would oversee and manage all its affairs. In advance of an appointment being made, however, it was recognised that the workings of the Development Office would need to be reviewed and a detailed specification of the responsibilities of the Executive Secretary of the ISE Trust would need to be developed. The funding for the post would also need to be put in place. Thus from January 2006 until April 2007, when Rev Canon Albert Ogle was appointed to the post of Executive Secretary, in the tradition of previous directors, I continued with the oversight and management of ISE Trust activities.

Financial Matters

Financing the extensive activities of the ISE Trust continued to create difficulties (of which more below). Many of the difficulties were foreseen by the Steering Committee during 2004 and 2005, though one, relating to the ISE's new building at 683 Antrim Road was not. At the official opening of the Belfast building in September 2005, following a few days of continuous rain, we were dismayed to discover water pouring through the roof. After a thorough investigation it appeared that, in addition to re-roofing the house, we would need to deal with an extensive dry-rot problem throughout. Eighteen months on, the work has been completed and the house radically improved through the excellent work of our contractor, but the cost of the repairs, which runs to more than two hundred thousand pounds continues to cast a shadow.

The tremendous success of the ISE's Education for Reconciliation programme in Northern Ireland created its own problems. This community-based theological education programme had grown dramatically and by 2006 was running in twenty-one centres in Northern Ireland and the border counties of the Republic, and involved over 1800 participants drawn from all sections of the community. It had been subject to external reviews, commissioned by the Community Relations Council in Northern Ireland, the most recent having been conducted by the Future Ways Project of the University of Ulster. The review was extremely positive about the reconciliation contribution of the Education for Reconciliation course and recommended that it be continued and expanded. However, funding for the programme was precarious. The funding climate had changed and although long-time donors continued to give their financial support, they did so to a lesser extent. Moreover, a major source of funding, the Peace II Extension fund, was drawing to a close. Consultants Peter McEvoy and John Sheils were tasked with raising funds to enable the programme to continue for a three year period, while a process of review was undertaken. A successful application to the International Fund for Ireland in June 2007 put the final piece of funding in place to support the programme through until August 2009.

In the eighteen months from January 2006 until June 2007 the Steering Committee devoted considerable energy and time to developing a strategy for the future of the Education for Reconciliation programme. This had two strands. On the one hand, the staff was working to identify how this programme could best develop in light of the changing political and cultural climate in Northern Ireland. In the process it reaffirmed its core mission, which is to enable the churches to deepen, strengthen and enhance their long-term institutional contribution to recon-ciliation. In the pursuit of this mission, however, the staff identi-fied four strands which would become priorities over the next number of years. These are: the establishment of a number of new local Inter-Church Fora; the extension of the 'Women as Peacebuilders' project; the creation of a fresh strategy for recon-ciliation-focused adult-learning in Northern Ireland to take ac-count of the new inter-religious and inter-generational chal-lenges; and dissemination of the outcomes of this inter-church work at the local level through a series of publications. There is no doubt that this is an ambitious developmental programme. Moreover it is clear this work can't be accomplished unless the long-term financial sustainability of the programme is assured.

Work on the long-term funding of the programme had begun while Kenneth Kearon was Director. At that time it was agreed that the ISE Trust would seek to 'mainstream' the fund-ing of this educational programme, much in the same way as had been accomplished for the graduate programmes. A work-ing-party, comprising Fergus MacAteer, Johnston McMaster, David Poole, Salters Sterling and myself, was set up and throughout the summer and winter of 2006 we met with senior civil servants from the Office of the First and Deputy First Minister, the Community Relations Unit, the Departments of Education and Skills, and of Employment and Learning as well as from the Northern Ireland Office. The purpose of these meetings was to acquaint the various parties with ISE's plan to develop the existing Education for Reconciliation programme to the point of a certificate/diploma/degree qualification of a professional kind for those involved in reconciliation work in the churches and community. We also sought advice on how the same kind of secure funding as had been provided by the government in the Republic of Ireland through the HEA could be achieved from the financial authorities in Northern Ireland. To date this work to mainstream the Education for Reconciliation programme is ongoing and without a clear resolution. The further and higher education sector in Northern Ireland is currently engaged in an extensive process of reorganisation, which is setting the pace. Nonetheless one is hopeful that particular structural changes in the sector will enable ISE, through an association with the Association of Colleges of Further and Higher Education in Northern Ireland, to progressively move towards an accreditation of this adult learning programme which is focused on the reconciliation challenges in the churches' sector.

Restructuring the Development Office
Alongside the task of developing an academic and financial strategy for the future of the Education for Reconciliation programme, the Steering Committee, under the direction of its Chairman Mr Henry Saville, began to put flesh on its plan to appoint a director of the ISE Trust whose primary role would be to oversee and manage all of its affairs. In advance of a recruitment process being begun, however, difficult decisions had to be made regarding the existing organisation of the Development Office of the ISE Trust. The Development Office had served the ISE exceptionally well over the three decades of its existence. However, it was clear that, with the additional university-related duties of the professor, and with the School's ambitions to grow

further, the Trust needed a person in a senior leadership role, whose work would complement the academic focus of the professor. Discussion and debate at the Steering Committee helped clarify the nature of this post, which would mean a major departure for the School in that, organisationally, it distinguished the Trust from the School in a manner that had not been done before. In terms of vision and mission, however, the two components of the organisation continue to be univocal. The post, eventually advertised under the title of Executive Secretary of the ISE Trust, is one that involves developing relationships between the School and individuals, churches and other bodies dedicated to ecumenism, reconciliation and peace, both in Ireland and abroad. It also involves, importantly, providing leadership and direction for the fund-raising activities of the Trust. A host of excellent candidates from many different countries applied and ultimately the committee recommended that Rev Canon Albert Ogle be appointed. A current student on the International Peace Studies programme, Albert was ordained in the Church of Ireland and is a Canon of the Diocese of Los Angeles. As I write he is less than three months in post, although the importance of the work he is doing in elaborating a role and identity for the ISE Trust is already clear to see.

DEVELOPING RELATIONSHIPS WITH TRINITY

Finances, Again

The OECD *Review of Higher Education in Ireland* (2004), together with changes to the manner in which the higher education sector will be funded by government in the future, has led to a process of academic restructuring and financial reform within Trinity. Behind these more immediate issues with which ISE, along with all other schools has been grappling, however, are deeper questions about the role of universities in Irish society and the meaning and purpose of education in a country in which the idiom of economy seems to have replaced that of society. Thus the higher education sector in Ireland, and indeed globally, is in a period of transition, with a host of issues about the future of universities as yet unresolved. Much of the reform has been necessary and the deliberative process in Trinity, though often fractious, has been impressive. As early as 2004 it was becoming clear that the Agreement of 2000 between ISE Trust and the Provost and Fellows of Trinity College Dublin assumed a structural and financial environment that was changing and that, by 2006, had disappeared. The new environment involves both new structures, i.e. involving fewer but larger schools, (of which more below) as well as new methods of allocating the diminishing core-funding from government. These have had a major impact on ISE, although at the beginning of 2006 the precise nature of that impact was as yet unclear.

The first major signal that the landscape had radically altered came in the guise of a discussion about ISE's finances within Trinity. The Agreement of 2000 included a clause that noted that the ring-fencing of the ISE's financial allocation from the HEA would continue for a period of 'not less than five years'. One interpretation of that clause was that from January 1st 2006 ISE's finances would no longer be ring-fenced and it was with this interpretation that the Treasurer's Office worked in the early months of 2006. Although ISE was working within its financial allocation from the HEA, the withdrawal of the ring-fencing around ISE's budget and the application of Trinity's new academic resource allocation model (ARAM) to ISE would result in ISE losing a considerable portion of its HEA allocation. Extensive discussions ensued, both internally and with the HEA and although the matter is not finally resolved, the interim conclusion is that the financing of ISE is to continue as is until the end of 2008 when the HEA will be introducing a new model of funding for the sector as a whole.

What accounts for the disparity between the HEA allocation to ISE and the funding model to be applied within Trinity? Ultimately the disparity can be explained by a combination of factors. One factor relates to the manner in which the 'no cost basis' of ISE's incorporation into TCD was calculated and how those costs should be interpreted within the new funding allocation model (ARAM). A second factor relates to the vagaries of government policy on funding third level and in particular how that is impacting on TCD. On one reading, many of the components of ISE's uniqueness, namely its cross-border location, its strongly international student profile, and its exclusively postgraduate orientation fit comfortably with aspects of the stated government policy on developing the university sector. And indeed there is no doubt that these particular aspects of the School are highly regarded and supported within college. Yet running counter to this stated aim, the new funding model being introduced by the HEA seems particularly to reward those institutions that are increasing undergraduate numbers, and this is having a serious impact on Trinity's capacity to further develop its postgraduate profile.

There is no doubt that the expectation that financial stability would accompany the integration of ISE into Trinity has been somewhat undermined by the changing funding climate. Nonetheless there are some reasons to be hopeful that the new funding arrangements will, eventually, be sufficiently flexible so as to enable ISE to continue to develop its mission. Trends in the third level sector in Ireland, namely the focus on graduate education, the plans to further internationalise the student body and the initiatives to develop cross-border co-operation between educational institutions on the island of Ireland, suggest that the range of educational activities with which ISE has traditionally been associated will become ever-more important. How government agencies will fund these stated priorities is still under review, and is a matter about there is much discussion between ISE Trust and senior academic officers within Trinity. Indeed many of the senior officers, and especially the Provost, Dr John Hegarty, have recognised the unique contribution that ISE can make to the university, have been extraordinarily supportive of the School and have been our partners in the effort to find a secure funding arrangement for ISE within Trinity. Yet the challenge of accomplishing this secure financial base still remains.

Restructuring within Trinity

In addition to changes in the financial environment within Trinity, major structural changes were also underway. For a time it seemed as though this restructuring would have a minimal impact on the ISE. However, midway through 2005 it became ever-more obvious that ISE would need to think differently about its position within the college structures, and most critically, would need to develop a closer relationship with a cognate area. By 2006 when ISE began to discuss this matter fully it became clear that the most fitting partner was the *School of Religions and Theology*, formerly the *School of Hebrew, Biblical and Theological Studies.* Although institutionally there had been difficulties between the schools on ISE's integration into Trinity, there were good personal relationships among many of the staff. As important was the fact that a significant convergence of disciplines and research interests already existed between the schools and so it was possible to envisage a confederal structure that would enhance our existing collaboration. Thus through the summer and autumn of 2006, encouraged by Professor David Dickson (Registrar), Professor Terence Brown (Dean of Arts and Humanities) and Professor John Scattergood (Vice-Dean of Arts and Humanities) staff began to consider the merits (and otherwise) of forming a confederal school with the *School of Religions and Theology*.

Eventually, after a stop-start process, in March 2007 the ISE and the *School of Religions and Theology* decided to seek the status of an aspirant School which will form part of the newly constituted Faculty of Arts, Humanities and Social Sciences. It will have an Interim Executive whose purpose would be two-fold, namely to create lines of communication with the wider college committee structure, and to develop a shared vision for the confederal school together with an agreed academic and resource plan. In an *aide-memoire* of a discussion that I had with Professor Andrew Mayes (*School of Religions and Theology*) on March 28th 2007 we noted that 'while both schools incorporate varieties of activity which co-exist in some tension, it was our judgement that such tensions could be creative in mutually enriching ways.' Importantly, from ISE's perspective, the *aide-memoire* recognises that the ISE Trust would continue to play an important ethos and support role in the life of ISE, although it was acknowledged that how such roles were to be associated with the confederal school would have to be worked out in their governance and management aspects.

As I write, the discussion about how the ISE Trust will relate to the confederal school is live and lively. Moreover it will almost certainly involve the ISE Trust and college in revisiting the 2000 Agreement, particularly in relation to the governance and management provisions that it currently enshrines.

Reviewing the Relationship between ISE Trust and Trinity
In fact the 2000 Agreement between the ISE Trust and TCD already provided for a review of the workings of the Agreement after five years. However, for a variety of reasons the review was deferred until May 2007. By the time it was underway the review had two purposes. One, already envisaged in the Agreement, involved an assessment of how the arrangement was working from the perspective of both parties. The other, necessitated by restructuring, involved examining the existing governance arrangements in the knowledge that they may need to be amended so as to allow for the creation of a new or analogous governance structure within the new confederal school. In advance of the review, the ISE Trust consulted with academic and administrative staff to canvass their views on the experience of integration. It was clear that from the perspective of ISE the experience of the workings of the Agreement had been, in the main, a positive one. Indeed, viewed especially from the perspective of academic development the integration has been overwhelmingly successful. ISE has seen significant growth in its student numbers, students have been able to avail of more facilities, academic staff had the opportunity to develop relationships with a number of different schools in college. They have been involved in college-wide research projects and with

joint supervision of research students with other departments. In addition, ISE makes available for moderation courses from its range of programmes to students from other disciplines. Academic and administrative staff also benefit from various staff development schemes. There continue to be challenges, however, most especially in terms of creating a good academic environment for staff and students on the Belfast campus. And of course those financial and governance issues to which I have referred have yet to be resolved.

RESEARCH AND SCHOLARSHIP

In addition to the on-going research on ecumenical and ecclesiological themes, research on reconciliation issues continues to be central to the individual and collaborative research pursued by academics in the School. Moreover, although this research has a strong theological dimension, it is also interdisciplinary in character. The themes of contested memories, forgiveness, reconciliation and justice emerge in the work of Denis Anderson, Gladys Ganiel, Cathy Higgins, Johnston McMaster, Geraldine Smyth and David Tombs. Understandably some of this work is focused on the context of Northern Ireland; however, comparative work is also important for all of the School's researchers, with South Africa, Zimbabwe, Sri Lanka and increasingly the Balkans being among the contexts that are of interest. More recently the School has begun to conceptualise a research project that widens the scope of our long-standing concern with reconciliation by exploring how the Christian churches on the island of Ireland (both old and new) can more effectively contribute to sustainable social and political reconciliation in the context of increasing ethnic and religious diversity. Indeed with the centenary of the 1910 Edinburgh conference in view, it is hoped that this research, led by Andrew Pierce, will provide the churches and theological colleges with social scientific and theological resources for approaching diversity and thereby for articulating a new ecumenical vision for the Ireland of the 21st century.

Research in the field of inter-cultural and inter-religious

ethics has also become prominent in the School over the years. John May has been to the fore here, and has been the leading Irish academic in this field. My own research has also become more focused on the multi-religious contexts in which ethical concerns arise. In recent years, I have been involved with two collaborative research projects in this area. One, funded through the *Institute for International Integration Studies* (TCD) and entitled *Interreligious Ethics and the Cultural Dynamics of Globalisation,* was conceived with Professor Maureen Junker-Kenny of the *School of Religions and Theology.* The research group includes Professor Nigel Biggar (*Religions and Theology*), and from ISE John May, Geraldine Smyth, David Tombs and Gillian Wylie. In this research we focus on the significance of religion in the cultural dynamics of globalisation. Through publications and seminars we have explored a host of issues including the role of religion in the processes of globalisation in light of their diverging memories, contested histories and legacies of violence; the role that human rights norms play in moderating the excesses of globalisation; whether the discourse of human rights can have an inter-cultural and inter-religious resonance; and how and on what basis religious voices can contribute to public debate in local and global civil society, and particularly in multi-religious liberal democracies. Among the visitors the research group has hosted are Professor Max Stackhouse (Princeton Theological Seminary), Professor John Kelsay (Florida State University) Professor Linda Woodhead, (University of Lancaster), Professor George De Schrijver, (KU Leuven) and Professor François Houtart. Much of my own writing has been focused on this area, and particularly on the latter two questions of the extent to which the discourse of human rights can have an inter-cultural and inter-religious resonance and the related question of how and on what basis Christian voices can contribute to public debate.

The theme of inter-religious ethics is also prominent in a second research project, on Health Policy Formation in a Christian Context with Religious Minorities. This research was intended to give a policy-related focus to the question of how the values and norms of different religious traditions can be accommodated in a multi-religious political sphere. The primary research was conducted by Dr Katy Radford, a social anthropologist, who has produced a challenging and discursive analysis of the emerging issues for the Irish health policy in light of the country becoming more religiously diverse. It has been funded by the Health Research Board, the Adelaide Society, AMICH (Adelaide and Meath Incorporating the National Children's Hospital) Tallaght and the ISE Trust and will be launched in 2008.

Of course it is always difficult to thematise the research that is pursued by academics in the School since there is also important work that does not fall neatly into the major themes but that is critical to the School nonetheless. Iain Atack's work on the ethics of peace and war, and increasingly on the ethics of non-violence, is a case in point, as is Bill McSweeney's work on the significance of religion in the construction of US foreign policy and Gillian Wylie's on human trafficking. Together with the themes discussed above, these critical questions continue to be analysed and debated. Our dialogue partners grow ever more diverse, both institutionally and geographically. Indeed the School is now part of a global network of academic and civil society organisations whose collaboration is premised on the belief that the academic, the political and the ethical are inextricably linked.

LOOKING AHEAD

Within these past eighteen months the School has seen a number of changes in terms of its staff and its Patrons. Eileen Gallagher was appointed to do inter-church fora work and Terry Duffy was appointed on a one-year contract to the International Peace Studies programme. Cecelia Clegg moved to a position as Director of the Centre for Theology and Public Issues at the University of Edinburgh, Yvonne Naylor completed her work on the SEED project, and Katy Radford's research on Health Policy Formation in a Christian Culture with Religious Minorities too came to an end. In addition two of ISE's longstanding and influential Patrons, the Most Rev Dr Robin Eames of the Church of Ireland and Rev Edmund Mawhinney of the Methodist Church in Ireland, retired from their roles as Patrons. They are replaced respectively by the Most Rev Dr Alan Harper and the Rev Donald Ker. On a sadder note, our friend and colleague Dympna Ryan, who had worked in the Development Office for many years, died in the summer of 2006, and we also lost a number of long-standing friends and supporters of the School, including the Rt Rev Monsignor Patrick Devine and Mr Gordon Buttanshaw.

This sadness notwithstanding, however, the past eighteen months have also been a time of considerable development and success within the School. Gladys Ganiel, Andrew Pierce, David Tombs and Gillian Wylie have all been successful in competitively tendering for funds from external sources to enable them to pursue their research. David Tombs was also awarded a prestigious Provost's Teaching Award, for teaching excellence within the university. Among the major events we hosted recently were a visit, in March 2007, from Rev Sam Kobia, General Secretary of the World Council of Churches and an international conference, organised by Gillian Wylie in July 2007, to mark the 200th anniversary of the *Abolition of Slavery Act*. The libraries in Dublin and Belfast have also undergone an important development programme. Bríd O'Brien and Sláine O'Hogáin have worked with librarians in Trinity to introduce a major computer-based re-cataloguing excercise that has linked the ISE catalogue to the main TCD system. Moreover currently we are working to develop the technology infrastructure with the intention that, by the beginning of the next academic year, ISE's campuses in Dublin and Belfast will be linked through video conferencing. It is anticipated that students in either campus will be able to attend courses in both Belfast and Dublin and that the cross-border communication between staff will be more effective, more frequent and less time-consuming.

The ISE is currently operating within an educational and political context in which many of the traditional expectations and norms of operation are changing. Moreover, some of these changes represent major challenges for the School. There is increased competition, nationally and internationally from other institutions. The types of interdisciplinary programmes traditionally associated with ISE are springing up in Europe and further afield. Indeed ISE is frequently approached to act as a consultant for such developments. There is no doubt that increased competition for public funds for humanities at third level, combined with diminishing EU and philanthropic funds to support reconciliation and peace in Northern Ireland, is also posing a challenge for the School as it looks to the future. Critical here will be the efforts to mitigate the potential negative effects of these factors by moving quickly to establish a stable institutional environment, by refining our research strategy in a way that takes account of the current research environment and by developing alternative sources of funding to replace those that are diminishing.

Alongside these somewhat destabilising factors are a host of opportunities that suggest that ISE can hope to continue to flourish. There is no doubt that there is considerable and growing interest internationally in interdisciplinary programmes that bring the study of religion into dialogue with peace and reconciliation studies. This is evidenced in ISE by the tremendous growth in students who apply to do research degrees at the School. Nationally, three emerging priorities in the public sector also suggest that ISE can continue to make a social and political, as well as an educational contribution to Irish life. In the first place, there is a growing recognition in Ireland of the need for research and teaching programmes in the field of inter-religious dialogue and inter-religious ethics, particularly among policymakers and public servants. The government's decision to develop a formal framework for a structured engagement by the state with faith-based organisations suggests that we are entering a new phase in what would traditionally have been termed 'church-state relationships', but which is now transformed by the growing religious pluralism in the state. The new political dispensation in Northern Ireland also creates a new context in which ISE's work can flourish. Our aim here continues to be to make a real and sustainable contribution to reconciliation and, with our ecumenical partners to deepen, strengthen and enhance the long-term institutional contribution of the churches to these processes. Whether through local inter-church fora, through community theological education, or through graduate education and research, our shared concern revolves around the development of creative and sustainable approaches to the establishment of inter-generational reconciliation. Moreover, as we reflect on our work in the post-conflict context in Northern Ireland, we are confident that the ISE has the potential for greater collaboration with international partners so that we can learn from each others' insights and educational strategies. Thus we expect, over the coming years, to forge more extensive partnerships nationally and internationally in order to better understand the complexities of and the possibilities for reconciliation between and within traditions. This resonates well with the commitment that the Irish government has to 'internationalise the knowledge gained from the Irish peace process.' As recently as 7 July 2007 the Minister for Foreign Affairs announced the establishment of a new unit which will work with academic institutions to ensure that Ireland's experience and expertise in peace and reconciliation work is harnessed and shared internationally. Within ISE we are considering the role we might play, in collaboration with others, to develop the capacity of Irish civil servants, policy-makers, NGOs and their overseas partners in this field of reconciliation and conflict resolution. Allied to this development and drawing its energy from the new political dispensation in Northern Ireland is the commitment of the government to develop cross-border co-operation. With its long-established identity as a cross-border institution, one hopes that ISE will continue to be supported in its mission to be both an advocate of and catalyst for reconciliation in this context.

By way of (an interim) conclusion ...

As one reflects on the contribution that the ISE has made to the academy in the thirty-five years of its existence, it becomes clear that a critical feature of that contribution has been the way in which the ISE has reframed the concept of ecumenics so that we now conceptualise the field in terms of an intellectual paradigm rather than in terms of a discrete discipline. Moreover, the essence of this paradigm is that it places the encounters between distinctive religious, cultural and social worlds centre-stage, it reflects on the implications of these encounters for their respective identities and it promotes modes of engagement that are reconciling rather than conflictual. Thus whereas traditionally the *oikoumene* of ecumenics had been understood in terms of the encounters between Christian denominations, ecumenics as pioneered by the ISE is concerned not only with the unity of Christians but also with inter-religious understanding and with international peace and reconciliation. In this way ISE's characterisation of the field restores to ecumenics the full and proper meaning of the *oikos*, originally the household, that is, the one inhabited earth. Moreover, in defining the field thus, ecumenics uniquely reflects something that many people are only now beginning to realise, that is, that the complex religious, ethical, political and environmental issues facing our world will neither be understood nor resolved unless we are involved in serious interdisciplinary work and unless we engage with distinctive traditions, religious and secular, in a dialogical, ecumenical manner.

It is already evident that the globalised context, in which religious and cultural communities live and work in ever-greater proximity, has transformed the nature of the questions with which ISE has been concerned. Thus one is hopeful that a closer relationship between ISE and the *School of Religions and Theology* will enable us to develop further the academic infrastructure that will allow us to respond more fully to the manifold and complex challenges that we face. Both schools already have research strengths that would benefit from a more structured collaboration. Nor are these over-lapping interests confined to the theolog-

ical strand of ISE. Our work in the field of inter-religious dialogue, reconciliation and international peace would be greatly enhanced if it were to be developed in light of the *School of Religions
and Theology*'s Jewish and emerging Islamic interests. Moreover
enhanced co-operation in these fields would enable both schools
to identify opportunities for further collaboration in the future.

As one reflects on the remarkable vision of the founder, Fr
Michael Hurley SJ, and on the manner in which that vision has
been elaborated and developed by successive generations of staff
and students, and by the many extraordinary individuals in the
ISE Trust, one is aware of just how creative and challenging is our
mission. Our subject-matter requires an approach that is both
multi and inter-disciplinary and depends on the mutual interaction of research, education and outreach. Thus the question for
the ISE now is how this mission can best be incarnated in the
changing and 'changeful' conditions of late modernity. Though it
has already undergone major reorganisation, the university sector in Ireland is likely to experience further structural and financial reform. In the future one is likely to see both greater institutional collaboration as well as greater competition. Moreover, as
has been suggested throughout this chapter, these factors will
continue to impact on ISE much in the same way as they do on
other schools in the sector. Nonetheless, despite the constraints
that the globalised, market-driven environment places on education, one is confident that ISE can continue to highlight the distinctiveness of its work, can deepen its impact, and can create
new constituencies for its academic and social mission. It is becoming increasingly manifest that the original vision of the
founder has the capacity to become exponentially greater and will
enable ISE to respond with vigour to the increasingly complex
issues of today. There is no doubt that many of the challenges facing the *oikoumene*, when viewed in isolation, seem overwhelming.
Yet one has confidence that they are capable of being conquered
by a combination of faith and intellect and in a context where the
institutional realities of ISE's partnerships become expanded beyond what must have been the dreams of Fr Michael Hurley.

Index of Personal Names